The Real Policeman

Also by Ron Owens

OKLAHOMA JUSTICE
The Oklahoma City Police
A Century of Gunfighters, Gangsters and Terrorists

OKLAHOMA HEROES
A Tribute to Fallen Law Enforcement Officers

JELLY BRYCE, LEGENDARY LAWMAN

MEDAL OF HONOR
Historical Facts and Figures

The Real Policeman

Ron Owens

iUniverse, Inc.
New York Bloomington Shanghai

The Real Policeman

iUniverse books may be ordered through booksellers or by contacting:

iUniverse
1663 Liberty Drive
Bloomington, IN 47403
www.iuniverse.com
1-800-Authors (1-800-288-4677)

Because of the dynamic nature of the Internet, any Web addresses or links contained in this book may have changed since publication and may no longer be valid.

ISBN: 978-0-595-48357-0 (pbk)
ISBN: 978-0-595-60447-0 (ebk)

Printed in the United States of America

To all those, of all generations, who defy
reason by running *toward* the sound of gunfire.
The times and names change.
The risks remain the same.

And for Lorne and Cash.
When you're old enough, maybe this will
help you understand why Pops was a
little different from other grandpas.

Policemen are soldiers who act alone;
soldiers are policemen who act in unison.

—*Herbert Spencer*
Social Statics (1851)
Chapter XXI, § 8
The Duty of the State-

People sleep peaceably in their beds at night only because
rough men stand ready to do violence on their behalf.

—*Attributed to George Orwell-*

Contents

Prologue

Mary was sitting under the tree in her front yard playing with her doll when Johnny came running down the sidewalk pulling his little red wagon and letting out piercing yelps at the top of his lungs.

"Wooooowooooowooooowooooowoooo."

"Whatcha doin', Johnny?" she asked.

"Playing policeman. This is my police car. Wanna ride in it?" he answered.

"Sure," she said as she climbed in the little red wagon.

Johnny vigorously pulled Mary around the house twice in his "police car" before they came to a halt far out behind the garage in the rear of the house. Stopping to rest, he sat down heavily in front of the wagon, arms and legs akimbo, breathing rapidly through his mouth.

"That was lots of fun, Johnny," said Mary. "Thanks for letting me ride in your police car."

Johnny didn't hear the words because his eyes were riveted on the wondrous sight in front of them. Mary's feet were still propped up inside the corners of the wagon and her dress had blown up above her knees. Johnny didn't understand exactly what had him so mesmerized but he stared unblinkingly up her dress.

Mary saw where his eyes were staring and she smiled coyly with a wisdom somewhat beyond her years. Mary had two brothers and Johnny was an only child.

"Ever seen anything like that before, Johnny?" she asked.

Hypnotized, he could just manage to shake his head without altering his gaze.

"Would you like to touch it?" she smirked.

Johnny nodded his head slowly and gingerly reached out. Gently, carefully, he touched the funny looking place between Mary's legs. It was alive and warm. He drew his hand back rapidly as he realized it was part of Mary.

"Would you like to put your finger in it, Johnny?" Mary asked.

Once again, Johnny slowly nodded and reached out. Extending his forefinger, he pushed it toward the magical place. Again he rapidly pulled his hand back.

"Would you like to kiss it, Johnny?" Mary asked.

Johnny blushed.

"Aw, Mary, you know I ain't no *REAL* policeman!"

—Related to a police academy class by
a veteran sergeant in January, 1970—

How and Why This Book Was Written

Dear reader, if you are considering reading this book hoping to be treated to an exposé, a public washing of dirty laundry, a revelation of closely held secrets or the ranting of a disgruntled former employee, you will probably be disappointed. My reasons for writing it are quite the opposite. After my family, my service with the Oklahoma City Police Department (OCPD) is the proudest, most satisfying achievement of my life and I doubt if I will ever surpass it.

Something else you won't be treated to is political correctness. When I first began making police reports in 1969, the abbreviation "WM" meant White Male. Caucasian was a term for anthropologists, not cops. We were just beginning to make the transition from "NM" for Negro Male to "BM" for Black Male, "IM" meant Indian Male (the prefix 'American' was understood, especially in Oklahoma) and "OM" meant Oriental Male. This terminology will be used throughout this book. It is meant without offense. If it offends you anyway, try to get over it. If it permanently damages your self-esteem, write to me for an apology and hold your breath until you get it. I don't object to all of society's rule changes, just the vacuous or obsequious ones. I'm not trying to dazzle you with my vocabulary. I just thought that was a slightly nicer way of avoiding saying "stupid" and "ass-kissing." I usually don't go to the trouble.

A book much like this could be written by just about every cop in America. In fact, most could probably tell stories very similar to each one recounted here and many more bizarre. Most of the cops I know say that they wish they had started a journal their first day on the job and had just written a little in it every night. Very few, if any, actually do. Some start a scrapbook whenever their photo and/or name start being printed in the newspaper but most grow weary of it. Eventually the scrapbook just stops with no explanation.

I waited two years before I started writing things down on an old manual typewriter so, in a sense, I started writing this book in 1971. As college, marriage, fatherhood, extra jobs and other responsibilities began accumulating, the stories got written down less and less. Every transfer or promotion to a new assignment spurred a renewed enthusiasm for the writing as new experiences came but eventually, as before, the responsibilities just eroded the time available. Not all of these events happened to me personally, therefore this book isn't strictly autobiographical. Essentially, this is an extension of my own journal along with the inclusion of what would have been other officer's journals who never wrote their own.

What follows are a series of what cops call "war stories" although few of them have anything to do with actual physical combat. They are actually a series of vignettes that are meant to illustrate the complexities, comedies, tragedies, peculiarities and unique experiences of being a police officer in a large American city several decades ago during a period of social and racial unrest that has not been experienced by anyone in this country currently under the age of thirty.

For those readers who are veterans of law enforcement, perhaps this book will bring back memories of your own career. For younger members, perhaps this will provide a preview of sorts of your future experiences and give you a look back over your shoulder at what has gone before. If you're a civilian looking for a closer view of reality than the extremes provided by Jack Webb, Dirty Harry or more recent Hollywood efforts, perhaps this will achieve that purpose.

There is more space devoted to Patrol and Homicide and there are two reasons for that:

1. Those are the two places where I spent more of my career than in any other assignments.

2. Those are the two assignments where I enjoyed my job the most, where I made my closest friends and where I believe I made the most of whatever small contributions to society I could.

More limited sections are given to Traffic (because I was never there) and to Vice, SEU, Narcotics and Sex Crimes, where my assignments were correspondingly shorter.

Other considerations are space and relative relevance. I spent eleven years on the Hostage Negotiations Team as a detective, sergeant and lieutenant. I didn't keep count of the exact number of hostage and barricaded suspect situations I was involved in or present at but it was quite a few. Needless to say, an entire book could be written about those experiences alone but, ultimately, hostage negotiations is a sideline specialization of police work and not part of the mainstream of police operations like patrol and criminal investigations. Therefore there are only a few stories dealing with that specialty.

The observations and opinions are mine and mine alone although I believe a lot of my colleagues would probably agree with them. As I said before, a book much like this could be written by any police officer in America. Perhaps, with certain cultural differences, by any police officer in the world. This one just happened to be written by me.

Some liberals, lawyers, academics, Constitutional scholars, leftists, mealy-mouthed politicians, human rights activists and many others with very soft, clean hands will probably view some of the following stories with horror and spout crap about how these are the kinds of things that could "cause the Republic to fall." In that light, I fervently wish Washington, Jefferson and the rest of the boys could come back for a few days, look around and give their actual opinions about what they see going on around here. Nevertheless, these were a few of the things a few good men and women did to try to protect many times their number at one time and some of the ways they dealt with those situations and those stresses. And the last time I checked, the Republic was still standing.

One of many old cop truisms is "Fairy tales begin with 'Once upon a time' and cop stories begin with 'This is no shit—'."

All cop stories have to be measured against a certain amount of embellishment (i.e., "bullshit factor".) Some of these stories happened to me. Some of them I witnessed directly. Some of them were told to me by others who were involved or witnessed them directly. Lastly, some were told to me by people who were told by reliable witnesses. The first two categories have been related as I experienced them, therefore a zero per cent bullshit factor. Well, maybe five per cent. Okay, ten per cent. Hey, I'm only human. The other two categories probably range between 80 and 90 per cent accuracy. Some literary license has been taken to present them in this format. Some dialogue is taken verbatim from official police reports or court testimony and some is paraphrased based upon many conversations I've had with other officers.

As previously stated, this is not an exposé. Some real names have been used but others have been changed because I have no desire to cause public embarrassment, arguments, divorces or shootings so you'll find some generic Joe's, John's, Smiths and Joneses in here. Some people with personal knowledge of a few of these incidents may wonder whether I just got my facts mixed up or if it is part of the aforementioned embellishment factor. The answer is neither. A few of these characters are composites of two or more very real people and a few experiences are composites of very real occurrences. In each case, this literary license has been taken to make a point. If you were involved, you can be the judge if I made my point and if it was worth making. I realize that some of these vignettes might almost rise to the status of urban legends but one should remember that sometimes urban legends have a basis in fact. Just remember that cop stories aren't like rumors—a small amount of embellishment does nothing to detract from the core of truth at the heart of the story.

For any who might object to my use of the word "cops", I grew up in an era when the word was neither pejorative nor disrespectful. I don't know if it was derived from the copper metal once used in the badges or as an abbreviation for Constable On Patrol or any of many other explanations but I have always used it synonymously with "police officer" including when applied to myself.

Incidentally, the title of this book is generic and doesn't refer to the author. It also isn't intended to be gender specific. It refers to hundreds of thousands of men and women who did and still do a very difficult job the way it should be done. And in that era, most of them did it most of the time without bulletproof vests or body armor, with nothing between them and harm but a thin layer of blue or gray cloth and each other. I am honored to have worked with some of the best of them.

This also needs to be said. This book could be viewed as history and if so, it should be viewed as *ancient* history. A few of these stories took place in the 1960s, most in the 1970s and a few in the early 1980s. Therefore at least a quarter of a century has passed since any of these events occurred. So don't equate any of these tales with the OCPD officers of today. Much more has changed than the times.

The OCPD of today is very different from the one I joined in 1969, much for the better in most ways. As a general rule, today's officers are better educated, better trained, better disciplined and better equipped than we were. They have social problems to deal with and expectations placed upon them that we did not. On the other hand, we had some problems they did not and different expectations upon us thus we were sometimes given more latitude in solving those problems. As a result, most of the stories in this book could have and should have occurred only in the time frame they did. As I was nearing retirement, some of the young officers in my unit used to good-naturedly kid me by saying things like "Old man, you probably couldn't even get hired under today's standards." My reply was usually something like "Maybe not. But I'm not sure you could do the job I was hired to do in 1969."

To the best of my knowledge, most if not all of these stories are true. If they aren't, they should be.

The Temper Of The Times

When I was a kid, I hated math. In grade school, learning the principles behind the decimal system almost killed me. In junior high school I had a similar problem with understanding the concept of the unknown "x" in algebra equations. Part of it was possibly the limitations of the teachers involved. An algebra teacher told me "x" stood for anything I wanted. I pointed to my incorrect answer to the problem and told her that was what I wanted "x" to be. I then discovered that "x" wasn't what I wanted it to be, it was what she said it was. A better math teacher later taught me that wasn't accurate either. Future math teachers taught me to make games out of math. It made it more fun, easier to learn and helped me overcome my fear and loathing of it. It became a lifelong mental diversion.

When I retired from the Oklahoma City Police Department on January 1, 2000, I had been alive for 20,150 days. For those who don't enjoy such mental diversions, that was two months past my fifty-fifth birthday. I had been a policeman for 10,989 of those days, about 55 per cent of my life up to that time. That figures out to 30 years, 1 month and 1 day. Somehow it didn't seem that long.

When I was hired as a patrolman by the OCPD on December 1, 1969, this world was different in some ways and the same in others. In both cases, it was a matter of degree. To put these vignettes in the proper perspective, the reader needs to understand some of these differences and similarities.

The recruiting brochures said the job paid $500 a month based upon a 44-hour workweek which figures out to about $2.62 an hour. The minimum hourly wage then was $1.60, gasoline prices hovered around 35 cents a gallon, a new car was about $3,000 ($88 a month for 36 months, as I recall) and a six-pack of beer was under a dollar so it was a pretty good job for a young man with a high school diploma and some college hours. Some college under your belt was a good idea but not required and you didn't get paid anything extra for it.

I say "young man" because at that time the OCPD was virtually an all-male province with all that implies. That includes the rivers of testosterone, macho posturing (false and otherwise), horseplay, genital scratching, flatulence contests, what is considered today to be gross political incorrectness and blistering profanity.

Regarding the latter, if a young man came from an ultra-religious background and had never heard or spoken a naughty word in his life, he would certainly hear plenty of them in this job, from witnesses, suspects, victims and colleagues alike. Some of the people he dealt with on a daily basis couldn't communicate without using profanity and he would learn to use it fluently to communicate with them. It often became a reflexive habit as well as a safety valve for stress. This is not a solely American phenomenon. During the Jack the Ripper murders in 1888, there was widespread dissatisfaction with the head of Scotland Yard and a London newspaper, using the English language the way only the British can, stated that "reporters have only got to talk to the first policeman they chance to meet on his beat in order to get his opinion of his chief, *often expressed with that tropical luxuriance for which the force is famous"* (emphasis added).

Back to the all-male province, five female officers had been hired as meter maids to write parking tickets in 1955 but only a couple of them were still around by the late 1960s and very few others had been commissioned in the interim. They were primarily relegated to duties as matrons handling female prisoners in the jail. One might occasionally be assigned to Planning and Research, Training or the Records Bureau. There were none in Patrol or Traffic and their only incursion into the Detective Division was an assignment handling juveniles in the Youth Bureau. It wouldn't be until late 1972 that fully commissioned and trained female officers would enter the Patrol Division and years later before they entered the all-male bastions of Robbery, Homicide, Narcotics and other detective units.

So the job was an attractive one in terms of financial and job security but they didn't give them away. Every time there were openings, there were at least ten times more applicants than openings and they made use of that fact. There was a ninety-seven per cent rejection rate. Only three out of every hundred applicants were hired. That was a much lower acceptance rate than West Point or the country's other military academies. It was a merciless selection process.

The first step in the process started with a lieutenant in Recruiting tossing you a personal history form (misnamed because it was actually a booklet a dozen pages thick, printed on both sides), sometimes with the admonition "—and don't lie about any of it!" You had to list every place you'd ever lived or worked, all marriages, divorces, military experience, education, subversive affiliations, debts, arrests, tickets, lawsuits and a complete medical history. You also had to sign it, swearing that you were telling the truth, the whole truth and nothing but the truth in every statement. Then you were photographed and fingerprinted.

What followed were one or two detectives checking the truthfulness of every one of those statements for the next month or two. Starting with the day you were born, they interviewed every relative, friend, employer, co-worker, teacher, neighbor and acquaintance they could locate concerning your fitness to be a police officer. Your grades and school disciplinary actions were checked all the way back to kindergarten. A single lie, half-truth or misrepresentation on any of those dozen pages was enough to instantly disqualify you. In most cases, a single arrest for anything, an unpaid traffic ticket or an unresolved debt had the same result. Ditto for any military discharge other than Honorable. In the past, any narcotics usage at all had been disqualifying but, as a sign of the changing times, a small amount of recreational experimentation with marijuana was accepted but that exemption was usually reserved for Vietnam veterans who had tried it while serving in a combat zone and had stopped once away from those stresses. The exception didn't apply to pills, heroin, cocaine or anything else. Your photo and fingerprints were sent to the FBI and teletypes went out to the police department in every town you'd ever lived in. Any and all contacts you had ever had with any kind of law enforcement were investigated. They checked for any record I might have had in a city I had lived in from the ages of three to six.

If you passed the background check, the next step was a polygraph (lie detector) examination but it wasn't like anything any criminal suspect had gone through. You were asking for a job in a position of trust so the normal rules didn't apply to you. You had voluntarily forfeited all your rights and would have to endure tactics and strategies no murder suspect ever would. The examiner was a crusty old detective sergeant in a cubbyhole on the second floor of Police Headquarters. The rubber respiration tube was tightened around your chest to an uncomfortable point and the blood pressure cuff on one bicep was inflated until all blood flow was cut off to your lower arm. You were then questioned aggressively about every day of your life, every job you'd had, every school you'd attended, every pencil and paper clip you'd ever picked up that didn't belong to you, every sexual contact you'd ever had with any male, female or barnyard animal. All this took place in a windowless room about the size of the average master bathroom which the examiner filled with clouds of pungent pipe smoke. If you coughed, he yelled "Don't do that!" When your arm started turning purple from lack of circulation and you wiggled a numb finger, causing a tremble of the inked needle on the graph paper, you were loudly admonished "Don't move that goddam finger!" Any other time the inked line wavered, he beat the pipe into an ashtray or pounded his fist on the desktop, screaming "Bullshit! You're a liar!" My test lasted for two hours and forty-five minutes. My right arm was the color of a rotten banana at the end.

I later learned that virtually every test ended the same way. The examiner ripped the tubes, electrodes and blood pressure cuff off in disgust and sent you out to sit in the hallway, not coincidentally about a dozen yards away from the steel door leading to the jail. As you sat there for a seemingly interminable time, watching officers leading handcuffed prisoners down the hall and slamming the steel door behind them with a bone-chilling finality, you fully expected to soon be led down the same hall and thrown into a dungeon with the Count of Monte Cristo for eternity.

Most were just sent back to the unemployment lines. If you were one of the three per cent, the Internal Security (as Internal Affairs was called then) detective handling your application came and got you, told you to your amazement that you'd passed and scheduled you for a physical exam. You later learned the true purpose of the test. They just wanted to know four things about you from the examiner; (1) Is he basically honest and truthful? (2) Is he heterosexual? (3) Is he easily confused, irritated or enraged? and (4) Can he hold his temper?

If you passed the physical exam, you appeared before an oral review board. It was chaired by either the Chief or Assistant Chief and had command level representatives (Captains or Majors) from all five of the PD's divisions (Patrol, Traffic, Detective, Headquarters and Special Services). They asked you a series of canned questions (Why do you want to be an officer? Could you take a life if you had to? What are your career goals?), looked you over, basically tried to see how easily frightened or intimidated you were and voted to hire you or not. The Traffic Captain went to sleep during my board. He was close to retirement and not many new guys volunteered for Traffic anyway. The Headquarters and Special Services Majors also didn't get many new officers and the Detective Major knew it would be years before I had any hope of working for him. The Patrol Major, I.G. Purser (who would become the Chief of Police four years later and a city councilman after his retirement), questioned me most closely because he got most of the new guys. Apparently I did all right. I passed five to one. Years later I got to look at their scoring sheets and the one Major who voted against me remarked that I had a "ho-hum attitude." I guess I had forced myself to relax a little too much.

I don't want to give the impression that the oral review board was taken lightly by any of us. In many ways, it was the most stressful event of the selection process. Most of the higher-ranking commanders at that time were very highly respected and justly so. One lieutenant had begun his career chasing gangsters in 1937. The major in charge of the Traffic Division was an old China Marine, had been captured in the Philippines in 1942, survived the Bataan Death March and three years in a Japanese POW camp. Many others could have produced an impressive display of Combat Infantryman Badges, Bronze Stars, Silver Stars and Purple Hearts from World War II and the Korean War. Believe me, the major who thought I had a "ho-hum attitude" was mistaken.

If he survived all these challenges and was hired, the department issued the new officer a silver-colored badge, a commission card with his photo and thumbprint, and two black plastic nametags. A Recruiting officer then escorted him to J.B. Battles, a local uniform supply store, and he was immediately issued three complete police uniforms compatible with the season; gray poplin shirts (long or short sleeved), dark blue trousers, a dark blue clip-on tie for wear with the long sleeved winter shirts, a dark blue "Ike" jacket for dress wear, a black foul weather jacket with fur collar for winter wear, a whistle and chain, a black plastic 18-inch baton (or night stick), one pair of handcuffs and key, and a blue steel Smith & Wesson Model 15 Combat Masterpiece .38 Special revolver with a four-inch barrel. The City paid the tab. Mine came to $186 and change. The Recruiting officer made sure I knew I was getting a good deal. Besides the City's initial $186 investment in my future, the department had only recently begun issuing service revolvers to new officers. Up until a few months before, new officers had to buy their own guns.

The rookie had a little choice in most of the items but some were dictated by tradition. He didn't have to worry about the correct placement of gold service stripes (denoting one year of service) or stars (denoting five years of service) on the left sleeve of his Ike jacket yet. Issued both a soft white uniform cap and a black and white fiberglass helmet, he could wear either in any uniformed assignment but tradition held that the white cap was usually worn by traffic officers and accident investigators while the helmet was usually favored by patrol officers. Black calf-high Wellington boots were usually preferred for street assignments over the shiny new Corfam shoes. They provided more ankle support for running and, occasionally, kicking. The knee-high Wellington boots were reserved for motorcycle officers as were the jodhpur-style pants. The thin yellow stripe down the legs of the pants of years past was gone. Patrol officers' pants were plain. Traffic officers wore a two-inch light blue stripe and supervisors (sergeants and higher) had a one-half inch black "command braid" sewn down the outer seam. The old Sam Browne belt was retained but without the diagonal shoulder strap. The strap had been deleted for the same reason the ties were clip-on's now, so an opponent had two fewer things to grab and jerk an officer around by. The black leather belt, holster, twelve-round loop loader and handcuff strap completed the ensemble and usually indicated the relative seniority of the wearer. The "old hands" generally preferred a dull black basket-weave pattern while the newer guys were getting the shiny Corfam type.

Two more items were available that most officers opted for. One was a "sap" or "slapper". It was a flat, black leather, flexible truncheon about ten inches long with a strap on the handle and loaded with several ounces of lead on the other end. It slipped easily into a hip pocket and was flexible enough to stay there during an eight-hour shift of getting in and out of the car repeatedly. It was just as effective as the baton but less obvious and troublesome.

The other item was a flashlight called a Kel-Lite. A more thorough description of this item will follow later.

Thus equipped, the new rookie was ready to go to work. Unless his hiring was one of the few that coincided precisely with the beginning of a new Recruit School (as the Police Academy was then known), he was "placed on rotation." He reported to work at once, usually on a night shift, and began rotating through different areas of the department on a weekly basis. Depending upon how much time he had before the next Recruit School started, this rotation might include a week each in Records, the Jail, Traffic Division, Detective Division (covering several units in the week) and ending in Patrol. When he arrived in the Patrol Division, he stayed there until the next Recruit School began. During this time, he was assigned to ride with a senior partner, "senior" usually meaning he had completed recruit training and had over one year on the force. This was before the Master Patrolman rank was created and before there were formally trained FTO's (Field Training Officers).

The city was divided into five sectors for police purposes; four quadrants (northwest, northeast, southwest, southeast) and the downtown sector, each with their own distinctive character.

The downtown area was the central business district, skyscrapers bustling with professional activity during the day but nightly changing into a neon jungle of sleazy bars, flophouse hotels, pool halls and dark alleys populated mainly with pimps, prostitutes, and skid row drunks.

Southeast was mostly industrial businesses, oil fields, trailer parks and lower income residential housing. Northwest and southwest were mostly residential, ranging from impoverished lower income areas known as the Flats, Mulligan Flats and Sandtown along the banks of the North Canadian River that bisected the city from west to east, to high-priced suburbs the farther you got away from the center of the city. The northwest quadrant was the most upscale and wealthy at that time although in later years the southwest quadrant would give it more competition in that regard. Northeast was the primarily black area of town, a hangover from a previously segregated southern city. It followed the same general characteristics of the other quadrants, sleazy near the central city and getting nicer as you went further out. Among the cops, the near northeast quadrant was known simply as "the eastside".

Until the mid-1960s, all police cars in the city had been one-man cars. Increasing racial tensions and violence in that decade had resulted in one officer being killed and several being shot riding one-man cars on the eastside. Thereafter, all eastside cars were two-man cars on all shifts except under unusual circumstances. Therefore, most new officers began riding in a sector other than the northeast sector. Like everything else, that was a preference and not a rule, subject to changing circumstances.

Since Recruit School was ten weeks long (eight weeks of classes and two weeks on the firearms range), most officers of that period had from one to six months patrol experience before they ever received any formal training. The OCPD was still a decade away from decentralizing into suburban briefing stations and all officers worked out of the third floor lineup room in central headquarters.

The rectangular room was starkly businesslike. A wood podium stood on a raised platform at the front of the room, a full length mirror was on one door for officers to prepare their uniforms for inspection, a couple of tables along one wall held the latest radiograms for wanted persons and "hot sheets" of recently stolen cars, wanted posters for the FBI's Ten Most Wanted Fugitives were on the back wall and the rest of the wall space held historic photos of the OCPD. Fittingly, the color scheme of the room was black and white. The floor was tiled in white linoleum tiles with three lines of single black tiles running the length of the room. These were the lines upon which officers stood during their lineups, toes lined up along the front of the black tiles in a sort of informal parade rest position. When the new officer reported to his first lineup, he was quickly informed that rookies stood on the front row and the back rows were reserved for veterans.

The new officer would already feel pretty special just by having survived the selection process up to this point but it would be quickly pointed out to him that he still had a lot to prove. This was done silently by treating him like a lower form of life. There were no backslaps, handshakes or "welcome to the shift" greetings. He was an unknown quantity and was treated like he was a civilian in uniform which is essentially what he was at that point. They all knew and he was

The Temper Of The Times   15

to learn that he hadn't yet passed the *real* selection process. The one that took place on the streets.

Although he would be introduced to the shift by the lieutenant in command, the only people he could expect to speak to him were his sergeant (to introduce his partner) and the partner. Most of the senior partners introduced themselves with a short speech that went something like "Keep your eyes open, mouth shut, stay right behind me no matter what, don't touch the shotgun or the radio and no, you can't drive."

For those first few weeks or months, there was no formal training, grading, testing or evaluations. As in years past, "street school" preceded Recruit School. The only evaluation came just before he was scheduled to attend the next Recruit School and was equally informal. It was usually a series of questions from his sergeant to the senior partner along the order of "Is he worth keeping?", "Has he got any sense?", "Do you trust him?", or "Will he fight?" (i.e., "Is he a coward?"). Sometimes those questions were asked in front of the rookie with both the sergeant and the senior partner acting like he was invisible.

A negative answer to those questions wouldn't keep the rookie out of the next school but, if he graduated, he was probably not destined for the Patrol Division. One Patrol captain's son was going through the rotation and when the captain asked his partner about his progress, the partner honestly told him "Get the boy off the streets before he gets hurt or hurts someone else." The "boy" spent most of his career in the Records Bureau and the Training Division, retiring as a captain like his father but much less respected. Another veteran officer, frustrated beyond words with his rookie on one graveyard shift, took him out to a rural lake in far southeast Oklahoma City, made him get out of the car and left him there. Calling his sergeant to meet him when he got back to the inner city, he told the supervisor "Your rookie's out at Point 19 on Lake Draper. If you want him, go get him but don't put him in my car again." Near the end of his Recruit School, unable to qualify with his pistol and facing termination, that young man transferred to the Fire Department.

To be certain you understand the dynamic at work here, patrolmen didn't dictate to sergeants and captains very often. But a respected, active officer with the seniority and experience to rate his own district had quite a bit of say about who rode in the car with him especially when the issue was officer or citizen safety and a supervisor ignored his warnings at his own peril.

Those informal verbal evaluations also decided whether the sergeant would recommend to his shift lieutenant if they should request the officer be reassigned to their shift when he got out of school or just let him be assigned by "the luck of the draw."

Either way those questions were answered, that allowed the rookie to begin eight weeks of training in the third floor classroom where the Chief's reception area is now located. Most police academies including the OCPD have long since adopted a special uniform for recruits, consisting of coveralls or something to distinguish them from regular officers. At that time however, OCPD recruits wore exactly the same uniform as every other officer and that was the uniform they wore to class every day including handcuffs and a loaded sidearm.

The OCPD also provided training for other agencies and most recruit schools included several officers who were Airport Police, Lake Rangers or military police. A rigorous uniform inspection every day was followed by college-level classes on English grammar and spelling, police report writing, city geography, criminal ordinances and state statutes, medical and first aid procedures, patrol and specialized call procedures, criminal prosecution procedures, criminal investigations, familiarization with other law enforcement agencies and their responsibilities, the mechanics of arrest and dozens of other specialized subjects. Weekly and sometimes daily tests were given and any grade below 75 per cent was failing.

Successful completion of the academic phase allowed the new recruit to move on to two weeks at the Police Firearms Range, then located west of the Lake Hefner Water Treatment Plant at Hefner Road and Portland. In that time he would fire thousands of rounds of .38 caliber ammunition through his revolver (no automatics were allowed then) along with rifled slugs and double-ought buckshot from Ithaca 12-gauge pump shotguns until even the youngest, most muscular shoulders turned black and blue. Distances ranged from fifty yards to seven yards. He would be trained to fire accurately with both hands in case the strong hand was wounded or disabled. He would be trained to shoot aimed fire at eye level and un-aimed, instinctive fire from waist level. He would learn to fire 12 rounds in 25 seconds, firing six, reloading (one round at a time, no speed loaders) and then firing those six. It's a lot more challenging than it sounds. He would shoot in daylight, low light and near total darkness conditions in whatever weather conditions prevailed. This wasn't a baseball game. It wasn't called off because it wasn't clear and sunny. You shot in rain, snow, sleet, hail, fog and anything else that presented itself including the infamous Oklahoma winds. They also might run you around for a while just to make sure you're gasping for air while you're trying to aim.

Winter classes, as mine was, made it even more interesting. If you think it isn't a challenge to try to hit a target area smaller than a dinner plate from fifty yards with a revolver when the temperature is below freezing and half-dollar sized snowflakes are blowing horizontally in front of you in a thirty-mile-per-hour wind, try it sometime. To give you some added incentive, if you don't hit it at least 70 per cent of the time, you lose your job.

Passing the firearms phase meant graduation and a return to patrol unless you volunteered for traffic, motorcycles, the crime lab or another specialty. This was rarely allowed in those days and most rookies started in patrol.

While graduating from Recruit School endowed the rookie with no small sense of accomplishment, little did we realize that was only the beginning of a winnowing process that would continue for years and become even more Darwinian. Of the 25 OCPD officers who graduated in my class, only 12 would complete careers of 20 years or longer.

At that time, Oklahoma City was the largest city in the United States in land area, some 600 square miles depending upon what the city fathers were annexing or de-annexing at any given time. The city had a population of a little over 368,000 that spilled over into five counties and the metropolitan area population reached nearly three-quarters of a million. In the next decade, the city population would go over 400,000 and the metro area would exceed 860,000. By the end of my career, the city would exceed half a million and the metro area over a million.

In addition to the permanent resident population, Oklahoma City is the crossroads of three major interstate highways that bisect the nation in three directions. I-35 and I-40 intersect just east of the downtown area while I-44 bisects the city from southwest to northeast. Many of the transient travelers on those arteries stop in our city to avail themselves of our tourist attractions, hotels, motels, restaurants, prostitutes, narcotics and all the other amenities of any large city.

On the day I was hired, my Internal Security detective told me I was the 478th active duty officer. Seven and one-half years later that detective, Ted Gregory, would be my first lieutenant in the Homicide Unit.

We were given organizational charts in Recruit School that indicated there were 211 Patrolmen but that was based on a departmental strength of 347. They had been hiring a lot lately so, if Ted Gregory was right, there were probably about 290 patrolmen then.

When I retired thirty years later, the department had grown to nearly 1,100 officers and over 300 civilians operating out of sixteen satellite facilities.

Regardless of the actual body count, patrolman was a rank, not an assignment. Some of them were assigned to the jail, Training, Traffic and Headquarters Divisions. The remainder that staffed the Patrol Division was divided among four shifts to cover the city around the clock, seven days a week, 365 days a year. In addition to its complement of patrolmen, each shift had five sergeants in charge of the individual sectors and was commanded by a lieutenant. The three regular shifts rotated counterclockwise monthly: that is, one month on days, one month on graveyard, one month on swing and then back to days. Day shift worked from 7:00 A.M. to 3 P.M. for the odd-numbered cars and 7:30 A.M. to 3:30 P.M. for the even numbered cars. Swing shift worked from 3/3:30 P.M. to 11/11:30 P.M. and graveyard from 11/11:30 P.M. to 7/7:30 A.M. The staggered half-hour between odd and even numbered cars kept half the manpower on the streets at all times, at least that was the theory. The three regular shifts were supplemented by one permanent shift, originally called the "Four Shift" because the radio prefix code One designated days, Two was swing and Three was graveyard. Later One, Two and Three Shifts were re-designated Adam, Baker and Charlie respectively, and the Four Shift became "Delta" shift. This shift worked from 6 P.M. to 2 A.M. and was intended to add manpower during the busy night time hours when more critical calls came out. Officers who volunteered for the Four or Delta shift were usually going to college during the days.

Everyone on the patrol shifts got nine days off a month regardless of rank and also regardless of whether the month had 28, 29, 30 or 31 days. There were three sets of days off. On graveyard shift, you got all nine days off in a row but on days and swing, everyone had two separate blocks of days off, one block four days long and one block five days long. If you had the middle set of days off, you also got blocks of four and five but you were always working the first week and the last week of every month. So on the last day of the month, when you got off duty you had to be back eight hours later because the shift had rotated. Not surprisingly, most rookies got the middle set.

In 1969, the city was divided into 27 patrol districts; seven northwest, six northeast, five downtown, five southwest and four southeast. The six northeast cars were two-man units (when possible) and the other 21 were usually one-man. So it took a minimum of 33 patrolmen, five sergeants and one lieutenant to fully man a shift, a standard that was only achieved for a few days in the middle of each month if no one called in sick, took a vacation day or was put on a special assignment like guarding a prisoner at a hospital. Very rarely was there a car in every district. During the peak crime hours when the Four Shift was on duty between 6 P.M. and 2 A.M., they might field another dozen officers. Therefore, even on the rare occasions when a full shift presented itself and the Four Shift was working, the Patrol Division had fewer than 50 cops on the street.

The entire PD operated on one radio frequency. A second frequency was available for semi-private conversations and records checks but all police calls were dispatched on the primary frequency so everybody could hear what everybody else was doing and saying.

Times were different and so were the laws. A lot more was dictated by the individual officer's discretion and judgment than by written policy. Shooting at fleeing felons was legal whether they were armed or not and whether they were presenting an immediate danger to someone or not but it was against department policy to fire warning shots. Go figure. The rumor was that this reasoning was because one of our commanders had heard that sometime in the distant past a New York City cop had fired a warning shot in the air and the bullet ricocheted off a fire escape above him and killed an innocent citizen.

Vagrancy laws were still on the books but weren't applied to keep the bums off the streets like they were in some cities during the Depression. They were usually applied to traveling criminals when the phrase "no visible means of support" meant if the means were visible, it would be illegal. Pimps, hookers, gamblers, bootleggers and professional thieves don't usually have a business address. There was also a charge for "Loitering On The Streets After Midnight." When you ran across someone who was acting suspiciously with more money in his pockets than he had any legitimate excuse for having (and thus obviously enough to bond himself out immediately on something as insignificant as a vagrancy charge), he could be arrested for "Investigation and Hold" to give the detectives 72 hours to see what he had been up to locally or if he was wanted somewhere else.

No doubt many of the professional and amateur legal scholars out there will be slobbering at the mouth to point out why these laws no longer exist. Like any other power, they could be and occasionally were abused but, in my experience and observation, they were usually applied with discretion and justification. Whether the legal scholars like it or not, the existence and application of these laws solved a lot of crimes and prevented untold others.

Tremendous authority and discretion were placed in the street officer, much more so than today. Many street officers today are trained to call their supervisors at the slightest hint of some kind of weighty decision coming to the fore. Some of them merely take refuge in that option for virtually any decision that isn't covered by their increasingly voluminous policy and procedure manuals. So the officer calls the sergeant who calls the lieutenant who sometimes calls the captain. Then they have a little conclave, policy books in hand, and try to figure out what the hell to do and then, most important of all, who's going to be responsible for this decision. As I've always said, in three decades of doing that job, I've been hurt and I've been scared but it was never by an ass-chewing or a piece of paper. But that was an attitude fostered by our commanders at the time.

There are many factors accounting for these differences. The draft was still in effect then and most healthy young men in those days came to the police department with at least some military experience. Even the reservists and National Guardsmen had at least six months of active duty which included basic training and advanced infantry training. And there will never be a Police Academy that can compete with military training when it comes to making men out of boys. But this isn't about sociology so I see no point in discussing most of these factors here.

Several decades ago, sergeants were the first line supervisors and you called him for very few things; to authorize placing a felony charge on someone, to notify him you'd been hurt or hurt someone in a fight, to notify him you'd been involved in a shooting or damaged your police car. Beyond that, it better be something pretty special. On a first offense of asking your sergeant to make a decision you should have made yourself or asking him a question you should have known the answer to, he might just look at you a little funny. On the second offense, he might ask you if you're working too many extra jobs. The third time he's liable to ask you if you were sure you wouldn't be more comfortable making decisions in Training, Records or Planning and Research. And if you called the lieutenant (shift commander) for anything, it better be because the sergeant is on a day off, busy or dead.

The prevailing theory was that the patrol shift lieutenant on duty at any given moment was the Chief of Police as far as police operations went, the sergeants were the Chiefs in their sectors and each officer was Chief in his district. That kind of authority and power were passed all the way down in that manner but so was the responsibility and accountability. So if you chose to exercise it, you better be right, at least a hell of a lot more often than you were wrong. Your judgment was under scrutiny and question with every arrest, every report, every radio transmission, every call you handled. And those passing judgment on you were the harshest critics available—not the brass, not the media, not the citizens but your peers.

Another difference is you were expected to work. It was even called by that name. Police *work*. At its simplest, there were two kinds of cops—those that *rode* the streets and those that *worked* the streets. For those who *worked* the streets, the philosophy was simple—develop your instincts, check the cars that don't seem to belong in your district, check out the occupants, check your buildings for burglaries when they're closed, check your banks, convenience and liquor stores for armed robbers and take no crap from anyone, anytime. Now proponents call it pro-active policing and opponents call it profiling and/or police harassment. We called it common sense and doing our job.

You were expected to do more than just drive around "showing the flag." You were expected to do what you got paid for without being able to take refuge behind this Federal Act or that arbitration ruling. Not that everyone worked like sled dogs or there weren't slugs and shirkers but even they were expected to do *something*. And what cops did was quantified. You took radio calls, made written reports, wrote traffic tickets and made misdemeanor or felony arrests. Those were about the only excuses for your existence. Everyone was expected to do some or all of them every day. The supervisors usually allowed you the latitude of specializing if you brought in enough of your chosen activity to make the statistics look good. Some guys liked to write tickets but hated to arrest drunks. Some guys hated writing tickets but loved chasing felons. At a bare minimum, you were expected to take all radio calls in your district unless you were tied up on something else. If you missed a couple of calls in your district and you weren't doing anything, just didn't answer the radio or had your head up your butt, you'd hear about it before the end of the shift. If it became a habit, somebody from a neighboring district would probably end up knocking you on your ass one day after work.

That went along with the previously mentioned rivers of testosterone. Fist fights between officers and even partners were not that unusual an occurrence and they were never referred to Internal Affairs for resolution. It might be a difference of opinion about work or women or football or just a personality clash. Most happened after the shift ended in a wrecker yard that used to be across the street from the station but more than one occurred in the gas line while they were fueling their cars at the start of a shift and even in the halls or elevators of the station. A couple even escalated to two guys faced off like Old West gunfighters on the proverbial dusty street with their hands poised over their gun butts. Those usually never got to the point of drawn guns but there were rare episodes when one eccentric officer shot another one, usually his partner, perhaps accidentally, perhaps not. It was usually just a leg wound, intended to convince the partner he was very serious about whatever dispute they were having. Just like hitting the jackass between the eyes with a two-by-four, it takes more to get some people's attention than others.

The last bastion of the free love generation was ensconced in the Paseo area in the near northwest sector. Years later it evolved into a Taos-like bohemian arts and crafts enclave but in the late 1960s-early 1970s, it was Oklahoma City's version of San Francisco's Haight-Ashbury district. Smoking marijuana, speed-balling heroin and cocaine, snorting crystal meth and dropping LSD (*real* acid, not the phony crap that showed up later) made them try to fly off the building tops and fight the cops when they couldn't outrun them. By their calculation, anti-establishment equaled anti-Vietnam War equaled anti-police.

Like the rest of the country, Oklahoma City was suffering much racial unrest and violence in the same period. A substantial force of very militant Black Muslims operated out of a local Mosque and was occasionally augmented by visiting segments of the Black Panther Party which advocated the murder of police officers and had done so in New York, San Francisco and other cities. Several attempted snipings of officers were unsuccessful only due to bad marksmanship. Incidents where scout cars and officers were pelted with bricks, rocks and bottles became a constant threat in the primarily black northeast sector and certain housing projects in other sectors. Assigning backup units became automatic on all calls, no matter how innocuous. Sometimes the backup unit was necessary if only to guard the vacated scout car while the officers were away from it to prevent it from being stolen, vandalized, having the shotgun stolen out of it or, worse, used against the officers when they came out of the call. Fire trucks and firemen were shot at without injury on several occasions and there were several housing projects that the Fire Department would not enter to fight fires without waiting for a police escort.

Much of this racial strife and hatred was visited upon the most visible arm of the establishment, the police. They were treated like an occupying power by some (but not all) and black officers in particular were treated like traitors by those elements of their ultra-clannish society.

The dangers and violence were not limited to the black community. With the largest population of American Indians in the country, Oklahoma was ripe ground for the militant American Indian Movement (AIM), founded in 1968. After all, Oklahoma began as Indian Territory, was the destination of the Trail of Tears and its first large population influx had been as a *de facto* concentration camp for Indian tribes displaced by white expansion. A famous photograph from the 1973 siege of Wounded Knee, South Dakota, showed an Indian defiantly holding an AK-47 machine gun aloft. A few years later, several AIM members were arrested near downtown Oklahoma City and one of them had an AK-47. A rumor circulated that when the serial number was checked, it proved to be the same one shown in the famous photo. Maybe that's true, maybe not. But they were definitely AIM members, it was definitely an AK-47 and it was definitely loaded.

In fact, the 1970s would become and remains today the most deadly decade for American law enforcement. Nationwide, at least 2,215 officers would die in the line of duty during that period, 271 in 1974 alone, besting all previous records set in the Prohibition and gangster-battling days of the 1920s and '30s. Non-fatal assaults on officers also increased proportionately. The OCPD Homicide Unit tallied 353 incidents in which officers fired their weapons in the line of duty during that decade and the list is almost certainly incomplete.

Don't misinterpret those statistics. They include accidental discharges, warning shots (now permitted under restricted circumstances) and officer suicides among other types of incidents including missing the target. Nearly ninety per cent of those incidents resulted in no one being injured. No matter how good a marksman you are on the range, things change dramatically when the target isn't made out of paper or is shooting back. The cops weren't gunning people down without justification nor did every cop earn a Purple Heart but it is a representation of how urban America met the Wild West. The ordinary citizen suffered as well. Every category of violent crime (murder, forcible rape, robbery and aggravated assault) more than doubled from the previous decade.

All these facts taken together, the fact that we were fielding perhaps 50 cops per shift to cover the whole city and these numbers compared to the population figures gave rise to a "one riot, one ranger" mentality and a general feeling that Custer had pretty good odds after all. It was a tough town and a tough crowd, with and without badges. But it sure made it interesting.

For those of you who are cops, have been cops, have dated cops, married cops or have otherwise already been familiarized and demystified with the law enforcement community, you are now ready to proceed flipping the pages. However those of you who are approaching this book from a civilian perspective without having had that preparation might need to take a little extra leap of faith if you want to have a more complete understanding of what you are about to read.

So imagine you take a new job. A job with low pay, good training, excellent job security, lousy hours, a high sense of adventure and visibility, a low quotient of boredom and a *lot* of responsibility. They give you a uniform, a badge, a gun and a black and white car, all of which instantly gains you a lot of new enemies and very few friends. Your new bosses circle an area on a map and tell you that is your district—you and your partner or sometimes you alone. It's a few square miles with a few thousand people living there, a few thousand more working there and a few thousand others passing through every day. The bosses tell you your job is to try to take care of those people, try to protect them, try to keep them from getting assaulted, maimed, run over, raped, robbed, murdered, burglarized, defrauded, burned alive or any of countless other horrifying or illegal things that can happen to them any hour of the day or night. They know you can't do it because they themselves have tried as previous generations tried. It's like trying to empty the ocean with a teacup. No one can do it. It can't be done. They don't tell you that. They tell you "Try." And when those bad things inevitably happen, try to catch the people who did them and follow all the rules of law so they can't do it again. So you try.

Now you are in the right frame of mind to read on.

Patrol I

BE CAREFUL WHO YOU PICK ON

Back in the days when there was one and only one police station in a city, Station Captain was not a rank but more of a traditional position. The idea was that when a citizen came to the police station outside of regular hours (nights, weekends and holidays), the first person they met should be a senior officer with the experience to quickly evaluate their problem or complaint, know how to handle it properly and have the authority to get it done. There was no test, textbook or training manual for this position. Only decades of experience would do. The position was being gradually phased out during the late 1960s. But not yet.

Old Bill Marcum was the Station Captain that night. His job was to sit behind the Information Desk just inside the front door of Headquarters to answer or direct all walk-in citizen complaints and inquiries between the hours of 11:00 P.M. and 7:00 A.M. Since lieutenants were in charge of the patrol shifts, the Station Captain on graveyard shift was effectively the Chief of Police during those hours and answered to no higher authority. Since Chiefs, Assistant Chiefs and Majors don't like being unnecessarily woken up between those hours, the job required a man of experience, ability, judgment and decisiveness.

It was a good thing that Old Bill possessed all those qualities in abundance since the Chiefs and Majors thought he was far too dangerous to allow out on the streets. Tall and thin but with a voice like a tugboat foghorn, he had been a cop for nearly three and one-half decades. When Old Bill first began wearing that uniform, cops and gangsters were routinely blazing away at each other with Thompson submachine guns and police radios were a new gadget on which they could receive transmissions but not reply. Although the cars had radios, they didn't have luxury items like heaters. The officers heated bricks on the pot-bellied stove in a turn-of-the-century station and wrapped them in blankets on the floor of the scout car to keep their feet from freezing on long winter nights on patrol. Old Bill was one of the last of that breed still on active duty. He gave the impression of being the kind of man who struck the matches to light his cigarettes on the stubble of his jaw without blinking.

The night patrol shift usually assigned one of the newer officers to the Information Desk on a rotating basis to handle the modern paperwork. Old Bill's strong suit wasn't paperwork; it was using his head, thinking on his feet, sometimes mediating disputes, sometimes dispensing justice that wasn't available during the day. So the old Captain and the young officer complemented one another. Together they could handle anything that walked in the door for those eight hours, just as it was intended.

It had been pretty quiet for a Saturday night, now Sunday morning. A purse snatching victim had required calling in the night Robbery team to take a report. A few Saturday night drunks who had sobered up bonded out and came in to get their cars out of impoundment. Two burglary victims who had been called in by detectives came by to pick up their stolen property out of the Property Room. A few phone calls that Bill had handled with a series of grunts and growls. The young officer thought the rest of the shift would be spent dozing since it was almost 4:00 A.M. now but Old Bill was still patiently writing in the big ledger book about the night's incidents. The kid had tried starting a conversation a few times but it didn't work out. He wasn't unfriendly; it was just that Old Bill didn't waste a lot of words.

The large plate glass windows in the lobby rattled from the clattering engines of the two trashy old VW vans that pulled up in front of the station. The vacant silence of the downtown area at this hour only accentuated the noise. The streetlights threw shadows across a dozen figures that got out of the vans and started up the too-wide concrete front steps. The long hair and ponytails hanging beneath the bandanas on their heads was easily discernible in silhouette. Old Bill's head didn't rise from the ledger but the eyes cut upwards for half a blink. The young officer heard a metallic pop and looked sideways just in time to see Old Bill's hand return to writing on the ledger sheet. Below the level of the desk, the officer noticed that the retaining strap on Old Bill's holster was unsnapped now.

The younger officer followed Old Bill's example when he saw who was coming in the revolving door. An even dozen Hangmen, outlaw bikers wearing their colors; greasy, faded, frayed blue jean jackets with the sleeves cut out, an arc across the back embroidered with the name of their "club" on it above a hangman's noose. The various patches sewn on the jackets were of marijuana leaves, Nazi swastikas, the number "13", Harley Davidson emblems and winged wheels of various colors. Red, brown, black, purple. The young officer was trying to remember from his Police Academy lectures which sexual acts the colors of the wings represented when the group's leader stepped up to the desk. The officer noted that this one had four sets of wings, one of each color.

Old Bill looked down at him from the elevated platform. The man had a prominent black eye and dried blood was crusted in his shaggy beard. Silently surveying the group, he saw a variety of other damage. An arm in a sling, several pronounced limps, two bandaged heads, two hands in plaster casts, several more black eyes, swollen lips and a variety of cuts, bruises and abrasions. Like most people, the bikers were somewhat startled by the deep voice that rumbled out of the skinny neck.

"You boys have an accident?"

"We want to report a crime," the leader said.

"What kind of crime?"

"Assault and battery, destroying property and assault with weapons."

"Y'all the victims?"

"Yeah, all of us."

"I need your names and addresses. Probably be easier if you all just passed your driver's licenses up here."

That caused some hesitation in the group. They hadn't thought about that. After some uneasy glances among themselves, they all slowly put their ID's on the elevated desktop. Old Bill started copying the information in the ledger. "When did this happen?"

"Six, seven hours ago. About 9:00."

"Where?"

"West side of the lake."

"Which lake?"

"Overholser. Just off Highway 66."

Old Bill stopped writing and leaned back in his chair. "What happened?"

"We was just riding our bikes around the lake when these guys jumped us," the leader said.

"Yeah, no reason either," another one chimed in from the rear of the pack.

"Uh huh." Old Bill couldn't keep the skepticism out of his bass. "How many of them were there?"

"At least 20, maybe 30," the leader said.

"You know them?"

"No, all strangers. We was just minding our own business, ridin' around th' lake—"

"Descriptions? White, black, Indian?"

"All white, wasn't they?" the leader looked over his shoulder for support from his fellows.

"At least one of 'em was a nigger," mumbled an anonymous voice from the rear.

"Okay," the leader said. "I didn't see him but I seen the others. All white, about six feet, 180, 200 pounds, short hair, no beards, jeans and t-shirts."

"'Cept fur the ones in their skivvies," said another anonymous voice.

"Yeah, I guess some of 'em had been in swimmin'," the leader explained.

"So these guys just jumped you fellows for no reason while you were peacefully riding your bikes around the lake, huh?" Old Bill wasn't even trying to hide the sarcasm now.

"That's right, and they had guns, too."

"Anybody shot?" Bill scanned the group, addressing the question to all of them.

"No, but they had 'em. We all seen 'em."

"What kind of guns."

"How the hell should we know, it was dark."

Old Bill sighed like he was talking to a retarded child. "Rifles, shotguns,—?"

"Pistols, revolvers, black snubnoses."

Old Bill started riffing through a stack of impoundment sheets on his clipboard. Looking down at a report of a car impounded from a wreck a week earlier, he looked back up at the leader, fixing him with a baleful, unblinking eye.

"We might have something here that can shed some more light on this situation. We might have a witness to your case."

"A witness?" The leader's voice was doubtful but uncertain. "There wasn't nobody else out there 'cept us and them."

"Maybe not but this fella phoned in a report. Said him and his girl was parked under the 39th Street bridge playing slap and tickle. They saw what looked like a group of college guys over by the lake having a wienie roast, swimming, having a few beers and basically minding their own business when another bunch of guys with long hair started riding their motorcycles through the campsite, kicking things over and throwing up dirt over everybody. He said the college guys pulled the bikers off their motorcycles, kicked their asses and ran them off. Then they finished having their party and left. No car descriptions or tag numbers, he was too far off. That sound like your case?"

The leader's face was redder than the wings on his jacket but he was as silent as the rest of the group. Old Bill looked from one sullen face to the other, scanning the whole group before he spoke again. He looked over their heads at the two vans in front of the station.

"Where's your bikes?"

The pregnant silence continued for several long seconds before a dejected, sheepish voice came from the rear again. "They ran 'em in the lake."

The leader whirled angrily on his heel. "Shuddup! Let's go!" He reached up to the desk and gathered up the driver's licenses before stalking out through the revolving door with the rest on his heels. As the rickety old air-cooled engines sputtered to life outside, Old Bill went back to making notes in the ledger. The young officer looked sideways at him.

"Captain?"

Old Bill didn't look up, just kept scribbling. "Yeah?"

"You know about 20 guys graduated from the Academy Friday?"

"Good. We can use 'em."

"One of them was black."

"So?"

"I heard they were going to have their graduation party out at Lake Overholser last night."

"That so?" The only sound in the quiet lobby was the scratching of the pen on the thick ledger pages.

FIRST NIGHT

My first night in a patrol car was with Bob, a couple of years younger than me but a crusty old veteran of one year who had joined the department soon after returning from Vietnam. His uniform was immaculate and he gave every appearance of being the recruiting poster cop. We were riding Bob's district, Car 17, on a graveyard shift from 11 PM until 7 AM. This was in what was called Packing Town, named after the area of meat packing plants and stockyards that once rivaled Chicago and Kansas City in supplying beef to the nation.

He gave me a short version of "the speech" and we headed for our district, Bob driving, naturally. At that time of night, the only businesses open in that district were a few bars and a restaurant. Traffic was almost non-existent.

As we drove by the restaurant, Bob hit the brakes and stopped in front of the restaurant. He got his ticket book, slipped his Kel-Lite through the handcuffs on his belt and got out. Putting one foot on the rear bumper of a 1964 Chevy that looked legally parked to me, he began writing a traffic ticket.

In less than a minute, a man came out of the restaurant and approached us hesitantly. He was tall, skinny and had the furtive looks of a human weasel.

"What ya doin'?"

"Writing you a ticket, Frankie."

"For what? I'm parked, fer Chris'sakes!"

Bob took the Kel-Lite out of his handcuffs and methodically smashed every one of the car's six taillights. He then went back to finish writing the ticket, speaking aside to Frankie.

"No taillights."

Frankie started moving his lips like a guppy gasping for air but no sound came out. Bob turned and stood in front of him at arm's length. Speaking over his shoulder, he spoke to me.

"Frankie's a burglar. He's got no other job and no other skills. That's all he does, steal things from other people. Like most burglars, he only works at night."

Bob then started speaking to Frankie.

"The last time I saw you, Frankie, I told you to stay out of 17 at night, didn't I?"

Frankie, pouting and sullen, just stared and refused to speak. Bob handed him the ticket book and Frankie signed the ticket. I didn't need to be told that Frankie knew the boundaries of Car 17 as well as Bob did.

Frankie got in his car and drove off as soon as we did. I later checked his record. Bob, of course, was right. Frankie had dozens of arrests, most for burglary and its variations, breaking and entering, possession of stolen property and possession of burglary tools, more than a few of them by Bob. When he wasn't stealing, he was taking dope and had several prison terms for all of the above. Maybe breaking his taillights and writing the ticket were violations of Frankie's civil rights. Maybe it was a relatively minor penalty for ignoring Bob's warning. But there were no burglaries reported in Car 17's district that night.

EDUCATING THE EDUCATED

When I first joined the police department in the late 1960s, rookies were naturally not allowed to have their own district. The solace of knowing what district you would be patrolling, what car you would be driving and what your call sign would be was only allowed the veterans. Thus, all rookies "rode relief"; that is, he rode whatever district was empty due to sick leave or vacation or, if it was a full shift, he was doubled up with a senior man.

Having started my patrol duties on graveyard shift, I had already begun my re-education. For instance, having lived in this city for over two decades, I thought I knew the downtown area pretty well. These were the years when the downtown area was *the* business district, before people, entertainment complexes, theaters, shopping malls and businesses fled *en masse* to suburbia.

The downtown of my childhood was a maze of one-way streets that didn't always make sense to natives and must have been truly chaotic for visitors. The daytime streets were plied by street cars and diesel-belching buses, lined with historic old buildings and skyscrapers, and the broad sidewalks were crowded with men in business suits and women in fashionable dresses hurrying about their lives. In the early evenings, the streets were brightly lit by shop windows with elaborately dressed mannequins and the marquees of ornate old movie theaters doing a thriving business when televisions were a luxury.

Now however, the streets of downtown viewed from a patrol car on graveyard shift were very different. The buildings, streets and lighting were basically the same but the majority of moving vehicles were patrol cars, pimp-mobiles and lost tourists. The dark alleys, some cobbled with bricks half a century old, now smelled of urine, feces, vomit, cheap wine, sometimes blood and were primarily populated with rats. About the only businesses showing any activity were all-night restaurants, booze joints, pseudo-hotels/whorehouses that rented their seedy rooms by the hour and the all-night dry cleaners where all the cops got their uniforms cleaned.

After doubling back to swing shift at the first of the month, I would be introduced to the downtown of late afternoons.

A later Chief of Police was heavily into recruiting officers with college hours, degrees or aspirations toward achieving those ideals. He himself had several degrees and was aware he was presiding over a department with a few "fossils" with no college hours and, in some cases, not even a high school equivalency certificate. But, with years of seniority and exemplary records, they were "grandfathered" into his police department. Ironically, some of them had even helped to nurse him through his rookie years.

Many if not most of the newer officers looked down their noses at these less educated veterans because they said "I seen" instead of "I saw" and used words like "excape," "irregardless" and "lottering" (loitering). For a while, I was among them.

Then I had the privilege of riding a few shifts with one of these men. He was burdened with me because a new recruit class had just been dumped on the streets (including yours truly) so an extra-full shift created a two-man car out of one he had been riding alone since I was in grade school.

After I loaded my briefcase, night stick, ticket book and rain slicker (it was April) in the car, he started the shift with a kind but firm version of the "Keep your mouth shut, eyes open, etc. etc." speech. Working the evening swing shift, we left the station about mid-afternoon. We took a few calls and wrote a few tickets before the rush hour hit. I kept noticing him peering out of the top of the windshield. When I looked, I didn't see anything except some gathering clouds.

I noticed that, as rush hour approached, he kept drifting toward the southern boundary of our district, the boundary closest to the downtown area. Soon a single raindrop splattered against the windshield. Like a hunting dog that had heard a sound I couldn't, he immediately put the patrol car into a hard turn south and accelerated rapidly. I was, to use an expression I would later learn from him, "bumfuzzled." I hadn't heard anything urgent on the radio, I hadn't seen or heard anything to warrant his seemingly urgent response.

Resisting an incredibly strong impulse to ask what I somehow instinctively knew would be stupid questions, I just sat there and watched. The semi-high speed burst took us the two miles to downtown in less than three minutes. As he turned into the downtown skid row area, he slowed and began looking from side to side in the alleys as we passed. The raindrops were coming a little more frequently now but still didn't warrant turning on the wipers.

In less than five minutes, he hit the brakes, reversed the car and drove into an alley. He stopped the patrol car a few feet away from a drunk passed out in the alley. Before I could react, my partner was out of the door, fairly gently had the drunk up against the wall and was expertly patting him down for weapons. As I recovered from my astonishment and was getting out of the car to provide the illusion that I was covering him, my partner handcuffed the drunk and put him in the back seat. Off we went to jail, entering the booking area just as the raindrops became a shower.

I was now even more bumfuzzled. I had overheard some stories about my partner. Even thought he was an old fossil, he wasn't a ROAD (Retired On Active Duty) fossil. His reputation was that he wrote a few tickets when they happened right under his nose just to keep the sergeant happy but his specialty was burglars. He'd mosey all the way to a public drunk call, hoping the drunk would leave before he got there, but would burn the engine out of a brand new patrol car trying to be the first to a silent alarm. And he didn't need an alarm to find them, either. He almost seemed to be able to smell them. Several times a month you'd hear him call on the radio, saying he'd be out checking a building in his district. A few minutes later, he'd come back on the air, saying he was 10-15 (on the way to jail with a prisoner) and calling the sergeant for authorization for a burglary charge. He had a file full of commendations for catching them. Seeking out a lowly drunk arrest was rumored to be beneath his standards.

After waiting our turn at the booking desk and booking the drunk, we returned to the car about an hour later. He looked up at the clearing skies with a mysterious sense of gratification and we went back on patrol. After an uneventful hour, we got out for a meal break. That's when I finally got up the nerve to ask him what the hell had just happened that I had missed.

He silently studied me for a few seconds with shrewd but amused eyes over his coffee cup, then smirked paternally and gave me his reasoning, step by step, like I was a little slow. I'll paraphrase:

One, it's springtime in Oklahoma, well known for rain showers of little warning and brief duration. The low, thick, darkening clouds and the increase in humidity was probably evidence of one approaching. You don't need a degree in Meteorology to figure this out.

Two, when one of these spring showers erupts, the water mixes with the oil in the streets and makes them slick. It also reduces visibility and increases driver distraction, stopping distances and the ability to slide in creative patterns. But a lot of the good citizens will continue to drive like it's a fine spring day, exercising their inalienable rights to run at least ten miles an hour over the limit and right on the other guy's bumper. A large portion of the motoring public never seems to figure this out until they run into each other, literally.

Three, within minutes of the start of one of these showers, police calls start coming over the radio on traffic accidents. With the increasing tempo, all Traffic units are rapidly assigned and the accidents start getting assigned to Patrol units. That's us.

Four, now, which would you prefer (or, as he put it, "which'd ya druther?"):

A. Drive around until we get one of those calls and spend the next hour standing out in the rain, getting soaked to the skin in spite of the city-issue raincoat, measuring skidmarks, points of impact and taking measurements? Since it's raining, at least we probably won't have to break up a fight in the street between the drivers but you can never be sure. A man with a crunched Cadillac sometimes forgets the value of his suit. If we're lucky, it'll just be a two-car crash in an intersection with no injuries. If we're not so lucky, we could easily be dealing with multiple vehicles, perhaps on fire, serious injuries or, the worst, fatalities. The time, effort, complexity of the investigation and possibilities for court appearances multiply exponentially in those cases. Or—

B. Arrest the first drunk we can find (who won't bother pleading not guilty in court, will lay his fine out in the city drunk tank getting three hot meals a day where he won't have to sleep under a soggy cardboard box and gets out even faster if he wants to go to the trouble of becoming a trusty) and spend the next hour at the booking desk, warm and dry? By the time we get back out on the street, the shower will be over and all the wrecks will be assigned.

Five, there are several other ramifications of this situation to consider as well. You have to time the arrest just right so you have to know where to look. You also have to know what to look for. You don't usually grab the first drunk you see. You don't want a sick amateur who might puke in the back seat or get an urgent call of nature back there, leaving his aroma to remind you of him for days to come. After all, that car is your office. And you have to clean it, the drunk doesn't.

You also don't want an old professional who's jumping with body lice or is always on the verge of a bloody, liquid bowel movement that is usually beyond his control. Nor do you want one with tuberculosis, hepatitis A through Z or any number of other communicable problems you don't want to inherit or pass on to the family.

You also don't want one who's injured, bleeding or dying. If you happen upon one like that, you can't leave him but it means considerably more in time and paperwork than what you intended to invest initially. You also don't want one who wants to fight, thus forcing you to put him in the injured, bleeding or dying category. One that's too drunk to fight and too tired to run fits the bill just fine.

And this uneducated, antiquated old fossil, who had never even seen a college campus unless he got a radio call to one, thought of all this by himself. Not only had he thought of it, he had gone through steps 1, 2, 3, 4 (A and B) and 5 in the blink of an eyelid while looking at a passing cloud. And the college boy with 76 credit hours and a 3.8 (temporarily) grade point average watched the whole thing unfold before his eyes and couldn't figure it out without an explanation.

That was the day I gained a respect for the old street cops. It increased even more in the future years when I discovered it was damned hard to teach someone deductive reasoning and you absolutely couldn't teach common sense. When I eventually rated the title of veteran, I even publicly disagreed with a high ranking commander about that. Stating pretentiously that he wouldn't even bother to converse with someone with less than a Bachelor's degree, he contended that a college degree could make a good (meaning competent) cop out of a bad (meaning incompetent) cop. I disagreed, contending that a college degree could make a better cop out of a good cop but, beyond a certain point, precious damned little could make a good one out of a bad one.

Talking amongst ourselves as rookies do, I had the opportunity to tell that story to several of my classmates only to find out that many of them had experienced a similar learning experience, at least the ones who had been lucky enough to ride with a partner like mine for a little while. I also had the opportunity to tell the story to a few who were not so lucky or too impressed with their college transcripts whenever I heard them make a crack like "He thinks Longfellow is the star of a stag film".

And now, decades later, I'm one of the old fossils. And after answering thousands of radio calls, writing thousands of crime reports and making hundreds of arrests, having read Longfellow never helped me a damned bit in doing this job.

So, that night the educated rookie bought the old fossil's meal. Not to brown-nose or as an act of submission. Just because if you're going to teach when you don't have to, you ought to get paid for it. And it was a cheap, acceptable way to say thanks.

SLEEPERS

The rookie walked into the break room, got himself a cup of coffee from the vending machine and plopped down listlessly in a chair. Several of the veteran officers sitting around waiting for roll call took note of his mood. It wasn't a tired, worn-out kind of exhaustion but a dejected, resigned sort of lethargy. It was the way a man acted when he had spent too many years in a patrol car and he was extremely unhappy with his place and purpose in life. They had all seen it many times but very rarely in a man with less than a year on the Department. They all pulled their chairs closer to him.

"What's the matter, kid?"

"Nothin'," he said, staring down at the oily film on the surface of his coffee.

"Been working a lot extra lately?"

"Not too much."

"How's your old lady?"

"Fine."

"How you like riding with Joe?"

"He's a good officer," he said, taking a cautious sip of the coffee.

They all looked at each other. The first incongruous remark. Evidently he hadn't been working himself into exhaustion lately and his family life was all right. But if you enjoy riding with your partner, you don't just say "He's a good officer" and let it go at that. That's something you say to cover what you're really thinking. But in this department, like most, rookies are supposed to keep their mouths shut and their eyes and ears open. They're supposed to learn but deal with their feelings, opinions and ideas on their own time. Especially they are not supposed to criticize senior officers. You don't earn that right until you have sufficient background to warrant it and by then you aren't a rookie anymore.

"Does Joe still like to catch up on his rest on nights?" one of the officers grinned knowingly.

"Yeah," the rookie said smiling slightly.

So there was the problem. You take one officer who has years of experience in a patrol car and who has a habit of sleeping half the night on graveyard shift so he can be rested for his extra job the next morning. His years of experience have qualified him to be a training officer. Add a rookie who wants to work twenty-four hours a day. Everything is new and exciting to him and he can't experience enough or learn enough in the mere eight hours the department lets him work every day. He's having so damned much fun, he'd do the job for free if they let him. Put the two together and you have a combustible mixture. A tired old horse who wants to plod along chained to a young stallion who wants to run all day and all night. The veteran is driven to exasperation by the hyperactivity of his rookie and it has been so many years that he has forgotten what it's like to be new at this job. The rookie has to knuckle under to the senior officer. If he's lucky, he gets to do four hours of work on the night shift and spend the remaining four hours listening to his partner snore on the other side of the car. This can happen one of three ways.

The senior officer drives the first half of the shift while they take radio calls and do their jobs. Halfway through the shift, they switch drivers. The veteran sacks out and the rookie gets to drive, following some carefully laid out rules. Drive carefully and slowly, steer around the bumps and potholes, stay off of the well-lit streets and don't get into anything. Violate these rules and you violate your partner's rest. This leads to the second way. The punishment for these violations is the rookie drives the first half of the shift and when the veteran takes over, he simply parks the car in some dark hole and sacks out while the rookie fidgets for the rest of the night. The third way is that if the rookie really pisses him off, he doesn't get to drive at all.

One of the older officers (he must have been all of 27) spoke to the rookie in a low, confidential tone.

"I had a partner like that when I first came on the job. Old Jarhead. Ex-Marine. He's retired now. Here I was ready to grab crime by the tail and swing it and he would go to sleep every night just as we left the station. I drove every night and it didn't matter how I drove either. There wasn't a bump or pothole in town that could wake Old Jarhead up. We rode the paddy wagon on The Strip downtown for a year and a half. I'd get out of the wagon a dozen times a night and check those old joints down there by myself. There were some real bad asses in those joints then. I never got into anything I couldn't handle by myself and it's a damned good thing. Old Jarhead would still be snoring away in the wagon when I came back out."

"When I finally got off probation, I decided to do something about it. It was obvious they intended to leave me with him for a while after I got my rookie year in and I couldn't go on putting up with that crap. Sooner or later, I was going to get into something in one of those dives where I'd need a backup and Old Jarhead would be as useless as tits on a bull if he was sacked out in the wagon. So one night I got my hands on this HUGE firecracker. Must'a had a couple of ounces of powder in it. They're illegal now. Well, we left the station right after roll call and, sure enough, Old Jarhead crapped out right away. I drove around for a couple of hours over the roughest roads I could find but he never missed a snore. Finally, about two in the morning, I pulled into this alley off of Main Street. I called headquarters quietly so Old Jarhead wouldn't wake up and told them we'd be out for a few minutes. Then I unscrewed the mike from the radio and hid it under the front seat."

"Then I got out and went about fifteen feet in front of the wagon, right in the headlights. I drew my gun and laid face down on the ground. Then I lit the firecracker and threw it over by Old Jarhead's door. Just before it went off, I yelled 'Get him, Jarhead!', lay down with my gun in my hand and tried to look dead."

"When that thing blew, it sounded like a cannon in that alley. It was so damned loud, I was afraid it might have cracked some windows but it didn't. Old Jarhead jumped straight up out of his seat because I saw him hit his head on the roof of the wagon. When he saw me lying on the ground, he jumped out and took about two steps towards me with his gun out. Looking around and seeing no one, he jumped back in the wagon and started scrambling for the mike to call for help. I could hear him swearing a blue streak while he almost tore the dashboard apart trying to find the mike. He was still rummaging when I got up and walked up beside him. He was looking for the mike so hard, he didn't even see me until I tapped him on the shoulder. He went white as a sheet when he saw me, like I was a ghost or something. Poor old fart didn't know whether to shit or go blind."

"While he was still out of breath, I told him what I'd done. I told him that what he'd thought had happened hadn't but it could have and he'd have been in the same shape he was then. Except he'd be trying to explain how he didn't see whoever had killed his partner. He got the point. He was wrong and he knew it. He was the senior officer but I wasn't a rookie anymore, either. We rode together for another six months before he retired and I never saw him close his eyes on duty again."

The officer's narrative had been punctuated with laughter at the appropriate points but now the men lapsed into silence. The older officers were smiling slightly, one of them barely nodding his head, as they all mentally recounted similar experiences in their own careers. The rookie was grinning from ear to ear as if the weight of the world had been lifted off his shoulders. Finally he spoke, confessing his feelings to the group.

"Old Joe isn't quite that bad. We work like hell the first half of the shift. He's a damned good cop and I've learned a lot from him but it's only half what I could have learned. I always drive first but about 3:00 A.M., we switch and he always heads for that underground parking garage at Tenth and Broadway. He backs into a corner, cuts the lights and passes out. Even if a hot call comes out close to us, I can't do anything because he's behind the wheel! Hell, he's gone to sleep a few times while he's driving over there! Almost crashed a couple of times. It's driving me nuts!"

The other officers laughed but Old Jarhead's ex-partner was sitting quietly in thoughtful silence. After a couple of minutes, his face broke into a sadistic grin and he leaned across the table, speaking in a low, conspiratorial tone.

"I'll tell you what you do …"

After roll call, the patrol cars left the station like the spokes of a wheel, heading for their various districts. True to form, Joe and his rookie partner worked like dogs for the first four hours. Three drunks, two hookers and a burglar went to jail. Then, about 3:00 A.M., Joe told him to pull over and they switched positions in the car. He drove straight to the parking garage and was sound asleep in ten minutes. The rookie waited an extra half-hour to make sure he was out cold. Then, very slowly and quietly, he reached down and picked up the mike. Keying the call button, he spoke very low.

"Patrol One to Adam 14. Meet us on Broadway?"

"Clear."

The rookie replaced the mike on the dashboard quietly and sat back smiling to himself. He looked over at Joe slumbering peacefully behind the wheel. Hadn't heard a thing, he thought smugly. A few minutes later, the other patrol car glided silently down the garage's entrance ramp with its lights out, a slightly darker hole in the blackness around them. The sound of its engine was covered by the sound of their own motor idling in Park. The other car rolled slowly to a stop in front of their car, its front bumper positioned about three feet in front of theirs. The officer driving the other car stuck one arm out of the window and waved. The rookie waved back.

When the signals were completed, the other patrol car's four bright lights came on and the driver revved his engine up to a screaming pitch. The rookie turned towards his partner and yelled directly into his ear as loudly as he could.

"*JOEWATCHOUTFORTHATTRUCK!*"

Joe jerked upright in the driver's seat and grabbed the steering wheel by reflex. His mouth fell open in horror as his sleepy eyes focused on the four huge headlights three feet in front of his hood and the sound of the screaming motor pierced his ears. He automatically stomped the brake pedal and wrenched the steering wheel to the right with all his strength. It took a couple of seconds for the fact to penetrate his sleepy consciousness that the sound of the motor and the position of the headlights hadn't changed. Still the crash and explosion hadn't come. The shriek of the other motor subsided to an idle and the headlights went out. In the shadows of a distant streetlight coming from the entrance ramp, Joe could see the two officers in the other car collapsing with laughter. Joe whirled in his seat and saw his rookie partner sitting there looking at him with a perfectly straight face. Joe's face twisted in a fit of rage that slowly softened into understanding. As the other car backed up, Joe put the car in gear and drove out into the street.

A few weeks later, Old Jarhead's ex-partner was walking down the hall when he saw the rookie approaching him. As they passed, he spoke.

"You and Joe have sure been making a lot of calls late in the shift lately."

The rookie just smiled and kept on walking.

TRIAL BY FIRE

The sergeant at the booking desk looked up from his paperback western when he heard the hum of the jail elevator begin its two-floor ascent to the City Jail. He put the book down and stood up behind the typewriter on the counter.

When the elevator door opened, a huge Indian stepped out, his hands cuffed behind him. A young officer, at least half a foot shorter and thirty pounds lighter than his prisoner, walked behind him holding onto the chain between the handcuffs with one hand while his other never strayed far from the night stick hanging from his belt. A slightly pot-bellied older officer followed them out.

The sergeant stepped away from the booking desk and leaned around a wall where the other two night shift jailers were playing cards. "One of Joe's rookies is bringing in Stumbling Bear again." The two jailers exchanged grins and walked out to the booking area.

Even accounting for the potbelly, Joe was recruiting-poster sharp. Uniform clean, creases sharp and all the brass polished. The other two were somewhat the worse for wear.

The prisoner had a trickle of blood running down his forehead from beneath the hairline of his shoulder-length black hair. Another trickle emanated from one corner of his mouth. His clothing was as dirty and disheveled as you might expect from any professional drunk but a little more so tonight.

The younger officer was also a little mussed. One epaulet on his shirt was hanging down and the gold button was gone. Sweat stained the underarms and one pocket was partially ripped off. Several splatters of blood streaked the front of the gray uniform shirt. Since some dried blood was crusted under the officer's nose and at the corner of his mouth, whether the blood on his shirt belonged to him or his prisoner was problematic. Probably both. The dark blue uniform pants, which had undoubtedly been immaculate at lineup a few hours earlier, were now covered with blotches of dirt and mud.

The jailers knew the story without being told. Old Joe was an old timer who had spent his younger years walking a beat in one of the tougher areas. Joe had been a beat officer with all that title entails. Tough as a boot. A cop who held the line on his beat against all the drunks, pimps and others who would try you on a daily basis. As he got a little older, slower, fatter and tired of walking, Joe transferred to a patrol car.

Stumbling Bear was a Kiowa with a reputation for belligerence and the physical presence to back it up. Six feet six inches and 230 pounds of American Indian who hadn't surrendered yet and was still pissed off about what the white eyes had done to his people. John had only two passions in life—drinking himself insensible on Green Lizards Hair Tonic (75 proof) and fighting cops, whom he viewed as modern day cavalry.

Joe might be riding a patrol car now but he still liked to break his rookies in on his old beat. As Joe put it, if things got rough, he wanted to make sure he had backup. After the fight started was too late to find out you were riding with a coward. It had happened before.

Whenever the department assigned a rookie to Joe, he immediately drove to his old beat area and drove around until he found Stumbling Bear, always as drunk and testy as usual. Joe would instruct the rookie to arrest Stumbling Bear.

The officers would get out and confront John, who regarded them with a silent, baleful, bloodshot stare. The unsuspecting rookie would dutifully inform Stumbling Bear that he was under arrest for Public Drunk. Stumbling Bear would glance over at the old beat officer.

"That right, Joe?"

"If my partner says so. But if you can whip his ass, I'll let you go."

And the fight was on.

The young officer removed the handcuffs while the desk sergeant started typing the booking sheet from memory.

"Stumbling Bear, John, Indian Male, 36, Public Drunk, address City Rescue Mission, 523 South Robinson."

The sergeant looked up at Joe and then at the rookie.

"Adding Assault on an Officer?"

The rookie shook his head.

"Been by Mercy?" the sergeant asked as a matter of form, already knowing the answer.

"Refused treatment." Joe answered.

The sergeant looked at Joe and nodded towards the rookie.

"He a keeper?"

Joe smiled. "He'll do."

PATROL ONE

Every large police department of that time had a paddy wagon. Mostly they were used to patrol the skid row area of the city where the largest concentration of street alcoholics were and occasionally used to transport large numbers of prisoners in mass arrest situations. Ours was a regular van much like those used by many businesses for delivery and service calls but with some special modifications.

Like a normal police vehicle it was painted black and white, and had red lights and a siren. It had two doors in the front passenger area and two on the back, the rear doors having their inside handles removed, naturally. There were no windows along the sides except for those in the doors. The front area was separated from the rear by a black iron mesh screen. The rear area where the prisoners rode was simply two wooden benches along the sides. It was almost always manned by two officers and usually had the radio call sign "Patrol One."

Patrol One's primary duty was to arrest those citizens who fit the legal definition of Public Drunk, i.e. not just boozed up but making some kind of public nuisance of themselves, posing a threat to the public order or themselves.

The primary skid row area at that time was centered along the downtown streets of California, Reno and Sheridan. Some of that type of activity occasionally occurred in other areas, most notably on Commerce Street in Capitol Hill or Exchange Avenue near the stockyards but beat officers usually policed those areas during the day. Patrol One's usual beat was the downtown streets at night.

As with most large cities, this area was populated with a lot of very individual characters well known to the police. One of the harmless ones was Queer Charlie. Charlie lived downtown, walked everywhere he went and although flamingly obvious about his sexual orientation, he was discreet in his personal life and wouldn't bother minors, not that there were usually any children in the immediate vicinity of that area. Charlie loved cops because they didn't harass him, didn't judge him on his life style and they usually protected him from those who would prey on him.

There were, of course, dozens of others the downtown officers were on a first name basis with. One everyone knew was a chronic street drunk named Vernon. Vernon had had a hard life. He had one prosthetic leg and false teeth. The rumor was that he lost his leg by passing out with it draped over the railroad tracks and a passing freight train took it off. After drinking himself insensible on Green Lizards hair tonic, when the cops arrested him Vernon never went quietly unless he was completely passed out. When you arrested Vernon, the first thing you did was take his false leg and false teeth away from him. If he were conscious at all, he would take his false leg off and try to hit the officers with it. After they took that away, he'd grovel on the ground, making growling sounds like a wounded wolverine and try to bite their legs and ankles. Vernon was also very dirty and usually lice-ridden so the officers touched him only enough to make sure he had nothing else he could use as a weapon.

When someone called in sick or was on vacation, they often drafted officers from other areas of the city to fully man Patrol One, usually newer officers who didn't have their own district. I spent a very eventful couple of weeks in Patrol One with an "old hand" downtown officer. He was a full-blood American Indian who was quite a character in his own right. Outwardly very somber and usually without expression, he had a great sense of humor and was a very funny guy when he got to trust you. He also had a reputation for being generally genial and forgiving but, like everyone, he had limits.

To try to limit our exposure to lice, tuberculosis and God knows what else, we took turns making the arrests. Our first night together, we found a guy staggering down the middle of Reno Street with cars honking and driving around him. We motioned the guy over to the curb and pulled up behind him. We both got out and it was my partner's turn to make the arrest so he stepped forward. He told the guy he was under arrest for Public Drunk and reached for his arm to turn him around and start searching him for weapons. The guy took one look at my partner's very dark complexion and jerked his arm away violently. I stepped forward to back up my partner and the guy turned toward me, slurring his words badly.

"I'll go with you but I ain't going with no goddam Mexican."

Uh-oh.

My partner hit him once, right on the chin. Out cold. Call it 1970s sensitivity training. If you're going to live in Oklahoma, take the trouble to be able to tell Mexicans and Indians apart.

During the early 1970s, someone decided it would be a good idea to try to instigate some more higher culture into the downtown area. As a result, they constructed the Mummers Theater on Sheridan Avenue, just across from the Union Bus Station and dead center in the middle of skid row. We already had the symphony housed at the Civic Center Auditorium but the few blocks between those two locations were worlds apart.

A modern, almost Cubist construction, the new theater resembled the ductwork for a heat and air conditioning system built above ground. They would host plays and other cultural activities. They pretended not to notice the Terminal Lounge, Sweet Leona's and various other notorious places nearby.

One night the new Mummers Theater was having their grand opening. The sidewalks were full of bejeweled high society ladies in their expensive gowns and men in tuxedos and black ties. We were driving down Sheridan and, lo and behold, there was Vernon, passed out flat on his back in front of the Terminal Lounge, right across the street from the Mummers. The old money gentry were giving Vernon a wide berth, stepping around him and literally holding their noses until they got upwind.

We pulled the van over to the curb as close as we could get to him and got out. It was my turn. My partner stood at Vernon's feet (or foot) while I knelt down by him. I shook him and called his name. Nothing. He was snoring loudly. I took a bullet out of my belt loop loader, put it between two of his fingers and squeezed. Giving him a downtown handshake had no effect either. He was totally out.

If you've never tried it, it's not easy to carry someone with an artificial leg. You've got one less thing to hold on to and they're somewhat out of balance. It's also not pleasant to carry someone with lice jumping all over him. Add to that someone who sometimes doesn't bother to remove his pants to go to the bathroom and that limits your transportation options.

My partner went to the rear of the van and opened the doors while I grabbed Vernon by the rear of his coat collar. I started slowly dragging him along the sidewalk the ten paces or so to the rear of the van. Suddenly there was a piercing shriek behind me. I looked back and one of the society matrons on the sidewalk had her hands over her eyes, screaming her head off. A few yards behind us, Vernon's artificial leg had come off. I guess the old girl thought she was witnessing the cops dismembering poor Vernon right before her eyes.

We put him in the van, retrieved his leg, took his teeth out and went to jail. Vernon never batted an eye.

FREE MEDICAL ADVICE

The rookie pondered his unhappy lot in life. A fistfight in a Skid Row bar led to a trip to Mercy ER. Before he got there, his right hand was approximately the size and color of a rotten grapefruit. A couple of hours of surgery left him with a cast from fingertips to elbow with two stainless steel pins holding the bones together for the next seven weeks.

Since his right hand was also his shooting hand, he was off the streets. Since he couldn't defend himself or search prisoners effectively, he couldn't be assigned to the jail. Since his right hand was also his writing hand, he couldn't be assigned to Dispatch. Less than two weeks on the streets and here he was. A clerk in the Records Bureau on the night shift. The only job a temporarily one-handed cop was good for.

From the Records counter near the central atrium of the building, he could hear the graveyard shift coming out of lineup one floor up. The humming elevators were bringing the officers down to the basement to their cars. One elevator stopped on the second floor and one man got off. It was the man who had been his partner until two days ago. His training officer. The senior officer who was "breaking him in." The man who had waded into the melee of swinging drunks to pull him out two nights ago. The man who had taken him to the hospital and sat with him through all the x-rays and tests, and who had been sitting next to his bed in the recovery room when he woke up.

The officer walked over to the Records counter and set his briefcase down on the floor. He grinned as he leaned on the counter.

"How ya doin', combat?"

"OK, I guess." He smiled sheepishly and shook his head as he rested his cast on the counter. "Is this a sympathy call?"

"Nope. Just a continuation of your training."

The older officer could have said many things. He could have said that the human hand contains twenty-seven bones, none of them thicker than a pencil. He could have said it was a machine capable of amazing dexterity. He could have said that an elephant can knock down a house but it can't pick a grape. He could have said that our opposable thumbs and the brain that controlled them were what set us above the other animals. He could have said that our hands were what had enabled humans to fashion tools and turn them into weapons. He could have pointed out that the biggest, toughest professional fighters in the world wrap their hands in layers of tape and cushion them with thickly padded gloves before they fight. But, as a good training officer, it was his job to boil all these elements down to short, easily remembered lessons without any unnecessary preaching, lecturing or gloating.

He reached into his hip pocket and laid his leather-covered, lead-filled sap on the counter. He drew his nightstick out of the ring on his belt and put it next to the sap. He reached into the briefcase and laid his black, knurled aluminum Kel-Lite flashlight beside them. Then he flexed his hands in front of the rookie's face, wiggling the fingers.

"The police department buys you lots of things to hit folks with. *These* are for *feeling!*"

GROUPIES

When people apply to become police officers, they do so for all kinds of reasons, positive and negative. Some of the positive ones are a desire to help people, to perform public service without having to grovel for votes or go to law school, for a job with lots of action and adventure, a job that has a certain charisma (albeit mostly generated by Hollywood and television) or a job with a constant variety of experiences. Some of the negative ones are a desire for power, the right to carry a gun or a badge or have authority over people. All kinds of reasons, some stated honestly on their applications and some not. Very few if any expect to broaden their sex lives with the job but they quickly learn that is a reality.

Back in the 1970s, long before the military's "Don't ask, don't tell" policies and even predating female officers in some departments, one of the priorities used to be that the future officer be heterosexual. One of the first things a new officer used to be told was that the three things that could get him in trouble the fastest were "women, whiskey and debts."

Officers, good officers, were actually forced to resign or fired because they bounced a check before payday or because some merchant called the Chief to complain about an overdue bill. Others were actually forced to resign for living with a woman out of wedlock; this while the sexual revolution of the Sixties was raging all around them. These weren't the first indications that they were being held to a different standard than people in other professions but they made a more lasting impression.

The potential for whiskey, of course, is self-evident. Along with an above average potential for suicide and divorce, cops have a higher potential for alcoholism. The stresses of the job never seem to be enough without finding something worse to add to them. Many cops don't have a big enough desk or wallet to hold all the photos of their current family and ex-families.

Most officers, in my experience, never had a glimmer before they were hired that cops actually have groupies. They thought that was something that came with being a movie star or a rock and roll idol. "People don't like cops. People hate cops. People fear cops. People resent cops. Oh, they like you just fine when you're pulling them out of a burning car or saving their ass from a killer, robber, rapist, or whatever. But people sure as hell don't *love* cops." It turns out that some people do, however. And a lot of them are female.

After the new rookie gets hired, a whole new world opens up to them. Their new world became what fighter pilots call "a target-rich environment" and it didn't take them long to identify the targets.

There was plenty of opportunity inside the department itself. There was a whole class of females who were used to working with, for and around cops every day. You can't do that for long if you hate or fear them. Secretaries, receptionists, report clerks, records clerks, jail matrons, dispatchers, school crossing guards and, later on, female cops. A shared work environment breeds familiarity, perhaps respect and often physical attraction. The downside of this embarrassment of riches is more gets shared than the work environment. Just as not many cops limit themselves to relationships with only one police employee, many police employees enjoy the company of more than one cop. Between themselves, cops have a sardonic response to these circumstances. They call themselves "husbands-in-law."

Another phenomenon is the fact that some girlfriends and wives start acting like they themselves are cops. Like they have shared the experiences, dangers, highs, lows, rewards and deprivations of doing that job. The cops humor the girl-friends on a temporary basis and some of the wives on a more permanent basis but they all recognize that sitting home and worrying about a spouse involved in a gunfight or a chase isn't exactly the same experience as actually being in a gun-fight or a chase. Privately, the cops have another sardonic response for the people exhibiting this phenomenon. They call them "cops by injection."

In the world outside the walls of the department, the environment was even richer. Emergency room nurses, medical technicians, waitresses in diners and cof-fee shops (especially the all-night variety who work the same lousy hours as cops), paramedics working for ambulance services, secretaries and dispatchers for wrecker services, bartenders, hostesses and dancers in nightclubs. The names change between generations—Fuzzy's, PJ's, Copahabana, Don Quixote's, Jun-ior's, Chastain's, The Trade Winds, The Sports Page, The Bombay Club, Bosco's, Ichiro's, Chevy's, Sherlock's—but they're all the same, really. It got a lit-tle better when the cops started their own nightclub—or worse. I guess it depends upon your viewpoint. At least they were more isolated from the citizenry when they drank, probably to the benefit of both groups.

Occasionally the environment even included witnesses and victims of crimes and, for those with extremely bad judgment, sometimes even suspects.

Always passed around was the old story, possibly apocryphal and possibly not (believe me, stranger things have happened), about the cop pulling a speeding car over. When he walked up to the driver's side door, a beautiful girl was driving.

"Where's the fire?" he said.

"Between my legs. Think you've got a hose long enough to put it out?"

Even if some guys thought they might have a better chance with certain girls afflicted with the man-in-uniform syndrome, it probably never occurred to them that they were getting into a job where women would aggressively try to pick *them* up.

The reasons for these attractions are many, varied and largely unknown. One is the "man-in-uniform" thing. But mailmen wear uniforms, too. Maybe the phallic symbols of the gun and tie, not to mention some people's fascination with violence or the potential for it. Most cops have had the experience of making a new acquaintance of a female and her asking *THE* question;

"Have you ever killed anyone?"

"You mean today?"

Maybe having to assert your will on people, some of whom will inevitably resist violently, makes your body produce more testosterone. One street philosopher even suggested something simpler. The world is full of kooks, inadequate personalities, serial murderers and worse. If a girl picks up a cop, she has a better than average chance of getting a guy who is relatively mentally, emotionally and financially stable, physically healthy, bathes and brushes his teeth at least once a day, probably won't demand anything *too* kinky from her sexually, and probably won't beat the hell out of her, dismember her or sell her into slavery at the end of the evening.

Just having men and women working together in close proximity produces extra potential for problems. With the level of these activities, the possibilities approach inevitability. Most of the following situations have occurred more than once and in more than one police department so it isn't necessary to name individuals.

An off-duty cop runs down the street, ducking and dodging, as his wife/girlfriend peppers the street around him with shots from his own gun.

A cop's wife/girlfriend runs down the street, ducking and dodging, as her cop husband/boyfriend peppers the street around her with bullets from his service weapon. This happens less frequently than the previous situation, simply because the cop is usually a better shot than the significant other and usually is unwilling to sacrifice their job/freedom for the satisfaction of shooting him/her. But there have been some near misses.

A cop strikes up an acquaintance with a lady and they decide to get to know one another better after he gets off duty. He goes with her over to her place where bad judgment, bad luck and worse timing collide. When they reach the point where he is down to his underwear, her estranged husband kicks in the door. Since this is a personal situation and not a professional one, discretion being the better part of valor applies. The cop bails out of a window and runs into a nearby city park. The enraged husband breaks the small badge parking tag off of the car parked in front of the house and calls the cops. He gives the tag to a supervisor. The tags are numbered and registered to the individual officer to allow them to park in police parking lots. The supervisor also collects the abandoned uniform, badge and firearm. Meanwhile the cop in his skivvies scurries out from the bushes in the park and jumps into a passing police car. Unfortunately it's another supervisor. Next stop—the unemployment line.

Then there was the detective who, for several years of his marriage, spent his eight days off every month with his wife. On the ninth day, he got up early, put on his suit and tie and left for work. Unfortunately, one day his wife found out that he got *nine* days off every month. Eventually she found out which girlfriend he was spending the ninth day with. Another notch on the divorce statistics.

Along with some of the cops, some of the women became legendary. One of the report clerks advertised her fondness for officers by having a personalized license plate on her car reading "KKC-867." While meaningless to the average citizen, every cop knew it was the FCC call sign assigned to the OCPD. There was Skeeter, who hung around the downtown area. There was Meguila, a very small Oriental girl who liked to hang around the Paseo area with the hippies in the early 1970s and had a big appetite for cops. It got to the point where every time Meguila saw a police uniform, she'd walk up to him and start spouting "You know Officer Smith? Officer Jones? Officer White? Officer Black?" She pronounced it "Off-i-sah" in a very fractured version of the English language. One of her unique qualities was after she got "acquainted" with an officer, she asked him to give her one of the bullets on his belt to remember him by.

Most of the girls either matured or married their way out of this stage of their lives. Some of them just faded away like Skeeter. Meguila went out with as much *panache* as she'd come in with.

What the guys didn't take into account was she'd been desensitized to the average person's standoffishness with cops. She'd been around so many cops, in the patrol car, in their personal cars, in the back seat, the front seat, on the hood, the trunk, grinding away in the dirt and the gravel, standing up in the alleys, she was like a wild animal that had lost their fear of humans.

One night, the shift commander decided to come by and check on the guys walking the beat on Paseo. This particular shift commander was unusual—a religious, straight-laced non-drinker, non-smoker and undoubtedly faithful to his wife, traits he didn't share with all of the younger men under his command. So he pulls up to the curb, knowing his men will spot him and be drawn to the black and white.

Without warning, the passenger door pops open and Meguila jumps in. In spite of her past familiarity with cops, she doesn't know the difference between a lieutenant and an admiral. She smiles at him ingratiatingly and starts her broken-English spiel—"You know Officer Smith? Officer Jones? Office White?" Then, determined to be friendly, she reached over and honked him. Got a handful of testicles and squeezed gently, just enough to let him know she liked him, a gesture that more than made up for her lack of fluency in her adopted language.

Off-i-sah Smith, one of the beat officers that night, under specific orders from the shift commander, had to put her in the County Jail for a mental hearing. What must have made it even more perplexing was that Off-i-sah Smith had been one of her "friends."

I heard that when she got out of jail, Meguila protested her treatment by showing up at the Patrol Division offices with a whole bag of bullets. Each one had a name written on it. The saving grace for all those names was that there were a number of supervisors' and commanders' names among them.

There was another girl, a very attractive blond, who drove around in a very easily recognizable Plymouth Roadrunner with the name "Scat Cat" painted on the side. I heard there was hell to pay when somebody spread the word that Scat Cat was only 17 years old. I also heard she was very mature for her age.

And then there was the lady in a lime green Camaro. Like Scat Cat, I never met anyone who knew her real name but her nickname was Head Job. With that, I think we've covered this subject sufficiently.

PEACHES

In the Neanderthal days of the 1970s, proactive police departments had different standards. After the Police Academy taught the rookie all the ordinances, statutes, policies and procedures, then came the street training. The street officers had different priorities than the Academy instructors. So the street training was boiled down to a simple formula—"Get him in a fight, get him a felony arrest and get him laid." In other words, make the rookie prove his courage, his aggressiveness, his common sense and his heterosexuality.

Doubtlessly there were homosexual police officers before the "Don't ask, don't tell" days but they camouflaged it. Proving one's sexuality was simpler than might be imagined. As the preceding vignette demonstrated and as fantastic as it might seem, cops have their groupies just like rock stars, lawyers, doctors, and politicians among others. At worst, cops were attractive to some women of the "Have you ever killed anyone?" variety. At the other end of the spectrum, a lot of women probably figured that cops were a safe target if only that they probably had some standards for personal hygiene, they had at least an average IQ if you decided to talk to them and they probably wouldn't torture you to death if you had a disagreement.

As in most professions, people thrown together in the workplace provided the most opportunity for liaisons. Cops just had a workplace that covered a lot of square miles. Frequent candidates included policewomen, police secretaries, meter maids, school crossing guards, nurses (cops spend a lot of time in ER's), waitresses in all night restaurants and coffee shops and, in a few cases, hookers and strippers. What can I tell you? All cops are human.

"Make the call now." The officer hung up the pay phone and walked back to the scout car. He got in, pulled the gearshift into Drive and drove off. His partner didn't say anything. Didn't ask him who he'd called or what it was about. Rookies didn't ask those kinds of questions. The senior officer turned the car onto Lincoln Boulevard near the State Capitol. Both officers maintained their silence until the radio broke squelch.

"Baker 5."

"Go ahead."

"Behind the liquor store at 35th and Lincoln, a prowler."

The senior officer reached for the mike. "Baker 4 to Baker 5, we'll take that call. We're 10-97. We'll advise on backup."

"Clear."

The scout car turned into the driveway. The rookie thought that was a little odd. His partner had taught him never to pull into a driveway on a call or park directly in front of the house. This also wasn't how he'd been taught to check for prowlers. The driver cut the lights and put the car in Park.

"You take this one."

"OK." The rookie opened the door and looked over at his senior partner, who hadn't moved.

"Aren't you coming?" You don't usually take calls alone in this district.

"Naw. I've made this call before. A woman lives here alone. You'll be OK. Just take the report and reassure her."

The rookie frowned a little bit. He'd never known his partner to be this casual on the job before. But he'd never steered him wrong either. You've got to trust your partner.

"OK." He picked up his report folder and flashlight. Maybe his partner just wanted to observe his procedures although how he was going to do that from the car was beyond him.

The front door was ajar a couple of inches and the light was very dim inside. He stood sideways with his weak side shoulder even with the doorjamb like he'd been taught. He put the report folder under his left arm and held the flashlight in his left hand. Keep the gun hand free. He tapped the flashlight on the door. It swung open a few more inches. He glanced inside. A light came from an open doorway at the back of the room. Strings of colored beads provided a barrier in the portal, reflecting the dim light beyond.

"Police officer. Did you call?"

A female voice came from the back room called out. "Yes, officer. Come on in, please. I'll be right out."

The rookie pushed the door open with the flashlight. As soon as it hit the wall so he knew no one was behind it, he stepped through. He immediately stepped sideways so he wasn't silhouetted in the doorway.

"Could you close the door, please, officer? I'll be right out."

He hooked the doorknob with the flashlight and closed it, moving a little deeper into the darkened room.

"Is there a prowler, ma'am?"

"Not any more."

She was silhouetted in the beaded portal. She was big—about 5-9, maybe 150 pounds. Whatever she was almost wearing was red and very thin. She stepped through the beads, smiling broadly. Her teeth were big, too. Now why in the hell had he noticed that? Her bare feet made no noise crossing the carpet. The next sound he heard was a zipper opening. And what she was wearing didn't have any zippers.

When he got back in the car, his partner didn't say a word. Didn't ask why he'd taken so long, didn't ask to see the report, didn't ask him why his uniform wasn't quite as sharply creased as it had been, nothing. And he sure as hell didn't say anything. He just wanted this shift to end.

The next day. As they were leaving the gas pumps, his partner gave him the day's game plan.

"How about sitting on a school zone? Maybe keep the kids from getting run over for a while?"

"Fine with me." It was the first time his partner had asked him if anything they did was all right with him. Maybe he was gaining some acceptance.

When they pulled over to the curb at 22nd and Dewey, he thought it was a little odd again. They were very obvious, not at all hidden from any potential speeders in the school zone. Besides there was a school crossing guard right across the street. When their tired brakes squealed, she turned around and waved at the black and white scout car. The wave was also accompanied by a smile. A big smile. With big teeth. His mouth dropped open. She sure looked different in something that wasn't red.

He felt eyes on him and turned to look at his partner. He too was grinning broadly.

"Welcome to the eastside."

MODUS OPERANDI

The three beeps on the radio signaled an emergency call.

"Adam 9, 5216 North Barnes, burglary in progress, shots fired."

"Clear. Almost 10-97."

It was after midnight and we were just a few blocks away. Steve put the gas pedal to the floor and we were there in less than a minute, rolling the last half block with the lights out. We both bailed out with our guns out and only made it a few steps before a guy came out the front door, carrying a rifle. We both skidded to a halt and aimed at him. He instantly threw both arms over his head, along with the rifle.

"*DON'T SHOOT! I LIVE HERE! HE WENT OUT THE BACK WINDOW!*"

"Put down the rifle! And go back inside!"

The guy laid the rifle on the porch and ducked back inside the dark house. We could hear a phone ringing inside. Steve headed around the house to the left and I went right. I cleared all of my side of the house and went across the back. Nothing. Then I turned up the other side of the house. A man's body was lying on its back about halfway up the side. Steve was standing next to him, pointing his gun down at the body. As I got closer, I could see Steve was standing on one of the guy's hands.

"Get up, asshole!" Steve glanced at me. "I think he's faking."

There was a large red stain on the guy's right shoulder. The location looked like a minor wound but I heard a little gurgle I'd heard before.

"I don't think he's faking, Steve. And I don't think he's getting up."

I was right. The guy was dead before the ambulance got there. There was nothing we could have done for him. One shot in the top of the right shoulder, no exit wound. While Steve stayed with the body, I went around to the front door. The rifle was still on the porch, a hunting rifle using .22 Hornet shells. I could see the owner sitting in the living room. He'd turned on a light so I went in, leaving the rifle where he'd laid it. A portable stereo, portable TV and some other electronics were stacked up just inside the front door. The phone was still ringing.

"You going to answer that?"

He just reached over, picked up the receiver and without even putting it to his ear, hung it up immediately. He gave me his ID when I asked for it and I started writing the information down.

"What happened?"

"I was sitting in here with the lights out and a guy started climbing in the back bedroom window and I shot him."

"Where did you have the rifle?"

"I was holding it."

"Let me get this straight. You were sitting here in the dark, holding a loaded rifle, when this guy came in the back window and you shot him?"

"Yeah."

I gestured to the stack of electronics at the door. "Did he do that?"

"I guess so. That's pretty much how the other guys said it might happen."

"What other guys?"

The homeowner had come home several hours earlier. He lived here alone. When he came in the front door, he found his electronics gear stacked up just as it was now. He heard a noise in the back of the house so he went back there and found a window pried open in the back bedroom. He called the police and a two-man car came out.

The officers from the previous shift found the pry marks on the rear window-sill and told him he'd interrupted the burglar.

TWO HOURS EARLIER

"Looks like you interrupted him," the officer said as he started writing the report.

Between providing the information for the report, the homeowner was asking questions.

"Do you think I'll be safe here tonight? Do they usually come back when they're interrupted like this?"

"Not usually. Sometimes but not usually."

"Why would he come back if he almost got caught?"

"You never know. He might be desperate for some dope money. Or he might be real stupid. Some of them are."

"But would he be desperate enough to come back to an occupied house?"

"Probably not. He'd probably try to make sure you'd gone first."

"How would he do that?"

The officer stopped writing and looked at the man. "First he'd probably drive by to see if your car was still here or if the lights were on. Then, if he put some thought into it, he might have gotten your number off your phone while he was in here. He might wait a few hours and go to a pay phone a few blocks away. He'd dial your number and see if anyone answers. If you answer, he'd just hang up and forget it. If no one answers, he'd leave the phone off the hook and come back here. When he comes to the house, if he can still hear the phone ringing inside, he'd figure the house was empty and break in again."

"Hmm. That's pretty clever."

"Not all of them are stupid."

After the scout car left, the guy moved his car down the block, then went back in the house, loaded his rifle, turned all the lights out and waited. After a little while, the phone rang. He didn't answer it and it just kept ringing. About fifteen minutes later, he heard a window being raised in the back bedroom. He went back there and saw a shadow crawling in the window. The guy was bent over at the waist when the owner fired, hitting him once in the top of the right shoulder. The guy gasped and fell back out the window. Then the homeowner called the cops again.

We waited for Homicide and the M.E. The Homicide guys agreed it was pretty cut and dried. The D.A. frowned on burglars invading occupied homes in his county. No charges would be filed. Probably give the guy a commendation.

Neither Steve nor I had ever heard of a .22 Hornet but one of the Homicide detectives had. It was a .22 all right but fired a round like an M-16, high-powered, traveled about 3000 feet per second. Lots of energy.

"Very impressive," he said.

He invited us to meet them down at the M.E.'s Office. We did and the M.E. showed us the X-rays of the dead burglar's body. The soft-nosed bullet had fragmented immediately and sprayed about a thousand pieces of shrapnel throughout his upper body. Those fragments had pierced every single organ in his chest and abdominal cavities. Like the man said, very impressive.

When we went back out in the car, we discussed whether we should make up a couple of fake warrants for Conspiracy To Commit Murder for the two officers on the previous shift but decided against it. It would be a lot of trouble since we were on graveyard shift. Then we got into a discussion about whether we could take credit for a burglary arrest.

TERMINOLOGY

Some guys turn into diamonds under pressure. Some don't.

I've heard police chases where the driver was reciting locations and directions into the microphone just as calmly as if he were sitting in his recliner reading the TV Guide out loud. But there's a lot of background noise—the wailing of the

siren, the groaning of tortured metal, the squealing of worn-out brakes, the rush-
ing air, sometimes gunshots. Noises that tell you he's driving a piece-of-crap
police car with more miles on it than Apollo 13, going over 100 miles per hour
when no one in their right mind would go half that fast in it.

The foot pursuits aren't usually as dangerous and some can be downright
comical.

Marmaduke is a comic strip dog, a good-natured Great Dane with the best
intentions but little self-control who leaves a trail of wreckage behind him everywhere he goes, the quintessential bull in the china shop. Marmaduke also used to
be the nickname of a cop. A good-natured guy and a good cop but one who was
very excitable and hyperactive, at least in his younger days. Those were the days
before the drug Ritalin had been invented but if we'd had it, we'd have given it to
Marmaduke.

One big difference between the comic strip Marmaduke and the police Marmaduke was that the cop wasn't lazy. If anything, he was *too* active. Like an over-
grown puppy with boundless energy and curiosity, sticking his nose into
everything within sight, sometimes he flushed out mice and chickens, and sometimes he flushed out rats and snakes.

One day Marmaduke was walking Patrol One, then a downtown foot beat.
The downtown foot beats were usually considered to be pre-retirement jobs,
"public relations" positions in the business district. Just stroll around the sidewalks, nodding to the hustling and bustling businessmen, showing the flag and
playing scarecrow. But sometimes you get to see some real crime.

"PATROLONETOHEADQUARTERS!(huff,puff)*I'MINFOOTPURSUIT-
NORTHONROBINSONFROMPARKAVENUE!*(huff,puff)

A downtown patrol car got on the radio, leaving off his call sign to save time.
"Description?"
Another nearby car chimed in.
"What charge?"

(huff,puff)*"PURSESNATCHING!BLACKMALEEARLYTWENTIESSIXFEE-
TONEEIGHT-YWEARINGABLACKTANKTOPBLUEJEANSAND A COCK-
SUCKER HAT!*(huff,puff)"

The broadcast was being monitored by dozens of police cars, a room full of
dispatchers, every police commander who was on the air, probably some officers
in suburban departments and highway patrol troopers, all the TV and radio station news rooms, wrecker and ambulance services, any interested citizen with a

police scanner and perhaps the Federal Communications Commission which licenses the police radio system. Even with all those ears out there, the air was eerily silent for several long seconds. Then an amused voice came on the air, deliberately omitting his call sign.

"What kind of hat was that?"

During every shift's lineup, the shift commander usually pointed out any significant arrests of the previous day. Today he told about Marmaduke's purse-snatcher, commending both him and the patrol car that helped catch him.

"We also have a memo from the Chief's Office. For the purpose of any future radio transmissions or police reports, any round, flat hat or cap with a short bill will be known as an English riding cap."

Marmaduke turned bright red while everyone else roared with laughter.

EQUAL JUSTICE

The patrol car sat idling quietly in the alley while the two officers surveyed the two-lane, one-way street. This area of the city roughly divided the upper downtown area from the middle class residential areas to the north. One block to the north the street was two-way for miles, all the way to the city limits but from here to the downtown area, it was one-way southbound.

This three-block length of the street housed the section variously known as "Hippie City", "Freak Street", "Flower Child Village" and various other names depending on which generation was doing the naming. Hippies, yippies, beatniks, whatever you called them, this was their natural habitat, this city's version of Haight-Ashbury. Three solid blocks of psychedelic bars with names like The Yellow Submarine, incense parlors, leather shops, record stores selling acid-rock and heavy metal, and "The Center", as they called it. A drug rehab center that provided social, recreational and psychiatric services for the hundreds of addicts, sociopaths, mental patients, runaways and rebellious kids that populated the area.

The alley ran the full length of the block between the acid-rock store and one of the more popular bars. Since several patrol districts intersected within three blocks of the location, it was a rare occasion when a patrol car wasn't parked in the alley. It was also a rare night when less than a dozen felony arrests were made on this street, mostly for narcotics and the rest associated with the outbreaks of violence between the peace and love generations. The officers had a running joke that there was an underground movement to put land mines in the alley but they were afraid of taking out the occasional VW bus.

As usual, tonight the street was a solid mass of humanity on both sides. The sidewalks swarmed with hundreds of garishly dressed, longhaired youngsters, most of them keeping one eye on the patrol car in the shadows. The older residents of the area had been complaining about the kids leisurely sauntering back and forth across the street obstructing vehicle traffic through the area. So some Traffic commander had dug up a forgotten ordinance. Since then, dozens of $25 tickets had been issued for "Failure To Yield The Right Of Way To A Motor Vehicle By A Pedestrian Not In A Crosswalk." The kids were now more judicious about crossing the street and the vehicle traffic flowed much smoother.

The two officers were casually watching two guys arguing about something, probably the price of dope, when they saw the new red sports car turn up the one-way street going the wrong way. The young, shorthaired driver in a business suit was obviously paying more attention to the sidewalks than the street signs. Probably a well-to-do jet setter trying to pick up a hippie chick and see how the other half lived. The area was constantly flooded with "tourists" who considered a drive through the area equivalent to a visit to the zoo.

The driver of the patrol car pulled out in the street, blocking the sports car's lane and turning on the red lights. The sports car braked to a halt as activity on the street virtually stopped and all attention was drawn to the pending confrontation in the street.

The officer riding shotgun got out with his ticket book in hand. Next to the car, he flipped out a citation and took out his pen. Suddenly several hundred spectators broke out in spontaneous cheers and applause. Both officers surveyed the crowd silently and looked at each other, grinning in combined amazement and amusement.

The officer took the red-faced young man's driver's license and began to write the citation as the cheers and applause continued to echo between the buildings.

ACCIDENTAL JUSTICE

Cruising around on a quiet day shift. Few calls and a quiet radio. Might as well go out on the Expressway and blow the car out a little. Five or ten minutes at 70 miles per hour will add a little to the top end if a bank robbery comes out, one of the few hot calls that happen on day shift.

Fives miles out and five back, the car runs a lot better and no calls have come out in the district. The patrol car is slowing for the exit ramp when both officers see the red Chevy float through the access road stop sign at about 15 miles per hour.

"1-Baker-6 is on traffic, X-Ray Adam Baker 728, red Chevy with six black males at the I-35 10th Street exit.

"Clear, 1-Baker-6."

The overhead lights come on as the patrol car settles in a couple of car lengths behind the Chevy. All the occupants look like teenagers. One in the rear seat looks around. He says something to the driver who checks his rear view mirror and started pulling over to the curb. The patrol car stops about a car length back and offset to the left. That way passing traffic will, hopefully, have to sideswipe the police car before hitting the officer.

The passenger officer gets out and stands behind his open door with his hand unobtrusively near his gun while the driver gets out with his ticket book. He stops a little to the rear of the driver's window and bends over slightly to look inside the car.

"May I see your driver's license?"

"I don't have one."

The officer opens the ticket book and flips out the top citation.

"Do you know why we stopped you?"

"Because we stole this car?"

The officer blinks a couple of times, then draws his gun and steps toward the rear of the car.

"Everybody out, slow, and put your hands on top of the car."

His partner also draws his weapon and sees his partner point to the license plate. Continuing to cover the three on the right side of the car, the partner reaches for the microphone. In about twenty seconds, he moves up towards his partner, nodding his head at him.

They handcuff their prisoners, call for another car to help transport them to jail and advise headquarters to contact the owner of the stolen car. It was taken about two hours ago in the southern part of the district but only reported about 15 minutes ago when the owner came out of the grocery store to find it missing. Dispatch hadn't even read it on the air yet.

They don't say a word about it until they leave the jail a couple of hours later.

"Good job." He said it with a straight face.

"Oh hell, you know I was just going to write them a couple of tickets and let them go."

They both started laughing.

SMILE, YOU'RE ON CANDID CAMERA

These days a female rape victim in a large city, if she insists upon it for her own comfort, can have her initial crime report taken by a female patrol officer backed up by a female crime scene technician and investigated by a female detective. Back in the Dark Ages of sex crimes investigations, this was not possible. In our city, she didn't even have a choice of hospitals.

Not all hospitals were created equal. Some had much better trauma centers than others, usually dictated by their proximity to the city's more frequent crime areas. Similarly, only a few of the city's hospitals were experienced in conducting rape examinations. There was no such thing as a standard-issue rape kit. Crime Lab technicians made up their own and carried them in their evidence collection boxes. At a minimum, they consisted of cotton swabs for collecting semen evidence, tools for scraping under fingernails and a sterile comb for combing the victim's pubic hair for samples of the suspect's hair.

The actual rape examination and the collection of the evidence samples was done by an ER doctor or nurse experienced with these procedures who would later be available to testify in court if a suspect was brought to trial. That was why the victim had to be taken to a certain hospital familiar with these procedures.

Eventually policies changed so a victim could be examined at any hospital she chose. The process of educating hospitals that had never seen a rape victim was sometimes a painful process.

The call came from one of the new hospitals on the call list. An excellent facility for medical care, it had been sheltered from most of the harsh realities of crime victims because it was only a few blocks from a much larger and more experienced trauma center.

The lady had just walked in and told the ER personnel she had been raped. They took her to a trauma room, made her comfortable and called the cops.

I got the call because both this hospital and the larger trauma center were in the district I was riding that day. I parked in front of the ER just as the Crime Lab van pulled up. The Crime Lab technician met me as we both walked in.

Charlie was a nice guy. Almost too nice a guy to be a cop. Very quiet, laid back, unassuming, almost shy, he'd have been great at undercover work if he'd wanted to because he didn't have the "cop look." The only thing that gave him away was the uniform since all our Crime Lab guys were fully commissioned officers. In a suit and tie he could easily have passed for a young banker, accountant or college professor.

We exchanged a few pleasantries as we walked into the ER. A uniformed cop never has to ask where to go in an ER, the medical people will automatically direct him to the trouble. This time, it was a grandmotherly-looking nurse in her sixties. She came over and beckoned us to follow her. Charlie and I automatically followed.

She stopped in front of one of the trauma rooms and told us the rape victim was in there. Charlie reached into his tool box and handed her a rape kit in a sterile plastic envelope. Anticipating the slightly confused look she gave him, Charlie asked her if she'd ever done a rape exam before. She shook her head so he explained.

"The cotton swabs are for collecting biological fluids from the oral, anal and vaginal cavities depending upon the circumstances of the case. They are in their individual containers. The tool in the other envelope is for scraping under the victim's fingernails if she scratched her attacker. The comb is for combing her pubic hair for samples of the suspect's hair. I have paper bags for the victim's clothing. Understand?"

She smiled thankfully at Charlie and nodded. She then retreated behind the curtain surrounding the trauma room. Charlie and I both began writing in our notebooks as we shared the information off the patient's admitting chart. In a couple of minutes the nurse stepped halfway out of the curtained area and nodded for us to come in, holding the curtain aside for us. Charlie went in first, looking down at his notebook for the victim's name.

"Miss Smith, I'm Officer ... uhhhhhh."

Charlie's voice trailed off into stunned silence as he looked up from his notebook. His reaction caused me to look up from filling in the Crime Against Persons report form in my notebook.

Our victim, a lady in her thirties, was lying facing us on a gynecological examination gurney. Both her legs were raised and spread wide apart in separate extensions branching off of the bottom of the gurney at forty-five degree angles. Her hospital gown had been pulled up to her waist and it was very obviously the only clothing she was wearing. Both she and the elderly nurse were looking at us expectantly. The nurse was holding the comb from the rape kit in one hand she was extending toward Charlie. Charlie looked like she was trying to hand him a live rattlesnake.

I recovered before Charlie did so I spoke first.

"Nurse, could we speak to you outside for a moment, please?"

When we got out of earshot of the trauma area, I spoke to her in as gentle a tone as I could manage.

"Nurse, I don't think you understand. *We* don't do the actual rape exam. You or a doctor does, in private with the patient. Then this officer collects the evidence and I interview the victim about the crime."

"But don't you have to watch, for some legal reason?"

"No ma'am, that's not necessary. We try to respect the victim's privacy as much as we possibly can. Since she's been the victim of a violent attack, she deserves as much courtesy and consideration as we can give her. Do you see?"

The nurse nodded and smiled sweetly at us, turning back into the trauma room, comb in hand.

When we were alone, I just grinned at the expression still on Charlie's face. I don't think he'd have been that surprised if she'd pointed a shotgun at him.

Undercover Vice

A philosophical old Vice cop once said that since ours was a country born in a revolution by men willing to fight and die for what they perceived to be their natural rights, no one would ever be able to tell an American that he couldn't buy a drink, place a bet or trade money for sex and make it stick. The best we could do was police it, try to control it within reasonable limits, try to minimize organized crime's control of it and levy fines against those who didn't pay taxes the way the rest of us did. You don't see many Form 1040's that list "gambler, bookie, bootlegger or prostitute" in the occupation box.

Under the vice-related laws of the time, city bars and clubs could not sell liquor by the drink. In other words, if you wanted to be served alcoholic beverages in a club, you had to purchase a bottle from a liquor store, bring it to the club, have your name written on it and be served out of that bottle until it ran out. Alcoholic beverages legally meant anything more than 3.2 per cent alcohol by volume (i.e., everything except beer).

The vice detectives could arrest a known prostitute just for hanging out on the street and soliciting business. They could arrest her (or him) for Loitering For The Purposes Of Prostitution, they'd pay a small fine and be released immediately with no jail time. But every few months they wanted to "trap" the prostitutes. That meant an undercover officer had to rent a room with her, get her to offer him sex for money, give her the money and have her begin disrobing to show intent to fulfill that bargain. Then they could arrest her for Offering To Engage In An Act Of Lewdness. This carried a much stiffer fine and some jail time, during which she would be subjected to a medical exam, checked for venereal diseases and treated if she had any. This was the only legal way of trying to protect the public who used their services from taking the clap home to mama.

In the early 1970s, our Vice Detail was a small unit, less than a dozen detectives. Since most had worked Vice for years, their faces and names were well known to the city's underworld denizens. Therefore when they needed someone for short-term undercover work, they resorted to drafting uniformed officers. They didn't actually "draft" them, they asked for volunteers.

Sometimes they took officers out of the Police Academy or ones who had just graduated. But their favorites were veteran officers with a year or two on the street but who had been assigned to areas of the city other than downtown. This meant they had some street experience but would minimize the chances of them being recognized. They also only used these officers for about a week so they wouldn't get too well known to be ineffective.

My partner and I were riding the predominantly black northeast sector on the Four Shift. We both had more than one year and less the three on the job, and we'd never ridden downtown so we fit the Vice Unit's profile. We were offered the chance to work undercover for Vice and we volunteered. It was a week we didn't have to shave (no facial hair was allowed for patrol officers then), could wear blue jeans and T-shirts to work, and it was a week out of the uniform and scout car.

TRAPPING AND GETTING TRAPPED

Our first night in Vice, we were each paired off with a single Vice detective. Each pair—one undercover patrolman and one Vice detective—would run their investigations independently and we'd meet up at the end of the shift. They said they'd start us off easy, busting clubs for liquor violations. Since it was winter and we were dressed warmly, hiding our guns, handcuffs and badges wouldn't be a problem.

They gave each of us a few "evidence bottles" and some marked money. These were small glass vials with plastic screw-on caps. We were to go into a club without a bottle and order an alcoholic mixed drink at the bar. If they refused to serve us, we were supposed to try to talk them into it, professing an ignorance of and disdain for the law. If they served us the drink, we'd watch them make it and take a sip to insure it contained alcohol, pay with the marked money and then drop the glass vial into it to get a sample for evidence. If we didn't come out within ten minutes that was the signal that we'd been served. The Vice detective would come in and the bartender would be arrested. The owner and waitress might also get arrested.

We started out in the downtown area. The Plastic Bar, Sweet Leona's, The Little White Cloud That Cried, the Talk of the Town, the Playhouse, the Terminal Lounge, the Tropic Club and others. As many as we could cover in eight hours.

The second night we moved farther afield to the joints bordering downtown and out on the Tenth Street strip. Little Abner's, the Swizzle Stick, the Scorpio Club, the Bunny Club, the Red Dog Saloon and others.

The third night we were told we had graduated to trapping hookers. This would be different in several ways. First, we'd still be going our separate ways but we'd each be with two detectives now. Second, we couldn't carry our guns, handcuffs or badges. Hookers would always give you a friendly hug and pat your butt while she was actually seeing if you were carrying a gun or two wallets. They knew a man carrying two wallets usually had a badge in the second one. The really smart ones would even run their feet up and down your calves to see if you were wearing an ankle holster. So the police equipment stayed in the back seat of the detective cruiser.

I'd go to a downtown hotel, the kind that rented rooms by the hour, and rent a room, even going through the farce of registering under a false name. They weren't about to ask to see your identification. I'd then proposition the desk clerk or whoever seemed to be in charge to send a call girl to my room. The Vice detectives would stake out the lobby until they saw the hooker go in. Then they'd come in, badge the desk clerk and check the register for which room I was in. One would stay with the desk clerk to keep him from leaving or making phone calls while the other would go up to my room and wait outside the door. When I'd made the case and money had changed hands, I was to open the door (the hookers automatically locked it behind them when they came in), let the Vice guy in and he'd make the arrest.

They told us they'd usually give us about fifteen minutes to convince the girl we weren't a cop, make the deal and exchange money. Another wrinkle was that the hookers in the city had recently become convinced that city cops wouldn't take a drink while on duty. This had a basis in fact because several officers had recently been fired for drinking on duty. That restriction didn't apply to undercover officers but the hookers hadn't figured that out yet. The hookers had developed a recent tactic of bringing a bottle with them, usually vodka, and insisting that the john have a shot or two with them before they got down to the sexual business. They thought this was a way of spotting the undercover cops because they wouldn't take a drink.

What the Vice guys didn't tell us was that they were watching us as closely as they were the hookers, just to be sure we didn't succumb to the girl's charms and forget our duty. They adhered to the fifteen minute time limit pretty closely. They didn't tell us that either.

So we hit the street. The Denver Hotel. Get a room, get a girl, have a couple of drinks, get her to offer sex for money, give her money, make the arrest, take her to jail.

Same routine in every place. The Kingkade Hotel, the Roberts Hotel, the Hudson Hotel, various other flophouses. Some hits, some misses. Some clerks got suspicious and wouldn't call a girl. Some of the girls were overly cautious and wouldn't make the necessary offer of sex for money. But eventually we had booked six girls into jail. The Vice guys decided we'd try the Black Hotel for our last stop that night.

I rented the room and the clerk called a girl. She came up to the room and I let her in. By this time I'd had a couple of shots of straight vodka with each of half a dozen hookers. I was no novice at drinking but nevertheless, I wasn't in the same shape I'd been in at the beginning of the shift. The Vice detective outside the door waited. And waited. And waited. Fifteen minutes went by, then twenty. Then, expecting the worst, he kicked the door in. And there we were.

She was sitting on the bed and I was sitting in a chair in the corner. Both fully clothed. Both with a drink in our hands. No sex. No offer. No money exchanged. No case.

We'd been talking. After about a pint of straight vodka and some conversation, I'd found out this girl was a pretty interesting person. She had no pimp and was strictly her own boss. The desk clerk got a small cut but she kept most of her earnings. It turned out she had a Master's degree in English Literature. The subject of why she did this kind of work naturally came up. She said she'd made $30,000 last year, hadn't paid a cent in taxes and damned little in fines. Although I didn't tell her, my annual salary at the time was about $7,000 and she probably knew it.

Then she got up, smiled and walked out, having committed no crime other than getting a drunken cop a little drunker. And a couple of amused Vice cops took me home.

GETTING CAUGHT NAKED (BUT NOT THAT WAY)

Everyone learned lessons from my previous experience. I learned to eat a full meal before going to work, keep it to one drink per hooker and act like I was anxious to get down to business. The Vice guys learned to have us only bust a couple of hookers a night so we weren't useless for everything else.

One night we went out and tried several flophouses without success. Either the clerks or the girls wouldn't go for it so we came up empty. Maybe the word was getting around, I don't know. After several hours of not being able to make a case or an arrest, we all met back at the station. The Vice detectives put their heads together and decided we'd try to bust some bootleggers. It was already well after midnight and the bars were closed so there wasn't anything more promising left to do.

They decided our first target would be Billy. Billy ran a gas station on Exchange Avenue near the stockyards but that was just a front. Billy was an old time thief who had progressed to being a small-time fence and bootlegger. When he wasn't pumping gas, he was buying stolen property over the counter and selling illegal whiskey out of the back room. Now in his fifties, Billy had a record stretching back three decades with five felony convictions. The Vice guys didn't think he'd sell to us because he was such a crusty, suspicious old bastard but we might as well give it a try.

So they put us in an old El Camino. I don't know if it was a seized car or one of their private cars or where it came from. They just told us to go to Billy's station and try to buy a bottle. So off we went. Too quickly, as it turned out.

Since we'd been out trying to bust hookers, we didn't have our guns or badges on us. They were in the back seat of the detective cruiser. We were rushed into our new assignment so fast and we were so used to being armed all the time we didn't remember to retrieve our guns first. The detectives would wait for us about a block away.

So we went to Billy's station. Put a couple of dollars worth of gas in the car and went inside to pay. Then we made a mistake. My partner started doing the talking. He was a short-tempered New York yankee and I should have known better. Billy naturally resisted his first efforts to buy a bottle and my partner got a little insistent. Billy got his hackles up and laid a .38 on the counter, telling us to hit the road. His fat, dumb helper seconded it by covering us with a shotgun from the storage room. So we hit the road. For about a block.

Turning the corner a block away after never getting it out of low gear, my partner slammed on the brakes next to the detective cruiser and we both got out, leaving the car idling in the middle of the street. While both the detectives were asking us what happened, neither one of us said a word. We were obviously pissed off. Having guns pointed at you will have that effect. We just got our guns out of the back seat and got back in the car. My partner then floored it in low gear again and we were back at Billy's station within a minute, the puzzled detectives in hot pursuit.

Leaving the car running with the doors open next to the pumps, we went back in the station and confronted a startled Billy and his helper. I stood off to one side while my partner laid his .357 Magnum on the counter and spoke to Billy through clenched teeth.

"Want to get that gun back out, old man?"

Instantly understanding, Billy just raised his hands. My partner switched his attention to the helper.

"How about you, lard ass? Want to reach for that scattergun?"

The helper looked like he was about to faint when the detectives came in. Billy and helper went to jail, their guns were confiscated and so were about a dozen cases of bootleg whiskey in the back room. The Vice guys couldn't have been happier. Instead of one misdemeanor arrest, they had two felonies.

Patrol II

EULOGY

Most of the officers in most municipal police departments are hometown boys or, at least, home state boys. A few take a more roundabout route. Mike took a more roundabout route than usual.

Mike was a New York City native and if it wasn't visible, it was damned sure audible with his brusque, nasal *New Yawk* accent. After he enlisted, the Air Force sent him to Great Falls, Montana, and Mike discovered he liked places where there was more grass than concrete and you weren't always elbow-to-elbow with thousands of people all the time. Meeting and marrying an Oklahoma girl along with his discharge brought him to the state capital of his bride's home state. The fact that he had three brothers on the NYPD determined his choice of employment.

In spite of the fact that he talked faster than some of the locals could listen, Mike became a hell of a cop. He was a self-starter who felt his job entailed more than just cruising around "showing the flag", eating donuts and writing a few tickets. He made a lot of stops for traffic violations but he was more likely to let them go if they didn't have criminal warrants. He took the radio calls in his district but in the meantime, he preferred chasing felons and he caught a lot of them.

Once one of his NYPD brothers came to town to visit. Mike and a few buddies took his brother out to a cop bar. Naturally the alcohol flowed freely and so did the war stories. Mike's brother told about how when they made calls in the tenement district, one officer watched the windows for snipers while the other watched the rooftops. It seems one of the favorite sports for the neighborhood kids was collecting old dead car batteries on the rooftops and trying to drop them on the cops ten stories below when they got out on a radio call at that building. At least one officer had been permanently crippled that way and had to retire. Mike's OCPD buddies countered with their own stories but at one point late in the evening, Mike's brother made the comment that "If you ain't been a cop in New York City, you ain't really been a cop."

As you might imagine, all of Mike's buddies took exception.

"That's bullshit."

"Yeah. So you've got 25,000 cops and we've got 500. So you've got 2000 murders a year and we've got 75. So what? It's just a matter of numbers."

"Just numbers?" he responded. "We get half a dozen officers or more killed in the line of duty every year. How many do you have?"

"Just one every two or three years and we're damned glad of it. But they're just as dead."

"Yeah," another piped up. "And why do you think our patrol guys wear the high-impact plastic helmets and the Traffic guys wear the soft white caps? Because getting hit in the head with a Coke bottle or a brick pitched from a two or three-story building at Second and Stiles isn't a hell of a lot better than a battery dropped from a ten-story building." Then several others took up the mantra.

"Even with eight million people up there, I imagine we've got a few things down here that you've never seen."

"Yeah. Ever seen a homicide with a bow and arrow? I have."

"Or pick up the bodies after a tornado? I don't remember reading about too many tornadoes in New York City."

"Or have cattle get out of the Stockyards? Ever try to herd cattle off an interstate highway with a patrol car?"

"Or drive through a residential neighborhood and see some kook who's got his eighteen-foot pet python stretched out in the front yard, sunning himself?"

"Or go into a bar *knowing* that nine out of ten people in there are carrying a gun? You've got some pretty strict gun laws in New York, right? Down here, gun control means hitting what you're aiming at."

"Or try to break up a knife fight at an Indian powwow after they've been drinking for three days straight? Not all the Indians down here have given up, you know."

Unable to get a word in edgewise, the New Yorker held up his hands in mock surrender. But he obviously hadn't changed his mind. The evening ended on a slightly tense note.

Time passed but the war continued. The groups on one side changed constantly. Students for a Democratic Society, the Weathermen, Students Against the Vietnam War, the Symbionese Liberation Army, the Black Liberation Army, the Black Muslims, the Black Panthers, the American Indian Movement, the Hells Angels, the Dixie Mafia, the Kansas City and New Orleans mobs trying to move in, *et al, ad infinitum*. But on the other side were always the cops. And the body count on both sides rose.

One night at oh-dark-thirty, Mike got flagged down by a security guard at a local hospital. He pointed out a Cadillac leaving the parking lot and said they had been driving around slowly, checking out the parked cars like they were looking for one to burglarize. Mike pulled out on the street and stopped them. There were eight people in the car.

Mike got the driver out of the car while his partner stood back, covering him. When the questions started coming faster than the answers, the driver took off running across the street. Mike caught him in a few strides and they both went down swinging. When Mike's partner ran to help him, the driver's brother stepped out of the car and fired one shot across the roof of the Caddy. The bullet entered Mike's side and went through his aorta. He couldn't have survived it if it had happened in an ER full of doctors.

Mike's partner shot one of the fleeing suspects but the other six, including the shooter, bolted in every direction. For the rest of the night, off-duty cops were filing into the station. Carrying every kind of personal weapon from shotguns to deer rifles, martial law was unofficially declared. The suspect was arrested the next day in a housing project across town.

Mike's three brothers from the NYPD came to town for the funeral. Being cops, they were given unprecedented access to the case information. The patrol guys, the homicide detectives, everybody opened their files to them and told them the whole story. The traffic stop, the fight, the shooting, the crime scene investigation, the hunt for the suspect, the arrests, the filing of the murder charges. Being cops, they'd have immediately spoken up if they'd seen anything they didn't like. They just gave it a cop's typically understated praise—"good job."

Some of the trappings of the funeral were familiar to any cop—the flag-draped casket, the honor guard, hundreds of dress uniforms in the pews, the black ribbons across the badges, the long line of police motorcycles leading the hearse, a line of black and white patrol cars behind the hearse, flashing red lights all the way to the horizon. But Mike's brothers weren't prepared to see the citizens pulling their cars over to the side of the road while the procession passed. They definitely weren't prepared to see some of the citizens getting out of their cars and placing their hands over their hearts as we passed. I guess you don't see things like that very often at a New York cop's funeral.

After the funeral, Mike's closest buddies and his brothers had the traditional cop's wake. Not a religious ceremony, it was an informal adjournment to a cop bar where everybody took turns telling war stories about Mike. Some philosopher said once that the only real immortality is when friends speak of you with humor and affection. Alcohol also helps dissolve tears. After several hours of this, one of Mike's friends got up to go to the bathroom. As he was washing his hands, one of Mike's brothers came in, the one who had come to town the year before. As Mike's friend started to leave, his brother spoke to his back.

"Hey." He turned back to him.

"You know what I said last year, about how you weren't really a cop if you hadn't been a cop in New York?"

"Yeah?"

"I was wrong." He stuck out his hand.

They shook hands and walked back outside to order another round of drinks.

"One night Mike and I were riding Baker Four on the Four Shift—"

THE BAKER ONE OLYMPICS

It's July and the annual three-digit heat is no particular surprise. This year, however, it's not the baking, dry heat of most years. This year the southerly winds keep saturating the air with moisture from the Gulf of Mexico. No rain, just the oppressive humidity. The temperature doesn't drop much below the three-digit level even at night. The combination of heat and humidity has turned the city into a sauna. Tempers are running especially high in the poorer inner city areas where there are fewer air conditioners to provide a temporary escape from the sweltering weather.

Most of the air conditioners in this section of the city are in police patrol cars. They don't give any relief to the citizens except for the ones who are handcuffed in the back seats temporarily and not much more to the cops in the front seat. When the cars are moving it's not too bad but most of the cool air goes out the windows because the cops have to keep them cracked a few inches so they can hear things they need to hear like sirens, screams, gunshots and breaking glass. About the best they can do is try to position themselves so the cool air goes by them on its way out the window. When the car stops, as it does frequently to handle the increased volume of radio calls, the air conditioner has to be turned off or the car will overheat within a few minutes.

This year the short-sleeved poplin shirts and lack of ties with the summer uniform are little consolation. The Police Uniform Committee is deluged with complaints about trying to find a replacement for the heavy, scratchy blue wool uniform pants.

The signs of the shorter tempers are everywhere but much more so in the poorer areas nearer to the center of the city. One of the poorest is a few square miles directly east of the downtown business district and north of the river that bisects the city from east to west. It's known by many different names depending upon whether you live there, work there or are on the city's Historic Preservation Committee. To the members of the police department, it's known by the designation of the patrol car assigned to the district, Baker One.

The general theory of manpower distribution is one patrol car for one district but that theory doesn't work in practice in Baker One. One car is assigned to a call but at least two always respond and half a dozen others are prepared to on a moment's notice. In any area where the buildings are more than a single story high, one car's officers get out to handle the call while another car watches the rooftops, looking for people who think that black and white fiberglass helmets make excellent targets for bricks and empty bottles.

Violent crimes have reached new highs. There have been four murders on one particular block in the last month. On top of everything else, police service and morale have reached a new low in the area. It all started three months before when a riot left about 20 officers injured. Since then, two cops have been shot, one stabbed and one was killed only two weeks ago. The arrest statistics show that more suspects have been armed than ever before. Every officer has had nothing but a hard time on every call for weeks. Phony calls have also increased alarmingly, making everyone tense, expecting an ambush where the projectiles are a little more destructive than bricks and bottles.

Resisting Arrest and Assault On An Officer statistics have gone sky-high again. A lot of the impetus for going "above and beyond the call of duty" has left the local patrolmen lately. They're more concerned with getting back to their families at the end of the shift than with the level of police service the local citizens get. They're well aware of the typical criticisms. "That's what I pay taxes for" and "That's what you get paid for" is a familiar refrain. Statements like that always come from people who don't risk getting a brick dropped on their heads or shot in the back when they're at work every day. Every cop accepts certain risks when he takes he job but as the risks rise to the level of eventual certainties, the dedication goes down. And anybody who thinks *anyone* gets paid enough to get killed is far too stupid to discuss it with.

"3-Baker-1."

"Go ahead."

"400 block East Second, mental patient causing a disturbance."

"10-4."

"3-Cruiser-4, back that unit in the 400 block East Second on a mental patient. The calling party requests a supervisor."

"3-Cruiser-4 clear."

"KKC867, 0115."

My partner and I are several miles from the call. Besides, we're waiting for a wrecker to impound the car of a drunk driver who ran into a tree. The object of our call is dozing fitfully in our back seat so we sit back and listen to the drama unfold over the police radio.

"3-Cruiser-4 to Headquarters."

"Go ahead."

"Reference this call on East Second, the mental patient is a 19-year-old male. His grandmother advises he is an outpatient of the state mental hospital and he was being treated for suicidal tendencies. He's climbed up an oilrig at this location and he refuses to come down or respond to our attempts to communicate with him. We need the helicopter and a Fire Department hook-and-ladder out here right away."

"10-4."

We both know the location. An oil derrick about 100 feet high stands right in the middle of a residential area, if you can call whorehouses, dope houses and corn whiskey joints that. We also both know the sergeant in 3-Cruiser-4 tonight. He's very excitable and has a tendency to get emotionally involved in the most everyday situations so he must be damned near hysterical over this deal. But he can't handle the situation alone and I doubt if he can expect many death-defying feats from his men tonight. Too many of them attended a friend's funeral last week and too many have had to go to a hospital before going home to their wives and kids this summer.

Our wrecker comes shortly and drags the drunk's car off. Since the oil derrick is between us and the city jail for which our friend snoring in the back seat is destined, we decide to stop by the East Second street call on the way in.

As we approach the area, we see that the street is blocked off at our end by a red Fire Department sedan and a patrol car. The other end of the street is blocked by two patrol cars. A hook-and-ladder truck is in the center of the block with its ladder slowly extending toward the top of the derrick. The cops and firemen are standing outside their vehicles, all eyes looking up at a shadowy figure in jeans and white T-shirt perched on the top of the oil derrick. The street is completely empty, everyone having been sent inside the buildings or outside the perimeter. The late hour on a weeknight helps, too. We can hear the metallic squeak of a bullhorn in the distance. Obviously 3-Cruiser-4 has decided to personally reason with the mental patient.

As we pull up to the patrol car, a Fire Department Battalion Chief in a white helmet is talking animatedly to one of the cops.

"—stupid bastard wanted one of my men to climb up the ladder and grab the guy while he distracted him by squawking at him through that bullhorn. And then fight him down a 100-foot ladder? I told him 'You gotta be shittin' me'. Is he always like that?"

The other officer grinned at me. I guess the Fire Department's dedication had slipped a little lately, too. They also had been the recent targets for bricks and bottles. Hurt their feelings, I guess. Everybody's supposed to love firemen. But not lately.

"I guess the Sarge is in character tonight?" I said to the officer.

"Oh yeah. Been running around like a chicken with his head cut off. He's got grappling hooks and ropes and all kinds of crap over there. Nobody'll go up the rig and the Sarge is too fat. So he's just been yelling at him through the horn for the last half hour."

The radio crackled with static. Obviously the sergeant's hand-held radio.

"3-Cruiser-4 to Headquarters, have you been able to get a helicopter yet?"

"Negative, 3-Cruiser-4. They're down for fuel."

The Fire Chief sneered.

"What the hell's he trying now? Going to drop a line to him from the chopper? He can reach the ladder if he wants to come down. Shit!"

The radio broke squelch again with the sergeant's panic-stricken voice.

"He jumped."

The body was already about 20 feet down when we looked up. He struck the side of the derrick twice before he disappeared behind the roofline of one of the buildings. The radio broke squelch with Headquarters' stronger signal this time.

"Attention all officers, Sykes Ambulance from Fourteenth and Kelly to the 400 block East Second, Code Three on a jumper, 3-Baker-1 and 3-Cruiser-4 on the call, KKC867 at 0149."

I put the car back in gear and steered around the patrol car. When we approached the other end of the street, one of the officers was backing his car up so we could get through. The other three officers were writing on their notebooks on the hood of the other car. As I pulled up beside them, they held the notebooks up toward us. Two of them had "10.0" written on them and the third had "9.5".

As we coasted by them, the third officer spoke.

"Didn't keep his feet together all the way down."

ROGER DODGER, OVER AND OUT

The noise in the lineup room had reached the level of a low roar as it always did when occupied by forty patrolmen just before shift change on a full shift night. Most were seated at three rows of long, narrow tables butted together that ran the full length of the room. The tables and chairs were a recently acquired luxury. The men had previously had to stand in lines along the three rows of black tiles placed in the otherwise white rubber-tiled floor.

Walking down the aisles between the long tables where the men were seated, one could hear snatches of conversations running the gamut of human interest in their all-male society; women, sex, football, sex, women, cars, police work, politics, sex and so forth.

"—so I clocked her at 60 in a 40. Pulled her over and, God, she was fine lookin'. So I says 'What's the problem, lady?' and she says 'I'm having trouble breathing. Do you know mouth-to-mouth resuscitation?'"

"So?"

"So I wrote her up. She wasn't *that* fine lookin'!"

"—third in the nation last year and blew it by three touchdowns! So there's five bucks shot to hell—"

"—wouldn't vote for that incompetent asshole even before I saw him work in court—"

"—so my back looks like I got caught in a phone both with a bobcat. I've tried to get her to trim her fingernails but she—"

As the minute hand on the wall clock touched the twelve, the hall door opened and the lieutenant walked in carrying a clipboard fat with papers in his hand. The roar subsided to a low growl. The lieutenant didn't take his accustomed place at the raised podium but stopped at the edge of the elevated stage in the front of the room. The door opened again and the Assistant Chief walked in carrying a portable tape recorder. Officers exchanged puzzled glances throughout the room. Assistant Chiefs didn't come to lineup very often, especially night shift lineups.

Not a well-respected man, he stepped up behind the podium as a low voice from the back of the room hummed the first few bars of *Hail To The Chief*. Some of the officers coughed into their fists while other merely turned their faces down to their laps while their shoulders shook with suppressed laughter. The noise stopped entirely when the Division Major, who *was* well-respected, stepped into the room.

As the Chief laid the tape recorder on the podium, he spoke to the group in a serious tone but without anger.

"Now that's a damned good example of why I'm here tonight. There's nothing wrong with a little cutting up and clowning around in the lineup room or anywhere else where there's nothing but policemen. We understand our own peculiar brand of humor, which is a little strange to the average citizen. But of all the places that humor does *not* belong, the first one is the radio."

No glances now. All knew they had been guilty at one time or another in varying degrees.

"There's been too much screwing around on the radio lately. It's not just this shift. It's been department-wide and that's why I'm making all the lineups to emphasize this point. I'm not accusing anybody and I'm not accusing everybody. I'm just saying that there's a hell of a lot of people out there who have police receivers besides us. Wrecker services, ambulance services, hospitals, suburban PD's, the Fire Department, some thieves and a lot of just plain interested citizens. They usually monitor the patrol frequency because that's where most of the action is most of the time and they can hear everything we say on that radio. That's also where most of the screwing around is done, unfortunately. You all know all communications traffic is taped on all frequencies around the clock. The cassette I have in this recorder is a selection of some of the traffic in the last week."

He reached over to the portable recorder and punched a button. The familiar sound of radio static filled the room as the officers at the tables leaned forward slightly to hear the tape.

"4-Baker-7 to Headquarters, do you have an ambulance on the way to this shooting on 80th?"

"10-4."

"Tell them to hurry it up!"

The tension and urgency in the officer's voice was evident. A microphone was keyed and the squelch was broken. Someone was drumming his fingers on the mike, making the clippety-clop sound of a running horse. A minute of silence followed.

"4-Baker-7 to Headquarters, this victim's DOA. I need a Medical Examiner and Robbery-Homicide at this location."

"10-4."

Another anonymous microphone was keyed and they heard another anonymous officer humming "Taps". There was little sympathy for the domestic shooting victim in 4-Baker-7's district that night.

"2-Adam-16."

"Go ahead 2-Adam-16."

"2-Adam-16, call Sally at 837-2961."

"10-4." A tone of slight exasperation.

There was a squealing sound as several microphones were keyed at once. In the turmoil, three officers' voices could be heard distinctly. One was hooting, one was panting heavily and the third was delivering a long, moist kiss over the airwaves.

"3-Delta-9."

"Go ahead 3-Delta-9."

"3-Delta-9, are you 10-6?"

"Hell, no!"

A few moments of uncertain silence. He could have just said he wasn't busy. The dispatcher's voice was hesitant when it came back on.

"3-Delta-9, can you take a call to 9826 South Agnew on a theft?"

"Headquarters, I can take anything you can dish out!"

They all knew this officer. He had been on this shift. He had also been working three off-duty jobs to try to pay for his wife's excesses in spending. He had also been taking her diet pills by the handful to keep himself going at that pace. The sleep deprivation and amphetamines had been affecting his mind. He had resigned the day after the incident on the tape had occurred.

"1-Adam-15 to Headquarters."

"Go ahead." Laughter in the background.

"What's the complainant's address on this call?"

"How the hell should I know, 1-Adam 15?" More laughter.

Then silence.

"1-Adam-15 to Headquarters, I can't find the complainant on my call. I'll be 10-8 until they call back with more information."

"Whatever you think, 15."

The dispatcher's voice was thick and slurred. He was obviously drunk.

"Attention all you motherfuckers, Gold Cross Ambulance from 49th and Classen to 30th and Penn on a stabbing. Anybody wanta take it?"

They all knew this dispatcher, too. Thirty years on the force and it had made a drunk out of him. He came to work a little drunker every night but it had never affected his performance before so his co-workers had turned a blind eye to it. But this particular night he had been on a two-day binge and was practically crawling when he came to work. Two of the other dispatchers thought it would be funny to put him on the radio in that shape so they did. The result had been disastrous for him but hysterically funny to them. They were the ones laughing so uproariously in the background on the tape. The old man had been retired the next day and the other two dispatchers were on disciplinary suspension without pay.

The Chief reached up and switched the tape recorder off before he spoke again.

"Incidentally, 'Roger Dodger, over and out' is not the same as '10-4.' So knock it off."

A few officers glanced cautiously at the red-faced officer who used that phrase to let the dispatchers know he didn't like the call they'd just given him.

As the Chief exited through the side door, the lieutenant stepped up to the podium.

"Taylor, Demoss."

"Here." The two voices answered as one.

"Baker 1, Car 68-127. Jones, Woodie."

"Here."

"Baker 2, Car 69-213. Torres, Rodgers."

"Here."

GOOD ALARMS, BAD ALARMS

As the title suggests, alarms come in two categories, good and bad. From a cop's perspective, a good alarm is one that only goes off when a burglary or armed robbery is in progress. A bad alarm is one that goes off when one of those crimes isn't occurring. After a little time on the streets, every patrol cop gets to know the odds of whether a certain alarm is a good one or bad one.

Alarms also come in two sub-categories, loud and silent. Loud alarms set off a bell, gong, siren or some other noisemaker that lets everyone within a block in every direction knows it has gone off. Cops don't usually consider loud alarms as good alarms because they chase criminals off instead of giving the cops a good chance to catch them. I suppose it has happened but I don't know of a single arrest ever made off of a loud alarm. A burglar would have to be nuts or deaf to keep working after the alarm starts clanging.

Of course, a cop can't always just shine the spotlight on the obvious points of entry (doors and windows) to make sure they're secure and then ignore the alarm. Trying to cut costs, the owner might have just wired the obvious points of entry and skipped interior motion detectors so you have to consider that the burglar might have "roofed" it, i.e. cut a hole in the roof which usually isn't wired for the alarm. The burglar also might have set the alarm off as he was leaving because he couldn't get back out the hole he made in the roof.

A lot of loud alarms also fell under the "boy who cried wolf" category. Many were so sensitive that they went off in high winds or thunderstorms, not a good quality when they're in the middle of Tornado Alley. In those days a lot of churches seemed to have very sensitive loud alarms. A pretty sad situation, not just that churches had lousy alarms but the fact that they had to have them in the first place.

Cops like silent alarms a lot better in some ways. The bad guys usually don't know when they've been set off. They're usually on businesses that have a higher risk of being burglarized or robbed like banks, liquor stores, convenience stores, gun dealers or high-end clothing stores. Businesses like the first three are a little more hair-raising because they are usually deliberately set off by employees, indicating that something is going on and you may be walking into a gunfight or a hostage situation. I said cops like silent alarms better "in some ways" because there's a good chance the crime will be in progress when they get there but nobody wants to walk into a gunfight in the middle of a bank lobby full of innocent citizens. Most patrol cops have made silent alarms on banks that were accidentally set off by the employees. They just smile sheepishly and apologize but they didn't have to creep up on the place wearing a nice big target of a uniform and try to figure out if one of all the people in the place is a bank robber with a Magnum in his pocket.

Businesses like the last two are usually motion detector alarms indicating a burglary in progress. Burglars aren't usually armed but there are always exceptions to the rule. If a burglar in a gun store isn't armed, he's not more than arm's length away from better firepower than the cops are carrying.

When everybody's on the same radio frequency, the entire shift learns which the good and bad alarms are or at least which are the better and worse ones.

One of the best ones in the early 1970s was on a gun shop on Classen Boulevard in the near northwest area. The last few times it had gone off, a burglar had been taken out of the building. It was in a converted residence that had two advantages for the cops and disadvantages for potential burglars—one front door and one back door. The last few burglars caught in that gun shop had not chosen to take advantage of all the armament around them but you never know when a criminal's level of desperation will exceed their good sense. Although in a northwest patrol district, the gun shop was barely a mile from several northeast districts and closer than that to the downtown districts. Any cop worth his salt will burn up a brand new scout car to get to an alarm like that.

"Adam 12, silent alarm, 3216 North Classen, on the gun shop."

"Clear, from 23rd and McKinley."

"Adam 10's at 18th and Classen."

"Baker 5's en route from 23rd and Broadway."

"Baker 6 from 36th and Santa Fe."

"KKC867 at 0243."

And probably several others who won't admit it on the air. The cops in Dispatch just grin at each other as they remember their days on the streets. On a quiet night, you can almost hear the four-barrel carburetors open up as gas pedals are mashed to the floor.

Almost 3 A.M. Virtually no traffic on the streets. No sirens, just the red lights if necessary. Headlights and brake lights switched off at least a block away. The patrol car's interior lights have already been rigged so they don't come on when the doors open. Radios turned down to low volume. Two black-and-whites coming up the back alley while two more are sliding into the small front parking area. One last radio transmission from one of the cars in the alley.

"Back door's been pried. Going in."

Drivers bail out with guns drawn, passengers grab the Ithaca shotgun out of the dashboard rack as they go out. The officers in front cover the still-locked front door and both sides of the building. All of these officers and many others have been in this store, on and off duty, and all know the interior layout well.

The two officers at the back go in the back door quickly, one to the right and one to the left. Don't backlight yourself in the doorway.

"Police! Come out before you get hurt!"

Silence. Not unexpected. Not many give up easily.

The driver has the only flashlight, the other's hands full of Ithaca twelve-gauge. Once inside, the officer turns on the flashlight, held a full arm's length away from his body on the opposite side of his raised pistol. Sweep the room quickly although in a room this small the flashlight lights the whole room without much sweeping. The rifles and shotguns in the wall racks look undisturbed, no gaps between the stacked weapons. That's good.

One moves to the left to look down the aisle behind the counter. Empty. The other one opens what used to be a closet door and is now used to store ammo, primers and cans of gunpowder. Nothing. One officer moves down the aisle behind the long side of the "L" shaped counter while the other trains the flashlight on the short leg of the "L" and trains his eyes halfway between the counter and the opening into the other room so he can instantly sense movement from either direction.

The one behind the counter peeks cautiously over the edge of the short leg of the counter, gun first. Nothing. His gun raising and aiming at the opening into the other room silently tells his partner that. Without exposing himself in the opening, the other officer shines the flashlight around the corner. From his position, the one behind the counter can see behind the stand-alone counter on the east wall. Nothing. He shifts his aim to the rest of the room and his partner moves the flashlight in that direction.

Another "L" shaped counter runs down the south and west walls. A large glass-topped display case about the size of a pool table, full of handguns, stands in the center of the small room. Without stepping into the opening, the officer with the flashlight can see behind the long leg of the counter in the adjoining room. Nothing. The one with the shotgun moves to his side of the opening and kneels, pointing the shotgun into the other room.

The handgun display case is not more than five yards in front of him. In the dancing shadows in the room, he thinks he sees a shadow a little darker than the others in the two-foot space below the case. He bobs the barrel of the shotgun slightly and his partner drops the flashlight beam lower. The shadow moved a little after the flashlight beam stopped.

A slight digression here for people who aren't familiar with police shotguns. Our shotguns were locked into a rack bolted to the dashboard that held the weapon upright between the officers. They were loaded at the beginning of each shift with four rounds of double-ought buckshot in the magazine, no round in the chamber. A twelve-gauge double-ought buckshot shell contains nine lead balls, each almost the size of a .38 caliber bullet. The reason no round was loaded into the chamber is because if you accidentally brushed the trigger, you might have a hole in the scout car's roof big enough to drop a bowling ball through. Also because the safeties weren't that reliable. One officer who pumped a round in the chamber while the shotgun was standing in the rack blew the red light off the top of the car and temporarily deafened himself and his partner. The trigger was never touched. Just slamming the slide forward hit the primer and fired the shell.

Most people who have seen enough movies and TV have at least a passing familiarity with the metal-on-metal "ca-chunk" sound of a live round being racked into a shotgun. Movies use it for dramatic effect with good reason. In a real situation, there are very few sounds that can raise the hairs on the back of your neck quicker. Even more so if you've ever seen what a shotgun can do to a human being.

A shotgun that isn't ready to fire is just a club. I don't know why the officer hadn't racked a round in when he got out of the car. I don't know why he spent five minutes pointing a shotgun that wasn't ready to fire around the gun shop. Maybe he forgot. Maybe he got caught up in an adrenaline moment. I'm fairly certain it wasn't for dramatic effect but that's the way it turned out.

Back to the gun shop.

He aimed the shotgun at the shadow under the display case.

"Under the handgun case. Come out if you want to live."

CA-CHUNK!

A little gasp of air comes from under the case. Then a gurgling sound. The shadow stirs.

"Hands first!"

The burglar crawls out, slowly, toward the officer. The partner steps over him, flashlight held under his left armpit, pistol pointing at him with handcuffs in his left hand. When he's cuffed, the officer steps over, unlocks and opens the front door, careful not to expose himself without waving a gray-sleeved arm first. The other officers walk in.

"What's that smell?"

"He shit himself."

"Why?"

"An Ithaca enema, I guess."

SOMETIMES

You get the call an hour before shift change. The last hour of the graveyard shift. It's still pitch black because it's the beginning of winter. A burglary in progress at a car lot.

You get there in a couple of minutes because there's nothing else on the streets at this time of the morning. The car lot has a security guard but he's the one who called. He steps out of his warm corner of the glass-enclosed showroom just long enough to get in your car when you pull up with the lights out. He saw the shadow moving out in the lot but he makes minimum wage, the temperature outside is one-third of his age so he calls the cops. You've heard this story before. So you get your flashlight, he goes back in his warm showroom and you start walking between the rows of cars. This car lot leaves all the outside lights off at night, probably for the same reason they pay the old security guard minimum wage.

Gun out, you use the button on the flashlight instead of flipping the switch on steady. You just flash it a second in the interior of each car to see if there's a body in there. Flashlight arm extended all the way away from your body so if the light draws gunfire, you might get hit in the hand or arm but not in the face or chest—if he's a good shot.

You get halfway down the second row when you see the quick flash of yellow light two rows over. A car's interior light. You quickly but quietly move to that row. When you get near where you saw the light, you get down on your knees. Looking under the row of cars, you see a shadow a little darker than the rest of the shadows a few cars away. The round part of the shadow is towards the front of the car. You get up and move down to the car's rear. You kneel down with as much of your upper body as possible shielded by a rear tire. You flash your light on the shadow and point your gun at his feet.

"Police. Show me your hands. Slowly."

He does.

"Crawl out."

He does. You stick him up against the car and frisk him. You've already got a bad feeling about this. You turn him around.

"How old are you?"

"Seventeen." He almost doesn't get it out because he's shaking so badly and it's not because he's cold.

You handcuff him and stick him in the car. Then you have to go back to walking the aisles. Five minutes later you find it. Four car radios lying between two cars. Now you have to check every car on the lot, find the four that have been burglarized and make a separate report on each vehicle. By that time it's shift change and you'll be late coming in.

And you'll be later than that. He's a juvenile. You have to notify his parents. Then check the stolen radios into the property room. Then you have to complete your arrest report in person, dictating it to a report clerk. You can't just record the report on a Dictaphone for later transcription because you have to have a copy of it in hand when you take him to the juvenile detention home. And half a dozen other special procedures because he's under eighteen. Cops hate kiddie calls, especially kiddie felons. It means an automatic three hours and maybe more.

You can't question him without his parents so there's nothing to talk about on the way to the station. He's stone silent, apparently because he's scared and not because he's a juvenile pro. So you have plenty of time to think.

You start thinking about whether it's worth it. You won't get to eat breakfast with your wife this morning. You won't get to take your son to school. You'll miss his school play this morning. He's a cowboy in the school's production of *Oklahoma*. And it's not the first school play you've missed. Or the first parent-teacher conference. Or the first T-ball game. And you know from talking to the other guys, it'll get worse.

Missed baseball games, football games, wrestling matches, soccer matches, missed dinners, picnics, movies, birthdays, anniversaries, parties, a thousand broken promises.

You run into guys who graduated from high school with you. They don't have Ph.D.'s from Yale or MD's from Harvard but they're still making two or three times what you do. They don't change shifts every month or work nights two-thirds of the time. They have every weekend off and never have to go to court on their time off. They never eat fast food and only see a sunrise when they go to Hawaii on vacation. They haven't been in a fight since high school and have never heard a shot fired in anger especially at themselves.

Of course they also don't have as much fun at their jobs as you do. They usually don't get much job satisfaction or feel like they've made a big difference in someone's life. They usually haven't had the chance to save someone's life nor had to deal with the possibility of taking someone else's. You love your job but you know how much it takes away from your family. Every day. Sometimes you just can't help but wonder if it's worth it.

You stick him in the juvenile holdover cell. You chew his ass royally. You explain his future. First offense? A few days in the Juvenile detention home. Another ass-chewing from a judge. Probation. Next time you're an adult. The joint. Anal sex. Oral sex. And not on your terms, on theirs. Bring your own wedding dress. He listens silently but not sullenly so maybe something's getting through. But you never know. You start your reports.

Five years pass. The State Fair's in town. You're assigned as one of the herd of the uniforms at the fairgrounds again. You're walking down the Midway, looking at the thousands of passing faces and comparing them to wanted bulletins, watching the carnies to see they don't entice the young girls into their tents, most of the time just serving the function of walking scarecrow.

"Officer!"

You stop and turn because he's used your name after the "Officer." A young man walks up, smiling. A girl carrying a baby is with him.

"What's the problem?"

"No problem." He's still smiling. "You don't remember me, do you?"

"Sorry. You sort of look familiar but I meet a lot of people."

"We met about five years ago. In a car lot on North May one night."

"Oh. Yeah. I remember. How're you doing?"

"I'm doing fine. Oh, I'm sorry, honey." He turned to the girl. "This is my wife, Angie, and our son Bobby. We've got another one due in about six months." Both of them were smiling, happily and proudly, the kind of smiles you can't help but return. "This is the officer who arrested me."

His last statement to his wife surprised me a little but their smiles didn't change any. "Congratulations."

"Thanks. I just wanted you to know something. I went back to school and graduated. Then I did three years in the Army. I met Angie right after I got home. I'm going to a Vo-Tech now and I've got a job as an apprentice welder at a steel plant. Joined the union and everything. Making pretty good money. We just bought a house. It's small but we'll do better in a few years."

"Well, that's great. Sounds like you're doing fine."

"We are. I just wanted to say thanks."

"For what?"

"For what you said to me that night. It straightened me out."

He held out his hand and I shook it. They went their way down the Midway and I went on my way.

That happened once in thirty years.

It makes you wonder if it's worth it.

Sometimes it is.

ENGLISH LESSON

"3-Edward-7."

"Go ahead."

"3-Edward-7, walking west in the 800 block of Northwest 32nd, a drunk."

"10-4."

The scout car turned into the 800 block of 32nd heading west at a snail's pace. As he entered the 1100 block, the officer saw the man staggering down the middle of the street. Still half a block behind the man, the officer picked up the microphone.

"3-Edward-7 is out on a subject in the 1100 block of 32nd reference my call."

"10-4."

The strategy was a trade-off. When you're sitting in a car, you're always at a disadvantage to someone standing outside the car. You're severely limiting the amount of area you have to move in and that can be dangerous if the other guy's armed. On the other hand, staying in the car sometimes discourages foot pursuits.

The officer removed his pistol from the holster and laid it in his lap, keeping his finger on the trigger. Steering the car to the right side of the street with his left hand, he pulled the car beside the man, stopping slightly behind him. As the police car's tortured brakes squealed in protest to the gentle stop, the man stopped and turned slightly to look behind him. His eyes shone large and moist in the swarthy face as he swayed a foot to either side on his unsteady feet. The officer stuck his left hand out of the window and beckoned to the man.

"C'mere, fella."

The Mexican belched and blinked before tottering forward, lurching badly. He stopped when his hip struck the left front fender and he steadied himself with one hand on the spotlight.

"Do you live around here?"

"Huh? *Que es esto?*" the man hiccupped.

Obviously an illegal alien. The officer's mind raced back to a year of high school Spanish ten years earlier.

"Got any ID? *Habla usted Ingles?*"

A broad smile of comprehension spread across the man's face as he heard his native tongue.

"Ah, *no senor. No hablar Ingles. Hablar Espanol.*"

"Yeah, that's what I figured. *Donde vive usted?*"

"*Mexico, senor. En Chihuahua.*"

The "x" came out as a breathy "h".

"Uh huh. Got any papers? Uh, *el pappel?* Citizen *los Estados Unidos?* Visa?"

The Mexican got a sheepish look on his face and shook his head sadly. The officer opened the car door and stepped out, holstering his gun.

"OK, *senor.* Turn around and put—there."

The officer put his hands on the man's shoulders and gently but firmly turned him around to face the fender, guiding his hands onto the hood. A frown crossed the dark face as the man began turning around.

"*Que es esto? No entiende—*"

The officer placed a hand on the man's shoulder and stopped him from turning any further. He held his hand up in front of the man's face and the man immediately stopped talking. The officer then pointed to his badge and shoulder patch.

"Police. You understand? *Policia? Federales?* Uh, Border Patrol. Savvy?"

Again the light of recognition passed across the man's features. He nodded and erupted with a volley of "*Si, Policia!*"

The officer turned him around again and began frisking him as the Mexican looked over his shoulder, smiling, and tried his best to explain that he wasn't carrying any weapons. The officer smiled and nodded while continuing his search. When he was satisfied the man was clean, he took him by the arm and led him to the rear door of the police car. Opening the door, the officer motioned for the man to get in the car. At this, the man jerked his arm away and began shaking his head violently while unleashing a torrent of Spanish. All the officer could understand was that about every tenth word was "no." The policeman sighed in resignation and reached into the front seat for his flashlight.

Since the police department didn't provide flashlights, each officer selected his own. Since the money was coming out of the officer's own pocket and they didn't seem to last long without damage on the street, some of the flashlights found in city police cars were the one-and-two dollar models from TG&Y. Cheap and easily replaceable.

But this was a very special flashlight. Called a Kel-Lite, it cost $16 and was made by a law enforcement supply company back east who had recognized a market when they found one. Coming in four and six-cell models, depending upon the number of "D" batteries they held, it was made from a knurled aluminum alloy and anodized a non-reflective black color. The large, bulbous head had a clear plastic lens. The four batteries this one carried brought its weight up to about five pounds.

While they were good flashlights, their main features were their sturdiness and versatility. Virtually the only thing breakable in the whole unit was the fifteen-cent bulb behind the Plexiglas lens. These flashlights had been dropped out of second-story windows, thrown through car windshields, run over by cars and used to break arms, legs and heads. None of this treatment had done anything more than scratch the paint.

You could call an officer's night stick a baton, night stick, billy or whatever other euphemisms you liked but there was no getting around it; it was a club and its primary purpose was to hit people. A Kel-Lite was a light source and a baton combined without the offensive appearance of the latter.

The officer turned the light on and aimed the beam into the back seat while pointing after it with his other hand.

"Get in, partner. You don't have any choice and neither do I. So why don't you just get in the car and make it easier on both of us?"

The officer knew the man couldn't understand a word he was saying but he hoped that his tone of voice would communicate his desire to avoid trouble. But the head shaking and the nonstop Spanish continued. So he took hold of the nearest flailing arm and tried to guide the man into the back seat. The man lashed out with his forearm and straightened up as he knocked the officer's arm away.

The officer brought the flashlight up and down in a short arc ending at the side of the man's head. The flashlight rebounded from the half-strength blow and the stream of Spanish stopped abruptly. The man was obviously unhurt as he froze and stared into the officer's eyes. For what seemed like minutes but could have only been moments, the two men stood in the middle of the dark, deserted street, each silently measuring what was in the other's eyes. After a few seconds, the man nodded mutely and got in the back seat.

"3-Edward-7 is 10-15."

As he got out of the car in the prisoner-unloading zone, the officer stuck his flashlight in his hip pocket before letting the prisoner out. Entering the jail, he locked his gun in one of the small lockers provided for that purpose. He kept the flashlight. As they got to the booking desk, a grizzled old sergeant chewing on a cigar stub took his place behind the typewriter across the chest-high counter. The officer placed his prisoner's hand flat on the counter before he started taking everything out of the man's pockets and laying the contents on the counter.

"What ya got?"

"Public Drunkenness, Hold For Immigration."

"Ah, *si*." nodded the sergeant as he started typing.

"Any Spanish-speaking officers on duty tonight, Phil?"

"No but we can get enough for Immigration's boys. Hey, *compadre, como se llama?*"

The man gazed blearily across the counter and belched.

"Pedro Gonzales, senor."

The sergeant's fingers started typing again. "*Como los anos?*"

"*Triente y cinco.*"

"*Gracias.*" the sergeant muttered as he typed "35" on the form.

"It looks like this is all he's got, Phil." Punctuating his statement, the officer threw a roll of $20 bills up on the counter. The roll appeared to contain well over $1,000. The booking officer shook his head as he put the money in a manila envelope.

"Considering what those assholes pay alien labor, it probably took him six months to earn that."

"Yeah, and it's probably every cent he's got in the world."

"We'll need that ring, Joe," said the booking officer, pointing to a plain gold wedding band on the man's left hand.

The officer reached over, picked up the man's left hand and reached for the ring. Before he touched it, the man jerked back his hand and began shaking his head vigorously while rattling off the machinegun Spanish again.

The officer took the flashlight out of his pocket and laid it upon the booking counter. The Spanish stopped immediately. The officer looked at the man and pointed to the place on his head where the flashlight had previously made contact.

The man stared at him for a moment, then nodded his head and took the ring off, laying it on the counter. The booking officer smiled as he put the ring in the property envelope.

"Looks like you two found another way to communicate."

LIVE FROM THE DEUCE

Many people have decried Hollywood movies and TV shows, especially cop shows, as being laced with unnecessary profanity. Admittedly sometimes it's overdone especially now that some cable TV shows are trying to compete with R-rated movies. Nevertheless the fact remains that many cops do use that kind of language, frequently and fluently. Sometimes it depends upon how much the individual officer uses that tactic as a method of relatively harmless stress release but it sometimes becomes a necessary second language for doing his or her job, depending largely on what area of town they police or the standards of the residents of that area.

The near northeast area of my city is now an upscale commercial area of businesses, restaurants, clubs and luxury condos. Nearly four decades ago it was the black downtown area of a segregated city, a combat zone and a center of militancy for competing groups like the Black Muslims and the American Indian Movement. One particular block, the 300 block of Northeast Second Street, was known as "The Deuce." It was a solid block of seedy bars, cafes, gambling joints, hotels and rooming houses that doubled as dope houses and whorehouses with a few legitimate businesses interspersed. Much of it was built during the early part of the century, not very well constructed in the first place and equally well maintained.

Among the local police, the area maintained a well-earned rough reputation. A popular joke was you could drive a police car down the single block of The Deuce, randomly spit out the window and hit a wanted felon three times out of five. When police made calls or bar checks down there, it wasn't uncommon to be pelted with rocks or old soda pop bottles from the tops of the two and three story buildings. One square mile with The Deuce at its epicenter probably had the highest rate of shootings, stabbings and homicides of anywhere in the state. The municipal ordinance against carrying a concealed weapon became almost meaningless on that block. One officer had a common practice of breaking his rookies in to that fact. Driving down The Deuce, he'd pull over at random and tell his rookie to check a certain man for weapons. The rookie would get out, search the man and inevitably come up with a small, cheap Saturday Night Special from the man's pocket or waistband. The senior officer, still sitting in the car, would then ask him "Why are you carrying a gun? Don't you know that's against the law?" The inevitable answer?

"Sho. But all these other muthafuckas got guns!", while sweeping his arm over the dozens of other men walking along the street. And he was right.

One day the brick front of one of the two-story buildings simply fell over in the street. Luckily the building was long abandoned but it was still used by homeless drunks for sleeping and dopers for shooting poison in their arms. Even so, the usual crowd was moving along the street when the cops and firemen showed up.

One of the local television stations had recently acquired their first remote broadcast van, packed with the latest electronics and surmounted by a telescoping twenty-foot tower with satellite dishes. It was their first experience with making live broadcasts from news scenes and they hadn't learned the lessons they have now. They also had a reporter manning it that day who wasn't familiar with the area he was in.

The reporter pulled the van as close to the scene as he could. Police and fire were still searching the building for any casualties or injuries but the falling bricks had hurt no one. As they interrupted their regular programming, the reporter started trying to interview the local denizens strolling by, gawking at the scene. Most bumped his outreaching microphone out of their way as they kept on walking but he finally got one to stop and talk with him. Aware this was a live broadcast incapable of being edited, a small group of cops gathered out of the camera's view to watch the show.

"Excuse me, sir, do you live in this neighborhood?

Smiling broadly, showing several gold teeth, the man replied cheerfully.

"Who, me? I stays over at Luster's." That was a rooming house/whorehouse a block to the north.

"Did you see this accident?"

"Yeah, I seen it."

"And your name, sir?"

The smile disappeared.

"Say what? Why you wanna know?"

"All right, sir, that's not necessary. Can you tell our viewers what happened?"

"Say lookie here, I'se going over to the Moonlight with my man Eugene"—he heavily overemphasized the first syllable, pronouncing the name You-Jean—"to get a Moon pie and strawberry soda pop. So we'se minding our own GOD-damn business when that muthafucka just fell down in the street. A coupla bricks goddam near hit my leg but I jumped back real quick and got outta the way but it goddam near killed Eu-Gene and we didn't know what the fuck was goin' on—"

Out of the camera's view, some of the cops were laughing, bent over holding their stomachs.

Suddenly spotting his friend in the crowd off camera behind the reporter, the man began yelling and waving wildly.

"*SAY, EU-GENE! MUTHAFUCKA, COME OVER HEAH AND GET ON TV!*"

One of the cops was laughing so hard he had to go sit down in his patrol car. The reporter, slack-jawed and stunned, finally recovered his aplomb and rapidly turned away from the screaming man. Looking earnestly into his camera, probably wondering how red his face looked on the thousands of color televisions tuned in to his demise in live broadcasting and mustering as much dignity as he could, he tried to bow out gracefully.

"This is Dan Olson reporting live from—"

He looked around and in a stage whisper that was much louder than he intended, he asked no one in particular "Where are we?"

His answer drifted out from the rear of the crowd.

"Sheeit man, you on *The Deuce!*"

"—live from The Deuce."

CHECK THE WELFARE

"Police Communications."

"Yeah, I wonder if I could get a cop to go by and see if my husband's killed himself?"

"Do you have reason to think he might have?"

"Well, I left him last month and he's been calling me about once a week threatening to kill himself. Personally I don't think he's got the balls but you never know."

"When's the last time you talked to him?"

"About five minutes ago. He called weeping and moaning again and then I heard what sounded like a shot."

"What's the address and phone number?"

"Where I am or where he is?"

"Both. Plus your names."

The dispatcher wrote down the information.

"Did you try calling him back?"

"No. Just have someone let me know what they find out."

She hung up and the dispatcher started dialing.

"Adam 10."

"Go ahead."

"Adam 10, 1418 Northwest Twenty-fifth, check the welfare of Thomas Nicks, white male 23. His wife was talking to him on the phone and thought she heard a shot. He's been threatening suicide for several weeks."

"10-4."

"Adam 10, this may be nothing. She seemed very casual about it. The phone is busy now."

"Clear."

A neighborhood of older, single family houses, clean and cheap. Red brick, small, single bedroom, big living rooms and dining rooms. Perfect for old people who've lived here most of their lives or students at the nearby university.

This one looked like a student. A ten-year old Datsun in the driveway, no curtains in the windows, no flowers or plants, yard a little neglected. The officer rang the front door bell and immediately followed it up with several sharp raps on the wood door. No answer. A cautious peek in the front picture window. Shelves of books, a small TV on an end table, a ratty sofa and recliner. No one visible. Another knock on the door and one on the window. No answer. A cautious turn of the doorknob. Locked.

The officer walked around to the west side of the house. No one visible through the windows, all locked. As he passed back through the driveway, he checked the car. Hood cold, windows up, doors locked.

Turning down the east side of the house, he walked up a few steps to the side door. There was a thick curtain over the window on this one. He knocked on the door several times. No response. He gently tried the doorknob and it turned. He pushed on the door and it opened but stopped when it hit something after a couple of inches. He spoke through the crack.

"Mr. Nicks? Police officer, Mr. Nicks. I'm here to see if you're all right. Your wife is worried."

Nothing. Through the small opening, the officer could see this was a kitchen. Old gas stove, metal wall cabinets, porcelain sink, much worn wood counter tops. The only sound was the irritating beep of a phone off the hook. He leaned a little of his weight into the door and it moved a little. Pushing a little harder, he could see the edge of a dark red pool of blood on the floor. Opening it until he could get his head inside, he looked around.

The young man was lying on his back, spread-eagled. Shoulder-length blonde hair, small goatee, white (and now red) T-shirt, blue jeans, sneakers. An old M-1 carbine with a five-round clip was lying between his legs, barrel pointing towards his head. A gaping red and black hole was where his right eye used to be. Gray and white tendrils draped themselves down over his bloody cheek. No point in taking his pulse. Twisting his head, the officer saw the phone mounted on the wall behind the door, the cord hanging down and the beeping receiver lying in the blood between the man's legs. The wall and phone were covered in a fine spray of high-velocity blood splatter, the kind caused from gunshot wounds. A single brass casing was in the blood pool on the man's right side. Stuck to the wall next to the wall phone at eye level (no pun intended) was the missing right eye, blown out by the gas pressure when the bullet went through the roof of his mouth.

The officer pushed the door open just far enough that he could enter the room, carefully avoiding stepping in any of the blood. It only took a minute to go through the rest of the house to make sure there weren't any more bodies. It wasn't necessary to touch anything. On a small table in the dining room, the man had carefully laid his driver's license and other identification in a neat row. An open billfold, cash still in it was next to the ID. And a plain yellow gold wedding ring. No note on first examination. All the windows and doors locked from the inside except for the one his body blocked when it fell. The officer went out the way he came and radioed for Homicide.

The tall detective was scribbling in his notebook while the shorter one talked to the officer.

"Looks pretty cut and dried. Got the powder burns in the right places, nick in his hand where the ejector rod clipped him before he dropped the rifle. Apparently he put some thought into it."

"Yeah. Books are all Physics, Calculus, and Electrical Engineering. No dummy, I guess. Hell of a waste."

"Most of them are. About the only way he could have been more considerate is if he'd done it in the bathtub."

"But then he couldn't reach the phone. No note, though."

"Yeah. Most don't leave notes. His note was whatever he said to the wife on the phone. Which reminds me, I've got to call the new widow. She called dispatch back a few minutes ago and asked us to let her know if he was bluffing again. Sounds like a cold-hearted bitch. Lab's all done, right, Mike?"

The last was spoken to his taller partner who nodded without a break in his scribbling. "Wagon's on the way." The Medical Examiner would take the body to the morgue before it was released for burial.

The short detective stepped gingerly, spreading his legs unnaturally apart to avoid the blood. Muttering under his breath "Only damn phone in the house", he picked up the receiver with two fingers, holding it by the clean spots. Using a knuckle, he punched the dial buttons. The other two listened to one side of the conversation.

"Mrs. Nicks? Ma'am, this is Detective Brown with the police."

Pause.

"No, ma'am, he wasn't bluffing this time. I'm with Homicide. I'm afraid he's dead."

Pause.

"Yes, ma'am. That was the shot you heard on the phone."

Pause.

"Yes, ma'am. The old carbine."

Pause.

"Well, ma'am, that's more of a question for a lawyer but since you're still married to him, I would assume all the property belongs to you."

Pause.

"Uh, it needs to be cleaned up a little but it's still a good rifle."

Pause.

"You don't? Are you sure?"

Pause.

"What'll you take for it?"

AND THE OSCAR GOES TO—

The lieutenant read the radiogram in front of the whole graveyard shift lineup. White male, 5-10, 175 pounds, short dark hair, clean-shaven, blue jeans, white cotton shirt, dark blue baseball cap with no logo, driving a late model Ford two-door, license unknown but Oklahoma tags. Will be in possession of a silver badge with the words "Police Officer" on it and a fake police ID card. Subject uses a red Kojak light to pull cars over driven by young white females who are alone. All the stops had been on the west side of the city.

The guy had pulled over seven girls so far, always at night, usually between the hours of 9 P.M. and 2 A.M. He accuses them of speeding or some other traffic violation and then starts hitting on them, offering to forget the ticket if they'll "go out" with him. None of the girls had fallen for it yet and the conversations had always ended with him "giving them a break" and letting them go. So far the guy hadn't done anything more serious than impersonating an officer or maybe cause a traffic hazard but the feeling was he was a budding sex criminal and would eventually escalate his behavior until someone got hurt. So everybody was told to watch for the guy. My partner and I heard it all but didn't think much about it since our district was in the northeast quadrant of the city.

It was a weeknight and everything was fairly quiet until a little after 1 A.M. We got a radio call to a Church's Chicken fast food restaurant on the far edge of our district. Trouble unknown but no ambulance running so we took about ten minutes to get there.

Cutting the headlights off half a block away, we drove slowly by the front of the business and looked through the front plate glass windows. No guys in ski masks holding shotguns or fresh bullet holes in the windows. The two employees we could see were behind the counter evidently going about their business normally.

A white guy was sitting in one of the booths, a black girl and three black guys were sitting in the next booth. Three cars were in the side parking area, a late model Ford two-door, an older Chevy and a Buick. Two more in the back where the employees park. Everything seemed normal so we pulled in, unsnapped our holsters and went in the front door.

The white guy was leaning on his elbows in his booth. He had a bruise under one eye, a little trickle of blood coming from one nostril and his hair and clothing were rumpled. He just glanced up at us once before returning to his hang-dog look.

All four of the people in the next booth started talking at once so we left two of them there and took the other two off into separate corners to get the story. Then we went back and did the same thing with the other two. After talking to the two employees, my partner and I got back together, both of us grinning.

The girl said she'd been driving down 23rd Street alone. She was a nurse, had just gotten off duty at University ER and was on her way home. The white guy had pulled her over with a red light on top of his Ford two-door. He showed her a badge and told her he was going to write her a speeding ticket. She immediately started her car and drove to the chicken place that was the only thing open around there. The white guy followed her into the parking lot and jumped out before she got out of her car. The three black guys were in the place eating and went outside. The white guy flashed his badge at them and, after a couple of minutes of conversation, they commenced kicking his ass and dragging him back inside the restaurant. One of them then called the police.

The stories of the four were remarkably similar, just stated differently enough to give them the ring of truth.

The girl said, "I've seen Oklahoma City Police badges before and that isn't an Oklahoma City badge."

One guy said he had had "lots of dealings with Oklahoma City detectives and none of them ever had to badge me to prove he was The Man."

Another guy said he also had previous experience with Oklahoma City Police in plain clothes and "none of them ever showed me a badge. Just attitude and a gun, in that order."

But the last guy was the most direct. "Sheeeiiiittt. One look in that boy's eyes an' I knowed he wasn't no cop."

"How's that?" I asked.

"Boy was scared. I ain't never seen a look like that in an eastside cop's eyes."

THE MATASSADOR

In the early 1970s, there was a popular joke about the experienced astronaut and the younger astronaut on his first trip into space. The veteran comforts his junior partner by saying they were "sitting on top of a missile with two million moving parts, all supplied by the lowest bidder."

It was one of those stories that if it wasn't true, it should have been. The joke was especially popular with government employees. Anyone with experience in military service or any job in the federal, state, county or municipal bureaucracies could appreciate their procurement processes. That included police departments.

Ranking at the top of a cop's equipment that he feels are central to his safety are his gun and his car. He is solely responsible for the condition of his gun but the City Garage is usually responsible for the condition of the car.

A new patrol car is a dream for most young officers. I knew one five-year veteran who, upon receipt of his first new car, said that it was the first time he'd sat in a police car with fewer miles on it than a NASA spacecraft and he wasn't kidding.

In the OCPD, it wasn't uncommon to put at least 100 miles on a car in an eight-hour shift and that was in districts of only a few square miles. It could be much more in larger, more rural districts. In the days before take-home car programs or mandatory trade-in schedules, cars were assigned to the districts, not the individual officers. At the end of his shift, an officer pulled the car into the gas line to be refueled, got his equipment out and went home. Many times the car was left running while the next shift's officer got in. It was entirely possible that the car was only turned off for the officer's meal breaks, on calls that required leaving it unattended and when it broke down. Cars easily accumulated more than 100,000 miles a year.

Like most police departments, the OCPD usually bought their cars from the cheapest models of the Big Three, Ford, GM and Chrysler. The bidding for replacements was renewed every year and went to the lowest bidder. Cars overlapped, sometimes by as much as ten years. In the early 1960s, it was Dodges, followed by several years of Fords in the middle of the decade and Plymouths at the end. The 1970s started with Chevrolets, followed by Dodges and Plymouths for the next three years. Although young patrolmen don't think about those things, it must have been a nightmare for the parts department of the City Garage. In 1974, some bizarre collusion between the police administration and City buyers resulted in two large breaks with tradition.

The contract was given to the American Motors Corporation (AMC) and the cars were to be solid white. Someone discovered they could save $50 per car by foregoing the traditional black and white paint job. The only saving grace was that the single red light on top of the cars, the old "bubble gum machine", was replaced by a clear plastic Visibar, the now familiar "Christmas Tree" of flashing red and white lights brightly reflected in mirrors. Possibly this was to increase visibility to compensate for the loss of the visibility provided by the black and white paint job. The old single light singularly lacked visibility. Sometimes when the air conditioner was turned on, the drag on the car's electrical system slowed the light down to the point where an officer could run around the car faster than the red light turned. In spite of the support for the Visibar, the troops bitched to high heaven.

Police uniforms were blue, police cars were black and white and that's the way God intended! They couldn't have raised any more furor if the uniforms had been changed to purple and green. And AMC? Some officers derisively called them "Nashes" after AMC's parent company that, 20 years earlier, had produced some of the ugliest cars in history, resembling overturned bathtubs with wheels. Nevertheless, the AMC's came in.

There were two models, the Matador and the Ambassador. Time passed. The cars had passably powerful V-8's but their maintenance record was lousy and they were still ugly and white.

Somewhere along the line, an Ambassador was totaled in a head-on collision and a Matador was hit in the rear. Some mechanical genius decided they could graft the undamaged rear end of the Ambassador onto the undamaged front end of the Matador and make one whole car out of this mess.

This was accomplished and the car was assigned to the Adam 11 district in the far western part of the city. John, one of the shift officers assigned to the car, saw an opportunity and took it. Rummaging around in the police car graveyard behind the City Garage, he came up with two of the chromed scripts that went on the rear of the cars. They were in the form of ornate cursive handwriting. One was for a Matador and one was for an Ambassador. He took them to a friend who owned a body shop. A little cutting, some tack welding and re-chroming and he had his new script. Since only three letters were changed, it even fit in the pre-drilled holes in the car's rear. Now John had the only "Matassador" on the force and very probably the only one in existence.

The troops thought it was hoot. The brass, if they ever knew, never cared. The next year, cooler heads prevailed. We went back into the Dodge, Plymouth, Ford and Chevy rotation. And the cars went back to black and white.

And what of the fate of the world's only Matassador? God knows. Probably driven into the ground on countless patrols and then sold at a City auction for $500. Then eventually abandoned or sold for scrap and now quietly rusting away in some auto graveyard.

JAILHOUSE JUSTICE

The radio call is down in the Flats, just north of the river. Mostly old, cheap, run-down clapboard shacks with plastic sheeting over the windows. No central heat or fireplaces in this housing edition. The upscale places have floor furnaces that sometimes go out and gas the occupants to death. Some still have potbellied stoves. Some have space heaters. Some have nothing. Winters are hard on everyone down here. Sometimes it's hardest on the kids.

The "man" of the house is a small time thief, which supports his primary source of nourishment, the cheapest rotgut whiskey available. As long as he gets his fill first, he shares this with his common-law wife. Unfortunately that doesn't leave much left over for the two kids as evidenced by a kitchen covered with dirty dishes, congealed grease and cockroaches. Neither one of the adults has any idea who the kids' father(s) are and they say so. The little girl is five but doesn't talk much yet. It's probably for the best. God only knows what she'd have to say if she could. The two-year-old boy just screams but he's entitled. Both his legs are broken and so is one arm. Compound fractures. That means the broken bones are sticking out through the skin. It seems he wouldn't stop crying, probably because he hadn't been fed anything for three days among other reasons, so the master of the house decided he'd give him something to cry about. The screams became so persistent even neighbors who were dedicated to minding their own business decided to call the cops. Both of the "parents" are mostly sober now. Badges in the house can have that effect in this part of town.

With great effort, the two officers on the call keep their cool and handle it by the book. An ambulance and DHS are called. The girl goes to a juvenile shelter and the boy goes to Children's Hospital. Mom gets to stay home because she can legally be as drunk as she likes in her own home but they explain to her their report is going to encourage a case against her for child neglect in the near future. After all, *she* isn't the one who called the police. The sullen man is arrested and handcuffed.

On the way to jail, the officers stop by Children's to check on the doctor's preliminary examination of the little boy. The driver stays in the car with their prisoner while his partner goes into the ER. The driver silently puts up with fifteen minutes of belching, farting and bitching from their prisoner in the back seat.

"You can't hold me. You ain't got any evidence."

"Them kids won't say nothing against me. The boy can't talk and the girl won't. Cause she's dumb. Dumb as a stump."

"You can't believe a damn word their momma says."

"I've gotta piss."

"What time do they serve breakfast?"

"What's my bond gonna be?"

"You gotta get me a lawyer, right?"

"I don't want no Public Defender. I want a good lawyer this time."

Eventually the partner comes out and gets in the car. Reading from his note-book, he doesn't wait for his partner to ask.

"Multiple compound fractures in both legs and the arm. Bones are splintered and there's nerve damage. Whatever isn't broken has deep bruises. Chronically undernourished and dehydrated, multiple infections from untreated lacerations. Best case is the kid will limp badly for the rest of his life and have a useless right arm."

The driver puts the car in gear and they head to the jail silently, jaw muscles clenched.

Well, almost silently. Mutters come from the back seat.

"Serves the little bastard right. I tole him not to keep falling out of that bed."

The jaw muscles in the front seat clench even tighter.

Out at the jail. Up the elevator to the second floor. The desk sergeant sees them on the camera monitor and activates the electric motor that opens the barred door as soon as the elevator door closes. One of officers takes both their guns and locks them in the small lockers on the wall. The other officer motions to the desk sergeant again, another electric motor hums and the door to the hold-over cell opens. When he takes the man's handcuffs off, the prisoner steps through the door. When the door shuts and locks with the ringing finality of steel on steel, the man turns and sees the cop standing behind him inside the cell. He looks around and no one else is in the cell. The partner is over at the booking desk chatting with the desk sergeant. A chill starts up his spine as the cop speaks in a low voice.

"Maybe you'd like to try to break my legs?"

Naturally he didn't take the cop up on it. Just stood there and wet himself. The cop even turned his back on him, giving him the best shot he'd ever have at an unarmed cop. But he wouldn't take it. After a couple of minutes of letting him seriously consider the future of his health, the cop gave up, brought him out and booked him. When they were finished with the process, the cop waved off the jail officer before he could get up.

"I'll take him up."

Another elevator. One floor up to the felony floor. As the jailer started out from behind his desk, the officer stuck his head into the small office.

"You want to go down and get a coffee? Just give me the key to the tank and I'll take him back."

The jailer nodded his thanks, handed over the key and got on the elevator.

The officer led the prisoner back to the large cell on the north side of the building. Taking up almost half of the floor space on that floor, it could comfortably hold up to thirty prisoners at one time. About a dozen very hard looking men were in the cell. Most had prison tattoos on both muscular arms. All were in on felony charges. Burglars, armed robbers, thieves, dopers, the dregs of a large city. The known killers and sex criminals were in cells by themselves but most of the lesser felons were housed together here. He inserted the key in the cell's lock.

"Away from the door."

The men, all very familiar with the jail's procedures, stood up and moved to the rear of the cell. The officer turned the key, opened the door and gave his reluctant prisoner a little shove through the door. Closing the door, he turned the key again and pocketed it. As he turned to go, he stopped and turned back in an afterthought.

"You fellas might want to be careful around this guy. He's a real bad ass. Permanently crippled a two-year-old boy tonight."

He almost made it back to the jailer's office before the screams started. Even thieves have some kind of standards.

TOUGH LOVE

When I went through the Police Academy in 1970, we received eight weeks of classroom training and two weeks of firearms training. Part of it was training in basic first aid, most of which was inferior to what a military recruit receives except emergency child birth procedures replaced most of the information on sucking chest wounds. We received little if any training on psychology, psychiatry, marriage counseling, grief counseling, dispute mediation or dealing with the mentally ill. Nevertheless our jobs would eventually encompass all these specialties and more.

As of 2005, that basic police training has almost tripled to twenty-six weeks. Perhaps some of the above subjects are covered today but, now as then, I suspect there is no substitute for experience and common sense, the hallmarks of a veteran street cop.

A cop soon learns that he is expected to be much more than a law enforcer, he is expected to be a problem solver, at least temporary solutions. Usually problems he didn't create and has very little control over. Not all of the solutions are as compassionate or subtle as might be hoped for but, by and large, most cops can probably impersonate a psychiatrist a hell of a lot better than a psychiatrist can impersonate a cop.

"Adam Nine."

"Go ahead, Adam Nine."

"Thirty-ninth and North Penn, Plymouth House Apartments, Apartment 132, possible attempted suicide."

"Clear."

"Adam Twelve to Adam Nine. Are you familiar with that address?"

"10-4. No backup necessary."

"Clear."

We all knew about Mary. Mary had problems. Middle aged but aging badly. Too many men. Too much booze. Too many pills. Low self esteem. Mostly just alone and lonely. Her cat was the only constant in her life.

Mary had discovered a way to get the attention she craved. Every few months or so, whenever the last guy had walked out on her, she'd pop a few 750 milligram Placidyls, chase them down with a few shots of vodka and when she started feeling drowsy, she'd call the cops.

Placidyl was a heavy-duty sedative. Alcohol exaggerated its effects, sometimes to a dangerous level. More than one person had committed suicide with them. Mary had increased her dosage of the pills and booze to the point where she depended upon the timely arrival of the cops to keep her from dying.

Mary didn't really want to die. She'd had many opportunities to kill herself if that was what she really wanted but she kept dancing along the edge. She always did it in the early morning hours in the middle of the week when she knew there would always be a few police cars near her district that wouldn't be busy. There would be very little traffic on the streets to slow them down and the nearest ambulance service would only be minutes away. She was also very careful to leave herself enough consciousness to be sure the dispatchers got her address right. The last tip-off was when an officer discovered a police scanner in her apartment next to the bed. Mary was waiting until she heard a car dispatched before she'd allow herself to nod off. She'd also give herself away to the cops and ambulance personnel by leaving a note asking them to make sure her cat had enough food and water for "a few days".

An ambulance would take her to the hospital, doctors and nurses would fuss over her while pumping her stomach, and she'd spend a few days getting around the clock care before they let her go home again to start down another cycle of spiraling depression.

The officer tried the door and, as expected, it was unlocked. Mary was in bed, fully dressed and snoring deeply. The ambulance came and hauled her off as always. The officer asked an ER nurse to give him a call when they got through pumping her stomach and she'd been moved to a room.

When the nurse's call came through dispatch, the officer returned to the hospital and put himself out taking a report. He'd never handled Mary before but he'd heard the drama recounted many times on the radio, in the patrol break room and several coffee shops. Entering Mary's room, he noticed that the other bed was empty for the moment. He pulled a chair up next to the bed. She was still drowsy and smelled strongly of the contents of her stomach that had recently been forcibly removed from her. She answered the questions for the report he was writing. As he finished writing, she rolled her head toward him on the pillow and peered at him through drooping eyelids.

"I don't know you."

"No, I just got transferred into this district. But I know you."

Her eyes opened a little wider. "You do?"

He nodded. "Yeah. I know about all the time cops, paramedics, doctors and nurses have to spend on you every few months. And I'll tell you what, Mary, one way or the other, it stops now."

"What do you mean?"

"I mean that I'm going to be the only cop in that district for the next few years. When a call comes out at your place, I'll get the call. The next call I get like this at your apartment, I'm going to disconnect the phone, lock the door behind me and go back in service. No ambulance. No hospital. The pills and booze will eventually stop your heart and you'll never wake up again. And when the cat food runs out, *you'll* be kitty's next meal."

Mary's eyes were wide open now. She wasn't drowsy anymore. The officer closed his notebook, got up and left.

Of course he didn't mean it but Mary didn't know that and he seemed *very* sincere. He rode that district for another two years and never got another call from Mary. A couple of years after he got promoted to detective, Mary's name came up over a few drinks with some old patrol buddies at the club. The next day, he checked Records on her. The last report on file was the call he had made that night.

THE CIVIC CENTER PETTING ZOO

Modern cops carry more equipment on their belts than a utility company lineman—automatic pistol, several ammo clips, handcuffs, a collapsible metal baton, a portable radio, a canister of Mace, flashlight and other things I can't even identify. Back in the Dark Ages, we were limited to a revolver, twelve rounds of ammo, one or two pairs of handcuffs and maybe a metal ring to hold the nightstick.

As a result, most of the cops I knew carried a briefcase. Many carried it to lineup with them, containing their portable daily necessities—report forms, ticket books, a couple of boxes of mug shots, a fifty-round box of pistol ammo, extra shotgun shells and so forth. It might also carry the stuff they didn't want to carry on their belts or in their pockets at lineup—flashlight, batteries, sap and/or nightstick. Those that didn't carry it with them left it in their personal car.

In either case, the first stop they made after lineup and the last stop before they came in at shift's end was their personal car. This is where the officers picked up their larger equipment—for the extremely organized, sometimes a portable console to ride in the center of the front seat or, for the two shifts that covered the hours of darkness, a personal weapon like a rifle, carbine or sawed-off shotgun. There was no SWAT Team to call. Every car was their own SWAT Team. "You be Task and I'll be Force."

There was a parking lot directly north of the police station that was reserved for officers' personal vehicles. Like everything else in the area, it was named for the surrounding civic center that included City Hall, Police Headquarters and other municipal government buildings. During the last ten minutes or so of every shift, this parking lot was littered with black and white patrol cars. In the winter, officers were warming their personal cars up before the drive home. Otherwise they were putting their equipment in their cars or waiting for Dispatch to call the cars in, signaling that the next shift had broken lineup and was on their way down. While waiting in their patrol cars and listening to their radios, many were in the traditional position—pulled up next to one another, driver's door to driver's door, facing in opposite directions. This way they could watch each others backs and drive off in opposite directions at a moment's notice.

It was after 11:00 on a weeknight. The swing shift's odd-numbered cars had already been called in, half of the graveyard shift was already on the streets and the swing shift's even numbered cars were just waiting out the last five minutes of their shift in the north parking lot.

Ray had just finished putting his briefcase in his car and was getting back in his patrol car when Brian pulled up next to him. When he saw the infectious grin on Ray's face, Brian automatically knew some deviltry was afoot.

"What?" he said, already starting his own grin.

Ray turned around in his seat looking over his shoulder.

"Watch this. Sleaze has been out to the zoo. They've got a present for Tom and Tommy."

Brian laughed as his eyes followed Ray's line of sight. About twenty-five yards in front of them, Baker Two was parked facing away from them. Tom was waiting in the driver's seat while Tommy was just returning from putting his briefcase in his car. Lurking one row over and preparing to pounce on them was Baker Four.

Baker Four was manned by two officers, David and Larry, who were renowned for their practical jokes. Larry was a former motorcycle officer who constantly had a huge wad of snuff stuck in his lip. David was a little, almost spindly guy especially when compared to his big, beefy partner but he'd climb over you to be the first one to a fight, shootout or chase. David's nickname was "Sleaze" and his sense of humor could only be duplicated by crossing a leprechaun with a hit man.

Baker Two was manned by two very different officers. Tom was a former newspaper reporter who had decided being a cop would be more fun than being a crime reporter. Tightly wrapped, animated, talkative, Tom was a contrast to his partner. Tommy was the much more lighthearted of the partners. Calm, laid back, soft-spoken and going to college studying accounting. Tommy had some relatives who didn't share his values. One of them, in fact, had been murdered in one of the local bars. Insulated, undemonstrative and highly intelligent, Tommy was somewhat of an unknown quantity to his shift mates until they got to know him well. What they *did* know he had was an extreme fear of snakes.

Baker Four's district covered Lincoln Park, where the City Zoo was located. One of the features of the zoo was a large man-made lake. Since there was no hunting, fishing or swimming there, the lake became a sanctuary for all types of wildlife. One of the types of wildlife that flourished there were some particularly large water snakes. Harmless, non-poisonous and protected from most predators, some of the reptiles grew to be over five feet long and several inches in girth.

Compared to some of the things Sleaze faced every night in Baker Four, a meek water snake was no challenge at all. As Ray was relating to Brian, Baker Four had finished their shift by catching one of these specimens at the zoo's lake. They had brought it back to the station in a sack they carried specifically for that purpose tonight. They were laying in wait now to spring their trap.

As Tommy got back in the car, he closed the door. Tom put the car in gear and started forward just as Baker Four rounded the corner. Baker Four stopped and the driver waved at Tom, gesturing for him to pull up beside him to talk.

Baker Four steered closer to the center of the aisle, forcing Baker Two to steer to their right, closer to the next row of parked cars. Tom had just barely enough room between his car and a pickup parked in the next row. When Baker Four pulled up alongside, the two officers in Baker Two would be trapped. With the driver's door up against Baker Four's side and the passenger's side just inches from a parked pickup's rear bumper, there would not be enough room to open either door far enough to allow either officer out of the car.

Tom dutifully pulled Baker Two alongside of Baker Four, his elbow on the driver's door almost touching the elbow of Baker Four's driver. When he saw the crooked smile, he sensed something was up but it just lasted a second.

"What's happening?" Tom said.

Sleaze reached down in his lap.

"Look what we found out by the zoo."

Even by the dim lights of the parking lot's overhead lights and twenty-five yards away, Ray and Brian saw Baker Four's driver throw the long, slender object into Baker Two's car. Tom's husky laugh had just started drifting back to them when it was drowned out by Tommy's rapidly rising scream of terror. Visible through the back window, the dim shadow on the passenger's side of Baker Two became much more animated. The car began bouncing violently and the passenger side door opened only a few inches before slamming into the pickup bumper. The door closed and opened again rapidly several times, slamming repeatedly and forcefully into the pickup bumper. Now the laughter coming from Baker Four was audible in the short breaks between the screams coming from Baker Two. Ray, Brian and several other officers in the parking lot were now also enjoying the sight. Then a strobe light went off inside Baker Two.

BOOM.

The muffled sound was recognizable to all of them as the report of a .357 Magnum loaded with hollow-point rounds. A plume of gun smoke began wafting out of the passenger side window of Baker Two.

BOOMBOOMBOOMBOOMBOOM.

The strobe light effect was even more pronounced now with the multiple flashes coming from inside Baker Two. Through the rear window, both figures in the car could now be seen to be much more animated, especially when silhouetted by the muzzle flashes. Baker Four jerked into gear and sprayed all the surrounding cars with gravel as it leaped forward several car lengths. Suddenly there was only one figure in Baker Two and Tommy came tumbling out the driver's side window. The burned cordite smell of gunpowder drifted over the parking lot as smoke poured out of the inside of Baker Two.

No supervisors were called. No reports were made. As with most of these cases, the men made their own investigation and it took a while to get the whole story.

Baker Four's driver had hurled the three-foot-long water snake through Baker Two's driver side window. Tommy would later fervently swear it was at least twice that size. The good news was it wasn't poisonous. The bad news was it was really pissed off from having spent the last hour trapped in a sack. The furious, hissing reptile landed right in Tommy's lap. His first reaction, not counting the scream he didn't remember, was to open the door and try to get out. The door only opened a couple of inches before it hit the rear bumper of the pickup truck parked next to them. Several more tries failed to budge the truck and only damaged the patrol car's door more. By this time, the furiously writhing snake had flipped itself over and off of Tommy's lap onto the floorboard at his feet.

Trapped with what looked like an anaconda that was growing larger by the instant at his feet, Tommy reflexively decided he wasn't dying without a fight. He drew his gun and emptied it into the floorboard at his feet. Remarkably, both the snake and Tommy's feet were unscathed. The snake took refuge under the seat while Tommy resorted to something none of them would have thought possible. In the cramped quarters of the front seat of the patrol car, Tommy *ran* across the seat, across his partner's lap and out the driver's window. When many of the guys refused to believe that a stocky guy like Tommy could do that, Tom had Tommy's dusty footprints across the lap of his blue wool uniform pants to prove it had happened that way.

When Baker Two's graveyard shift officers saw them the next night, they had one question.

"What the hell did you guys get into last night?"

All they knew was that the passenger's side door had several formidable dents in it; the door's arm rest had been ripped off and was found in the north parking lot, everything inside the car reeked of gunpowder and there were half a dozen bullet holes in the passenger's side floorboard. The swing shift guys told them the story and mentioned that they were lucky that the snake had been removed from under the front seat before they left the car.

Tom had to swear on his kids' lives that he'd gotten the snake out of the car before Tommy would even get in it again. It was rumored that Tommy had even considered transferring to another area of town so he wouldn't have to ride in Baker Two's car again. When Tommy asked, Tom told him he turned the snake loose by dropping it down the sewer grate next to the parking lot. Tommy would never park in the north lot again without looking around carefully, half convinced that the snake was waiting out there for him.

DON'T GET TOO COMFORTABLE

"Adam Twelve."

"Go ahead."

"Eight nineteen Northwest 44th. Loud noise disturbance. Complainant at this address."

"Clear."

"Unit to back Adam Twelve."

"Twelve to Headquarters. I'll advise on backup."

No need to take another unit out of service because some kids have pissed the neighbors off with their party or the dog was barking. He'd take the full ten minutes it took to cross the district to the call. No hurry. The call was the lowest priority.

Only three more nights of this crap. The armed robberies and burglaries in progress, chases, shootings, the action calls, that's what made Patrol such a great job. Unfortunately they were one in a hundred even in the hot districts. The rest of it was reports, vandalisms, loud parties, barking dogs and the myriad of other ordinances and statutes they were responsible for.

Sure, they were important if it was *your* kids being kept awake by the barking dog or it was *your* windshield that got busted in or *your* TV that got swiped. You felt for the victims but it didn't exactly get your blood running hot. Somebody had to do it—*you* had to do it—but it sure made the nights longer and it wasn't really what you took the job for.

Three more nights. Then four days off and his transfer to a plainclothes unit was effective. Five years of the uniform. Five years of the black and white car. Now he'd be dealing strictly with felons. No public service calls. No reports except arrest reports. He couldn't wait.

The scout car hadn't come to a full stop at the curb in front of Eight Nineteen before he had the call pegged. The passenger's side window was only cracked an inch but the vibrations of *The Who* coming from the house next door was rattling it.

He walked up to the door and rang the bell. A woman answered it.

"You hear?"

"Yes ma'am, I hear it. Have you asked them to turn it down?"

"It's a single guy and he drinks—a lot. The last time I spoke to him, he offered to solve my problem if you know what I mean. My only problem is him."

"OK, I'll take care of it."

He eyed the house as he crossed the unfenced yards. Lights on. Curtains drawn. Three steps up to a concrete porch, no railings, porch light on, a single naked 100-watt bulb. Grass four inches high. Big evergreen bushes on both sides of the porch. Bagworms. Guy wasn't into yard work.

He knocked on the door as the high points of the loud noise ordinance crawled through his brain. His mouth was already starting to form the words when the door opened.

He didn't see the man right away. He saw the shotgun. It was hard to miss. The barrel was two feet from the end of his nose and level with it. Twelve-gauge but the hole looked big enough to stick his head in.

It seemed like he looked down that barrel for a couple of minutes but it couldn't have been more than the blink of an eye. He threw the flashlight toward the shotgun, crouched, jumped sideways off the porch and drew his gun all in one motion. Just as he landed on his back in the evergreen bush beside the porch, he was bringing the gun up and grasping it with both hands. The front sight centered on the man's chest. Time stopped except for his trigger finger. He could feel the hammer coming back. Then time stopped again.

He tried to speak when he realized he hadn't taken a breath in a little while. He took a quick one and yelled.

"DROP IT!"

The man, wavering slightly on his feet, turned the shotgun upwards and sat it down next to the open door.

"OK. I'll authorize a Hold For State Charges. Pointing A Weapon." The sergeant sniffed the pungent alcohol wafting through the open window of the scout car. The handcuffed suspect was slumped over in the back seat, snoring and drooling. "But as tanked as he is, it'll probably get knocked down to Reckless Conduct With A Firearm. He's got no record, no dope in the house and the gun's registered to him. Just a paranoid, combative drunk who likes loud rock music."

"OK. Thanks."

The sergeant spoke softly. "Why didn't you shoot?"

"When I bailed off the porch, he followed me with his head but not with the gun. Like when you distract a drunk. Uncoordinated, you know?"

"Had you pretty cold, did he?"

He just nodded as stupidly as he felt. The old sergeant smiled with understanding.

"Don't get too comfortable out here—even in plainclothes."

NOBODY LISTENS

It has been my experience that most people aren't stupid. All of them act that way occasionally, cops included, but it isn't a permanent condition as it is with some. Like intelligence, people have varying degrees of patience, some more, some less.

One of the major stories of the twentieth century was labor unrest. When you think about it realistically, there was absolutely no actual reason why it shouldn't filter down to the cops eventually and it did. Most of the Boston Police Department went on strike in 1919, leading to a callout of the state militia to preserve order and accelerating the political career of Massachusetts Governor Calvin Coolidge. Earlier strife led to the formation of the nation's largest police union, the Fraternal Order of Police (FOP).

In 1975, labor unrest struck Oklahoma City. OCPD officers were making less than suburb officers whose primary duties were mollifying the residents of their six-and-seven figure mansions. OCPD officers were involved in shootings almost weekly while other departments rarely drew their weapons except on the firing range.

The FOP wanted a 10 per cent raise and the city offered seven and one-half. They went to arbitration and the arbitrators agreed with the cops but since the decision wasn't binding upon the city, they ignored it. An oblivious mayor backed up by an intransigent city manager and city council put everyone at loggerheads. The officers voted to begin a "work slowdown" by refusing to write traffic tickets, a major source of city revenue, or answer radio calls. Major calls were still answered but you couldn't tell it by listening to the police radio, silent except for the plaintive voices of dispatchers broadcasting messages out into a non-responding ether.

Naturally the local news media was having a field day. One TV station was pro-police, one was anti-police and the other just struggled to remain neutral.

After three days of the slowdown, it was obvious to everyone that it was not working and could go on indefinitely without resolution. Another meeting was called at the FOP Lodge Hall and hundreds of officers showed up along with a healthy representation from the local TV stations. Speeches were made, questions were asked, answers were given and the TV got plenty of pictures.

After a little while, the FOP president called for an executive session. That meant that no one could be present except members. The sergeant-at-arms went over to the media pool and politely told them they would have to leave for the executive session. Most of them picked up their cameras, folded up their note-pads and left. All but one TV cameraman who undoubtedly thought he was special. He began arguing with the sergeant-at-arms about the First Amendment and so forth and so on. The sergeant-at-arms patiently explained that the First Amendment didn't apply to this situation and he would have to leave. The cameraman started back on his filibuster. This was allowed to continue for a couple of minutes with him straddling his fifty-pound-plus shoulder-operated camera on the floor. All the while, a muscular patrol lieutenant known for a lack of patience was standing a few feet away, fidgeting uncomfortably.

Suddenly the lieutenant stepped forward, picked up the heavy camera with one hand and shoved it none too gently into the cameraman's chest with a single terse sentence.

"Get your shit and get out."

The cameraman probably saw the ticking second hand in the lieutenant's eyes, knowing his time was running out, and the only question left to be answered was whether he or his camera would be more heavily damaged when they went out the door. He turned and left immediately.

The sergeant-at-arms made a half-hearted protest to the lieutenant about media relations but both of them knew it wouldn't affect the quality of coverage they received that night. The cameraman was from the more anti-police station anyway.

"I think he would have left in a few minutes anyway."

The lieutenant wasn't sympathetic.

"The boy doesn't listen."

POST TRAUMATIC STRESS

Like everything else, the procedures when law enforcement officers are involved in shootings have evolved.

Many years ago, if the officer didn't hit anyone (deliberately or accidentally), no investigation or report was even made. Some cops have even been involved in as many as half a dozen shooting incidents but have never hit anyone so no official reports exist.

If someone was hit, an investigation and report were made, usually by two homicide detectives. These reports were forwarded up the chain of command and at each level the individuals in the officer's chain of command passed judgment on whether the shooting was within department policy and state law. Unless someone at the division commander rank (major) or higher took issue with the shooting, nothing came of it. In other words, no news was good news. If it was a bad (unjustified) shooting and the Chief wanted something done about it, it would be done. The end result was about the same as it was in later years, the main difference being that the officer was being judged by cops, some of whom had been involved in shootings themselves.

If someone was killed as a result of the officer's shooting and it was justifiable, charges of First Degree Murder were automatically filed against the officer. He would waive his right to a jury trial and within three days, the trial would be held in front of a district judge. The District Attorney would present the facts to the judge and if it were merited, the judge would acquit the officer and double jeopardy would make him immune to any further prosecution.

These procedures evolved into a Firearms Review Board that examined every instance in which an officer fires his weapon outside of the firing range. This board ruled on the justification and/or discipline in these shootings. The procedures progressed to today's massive response to every shooting by both Homicide and Internal Affairs, preparing for the inevitable lawsuit from family members and ambulance-chasing attorneys trying to get into the city's deep pockets. Now it has evolved into a Use Of Force Board that investigates everything from shootings to a prisoner's complaint that his handcuffs were too tight.

The PD made several tries at having a resident psychologist but they kept quitting. Some said it was low pay. Some said it was lousy hours. Some said the shrinks became frightened of the cops after they got to know them.

Not long after the inception of the Firearms Review Board, the PD decided they'd send officers involved in shootings for a psychological evaluation. Since the city shrinks kept quitting, they sent them to one employed by the state. They made these evaluations mandatory without considering that some of these cops had some pretty hard bark on them. Eventually they got to the point where they made the psychological counseling available to those who wanted it but didn't force it on those who didn't.

This is one of the reasons why.

The officer sat casually in the chair in the waiting room. No one else was there. He slumped in the chair, turning its straight back into a recliner, with one leg crossed over the other. Contrary to his laid-back attitude, his uniform was immaculate. Gleaming, spit-polished shoes, knife-like creases in his blue trousers, every piece of metal and leather highly shined, not a piece of lint anywhere. The badge on his white cap in the chair beside him showed he was in the Patrol Division. Two gold stars on the left sleeve of his Ike jacket showed that he had served a minimum of ten years in a patrol car. The nickel-plated .357 Magnum revolver in his holster was the reason for his presence here today.

His fingers were loosely intertwined across his lap. He hadn't picked up any of the magazines on the coffee table or turned on the TV in the waiting room. He also hadn't paced or dozed off. He just sat there with his eyes open but glazed over, obviously lost within his own thoughts but giving no outward clue as to what they were. It was almost as though he knew he was being observed through the two-way mirror on the wall.

After half an hour, the shrink finally gave up.

The connecting door opened and the psychologist stepped out, smiling pleasantly.

"Officer Green?" He held out his hand. "I'm John Elias."

The officer rose and shook his hand firmly.

"Good to meet you. I'm Karl Green."

"Come on in and make yourself comfortable." Elias said this casually, with no hint that he expected the officer to be anything but comfortable.

The psychologist closed the door behind them. The room was small, obviously not his primary office. An interview room. Two comfortable but standard government chairs facing one another. He let the officer have his choice, knowing he would choose the one facing the door, as he did. Elias took the other.

The officer immediately relaxed into his former position, butt scooted forward on the chair seat, back reclined comfortably, legs crossed and fingers intertwined across his waist.

Mildly surprised but not showing it, Elias picked up the sheaf of papers on the end table between them. He thumbed through them unnecessarily because he had thoroughly reviewed them before the officer ever arrived.

Elias was surprised because he had been conducting these mandatory interviews for several months now and he was becoming used to the behavior of the cops who were being forced to come see him. Most were angry, some were surly, all were uncooperative. He hadn't had one open up to him yet about feeling badly about the man he had shot but, on the other hand, he hadn't had anything but very justified shootings so far. This one was no exception.

The officer had received a radio call late at night on a "Trouble Unknown", a dispatcher's euphemism that could cover everything from a lost cat to a gunfight in progress.

The officer drove up and parked two doors down from the complainant's address. Unknown to him, he had parked right in front of the raging domestic disturbance that had caused the call.

As the officer got out of his patrol car, the enraged man came bursting out of his front door, waving a pistol in one hand and yelling about getting off his property. He had just used the pistol to whip his common-law wife into unconsciousness and still had his blood up.

The startled officer had reflexively crouched, drawn his sidearm and just got the word "Drop—" out when the man decided he'd point the gun at him. Three shots. One from the drunk that hit the ground a dozen feet in front of the officer, two from the officer that hit the drunk in the chest.

Elias flipped through the pages. The drunk was still alive in St. Ann's. Would probably make it if infection didn't get him. The officer was a good one. Ten years on the job, all in patrol, all in so-called combat zones. A dozen commendations, an Associate's Degree in Police Science, married, two kids, and three prior uses of force, all justified. This was his first shooting.

Elias looked up at the officer with a pleasant but neutral smile. The officer was looking back at him frankly but without hostility. He didn't bother to smile but at least he wasn't frowning or pouting. His gaze was directed at the psychologist's eyes with not much blinking. Pretty standard for cops.

"So, we're here to talk about the shooting."

A slight frown of puzzlement crossed the officer's features.

"What shooting?"

Elias let out a little laugh.

"No, seriously."

The officer's expression didn't change.

"I am serious. What shooting?"

"The shooting you were involved in last Friday night."

The officer relaxed, pursed his lips slightly and shook his head slowly.

"I didn't shoot anyone."

Elias was mentally flipping through his college notes on denial. He waved the sheaf of reports toward the officer.

"But I've got all the reports right here."

"They say I shot someone?"

"Yes. Yes, of course."

The officer shook his head again. "They're wrong."

Elias let out a little gasp of frustration. "Well, if you didn't shoot the man, who did?"

"He did."

The officer was pointing with his left hand toward his right hand.

Elias batted his eyelids rapidly several times. "Who did?"

"He did." Still pointing.

This was starting to sound like an Abbott and Costello routine, Elias thought. "Who? You were a one-man car. Who shot the man if you didn't?"

The officer raised his right hand, his gun hand. The fist was closed and held horizontally with the thumb forming a puppet mouth like some of the old ventriloquists in the early days of television. When the thumb moved, the officer spoke in a high, falsetto voice.

"*I didn't shoot him.*"

The officer looked down at his own hand, frowning, and spoke to it in his normal voice.

"Yes, you did."

"*No, I didn't.*"

"Yes, you did. Admit it."

"*NO, I DIDN'T!*"

"YES, YOU DID! ADMIT IT!"

"*No, I didn't! You're just trying to get me in trouble!*"

"Trouble? I'm the one who's in trouble! You better admit what you did!"

"*If you don't leave me alone, I'll tell him what you do to me at night when the lights are out!*"

"Oh for God's sake! Get the hell out of here!" Elias threw the reports on the table and stormed out of the room.

The officer got up, hitched up his gun belt and walked out, smiling the first real smile he'd had all day.

Selective Enforcement Unit

THE DEAD END GANG

The Dead End Gang, a nickname some of the members called themselves, was formed as an experiment in the police department "class wars" of the early 1970s. The Patrol and Detective Divisions were very much independent and separate fiefdoms. In each division, there were two distinct classes of individuals.

The first patrol group were those guys who just wanted to ride their district, take their radio calls, make the necessary arrests and reports, write a few traffic tickets and be left alone, competing with no one but themselves. The parallel group in detectives were those guys who just wanted to be out of the uniform, drive an unmarked car, work straight day shift with no nights, weekends or holidays, be assigned to a fairly innocuous, mostly non-confrontational unit and work the cases that the boss laid on their desk every morning. If members of the first group in patrol ever managed to be promoted to detective, they almost certainly joined the first group of detectives.

The other group in patrol was more driven. Besides doing everything the first group did, they picked up outstanding (i.e., still valid) felony warrants from the county sheriff's office to serve in their spare time, chased down people wanted on radiograms (internal wants on suspects issued by other officers), developed informants and even applied for and served their own search warrants sometimes. These guys competed with each other every month to see who could make the most felony arrests and most aspired to become detectives someday. The parallel group in detectives gravitated to what one major called the "more active" details such as Homicide, Robbery, Narcotics and Sex Crimes. They liked chasing bad guys, preferably dangerous bad guys who physically hurt people, putting them in jail and expected to work lots of nights, weekends and holidays.

There wasn't a lot of interaction between the first class of patrolmen and the first class of detectives except to say "Hi" when they passed in the halls. On the other hand, when the other class of detectives was looking for a fugitive, they frequently went to some of the other class of patrolmen who usually knew who the bad guys were in their districts, where they lived, where they hung out, who they were shacked up with and what they drove.

So someone got the bright idea of creating a small unit of half a dozen patrolmen from the second, more active group of officers and assigning them to the Detective Division as a sort of on-the-job training in detective work that would also supplement the Detective Division's manpower. A federal grant helped with the financing.

To disguise their status, the officers could work in plainclothes, set their own hours and could grow their hair longer along with facial hair. They were supplied with some outwardly shoddy unmarked vans with thick curtains covering the side and rear windows. The curtains prevented unauthorized people from seeing the array of cabinets built in the rear of the vans. The cabinets contained body armor, shotguns, a supply of double-ought buckshot and twelve-gauge slugs, tear gas guns and grenades, gas masks, night vision devices called StarTron scopes, portable radios (a luxury then provided only to supervisors), several different license plates and a selection of plastic magnetic signs. By slapping the signs on the doors, they could quickly become plumbers, TV repairmen, carpet cleaners, painters, construction contractors and any number of other innocuous covers identities.

It was dubbed the Selective Enforcement Unit (SEU) because the original idea was to target specific individuals that they knew were career criminals. They would follow these people around the clock and develop informants within their organizations or associates on the theory that the target couldn't keep his nose clean for too long under that kind of (hopefully invisible) scrutiny before being caught in a crime.

Unfortunately, it didn't work out that way. Under detective command and control, the unit began being used for too much of what the detectives thought of as "scut work." Long, unproductive stakeouts based on lousy informants, following known gamblers to locate their games or public relations assignments to impress influential people with having an entire undercover unit assigned to their particular problem. All eroded into the unit's intended function.

There was nothing wrong with the idea, just the way it was being implemented. In later years, when the department expanded to four decentralized patrol divisions, each one would have a FAST unit (Felony Apprehension and Surveillance Team) and these eventually evolved into IMPACT (Initiating Multiple Police Actions) teams. Both were based upon the SEU concept. But in its first year, it was largely wasted.

After a year, it was transferred back under the control of the Patrol Division and the individual officers were given a little more latitude in selecting their own assignments. Then things got interesting.

NOT EVERYONE BELONGS IN THIS LINE OF WORK

It's Christmas time and the SEU is doing the obligatory roaming stakeouts in mall parking lots, looking for burglars, car thieves and shoplifters. It wasn't our idea but we didn't bitch too much because it was a welcome chance to work days. Left to our own devices, we seemed to work a lot of nights. Great for activity but tough on families.

We needn't have worried about it being too good an assignment. Some genius in headquarters has decided to put two female officers with us this time. The fact that this was a very active unit that had a history of getting in a lot of hot spots didn't deter them. The headquarters genius probably saw a TV show that convinced him that undercover operations with a man and a woman in a van were less suspicious than two men.

Since female officers in patrol operations were still a relatively new innovation, there was still a lot of resentment and doubt about them among the male officers. Some of the women were working out very well and were gaining acceptance. But it was given to them just like it was the males—on an individual basis as they proved themselves. Compounding that was the simple fact that nobody likes to lose their partner, even for a day, to work with someone they don't know for a purely political motive.

One of the women assigned with us was one of the original five women in patrol and was establishing a good reputation as a working officer. The other one was newer and an unknown quantity. When you get a partner you don't know, male or female, you ask around to check them out. As far as I had been able to determine from the department grapevine, the only rumors making the rounds concerned her sexual talents. Since I was a relative newly-wed with a year-old son, I was more interested in her police-related talents.

The parking lot of this particular shopping mall completely encircled the mall. We were one of two male-female teams roaming the mall parking lot in our unmarked vans. Another team of two SEU officers was stationed at the far end of the parking lot. We alternated roles to reduce our visibility and to provide backup to each other.

To be as inconspicuous as possible, we tried to vary our routines. We'd roam the parking lot at random for a while, then we'd park for a while, then we'd get out and walk around inside the mall while the third unit took over our outside patrol. During one of our trips inside the mall, my confidence in my partner-for-a-day was shaken a little.

I decided to get a cup of coffee so I went to one of the fast-food vendors in the mall. Ordering the coffee, I took it, paid and turned away. My partner, right behind me, looked at me with a *Well!* expression I'd seen on other women's faces before—when she expects you to do something and you aren't cooperating.

Apparently I was expected to buy her coffee. I disagreed. We weren't *that* much undercover and this wasn't a date.

Somewhat miffed, she bought her own coffee.

Back outside, we drove around for a while and then parked. We tried a little small talk but it didn't work well so we just sipped our coffee. After about fifteen minutes, I saw something. Something I wondered if my partner had seen.

"The blue van." It was about three rows over in the next parking section, idling slowly down the aisle. Two white males.

"What about it?" she asked.

"That's its third lap through that section."

She shrugged. "Looking for a space."

"They've passed several empty spaces."

"Looking for a closer one," she shrugged again.

We lapsed back into silence. You develop certain instincts in this job. I wasn't encouraged.

The blue van turned back up the next aisle. Half way down it, it stopped behind a new Corvette. Obviously a quick braking, the van rocked a little from the stop. The passenger got out and the van drove off at a slightly faster speed. The passenger walked over to the Corvette's driver's side and looked around. White male, twenties, average height and weight, beard, dark parka. He immediately started shimming the Vette's door. I started the van.

He opened the door and ducked into the Corvette. I pulled out into the main aisle and idled in that direction, heading for the next row past him. As soon as he leaned over in the seat and disappeared from sight, I sped up, turned down the aisle and stopped one aisle north of him. As we approached the sports car, I motioned my partner to the rear of the car and I walked up to the driver's door. Drawing my gun, I held it down by my side.

The guy was leaning over the center console and working with some wires pulled out from under the dash. That's what the lawyers call probable cause. I opened the door with my left hand and he looked up at me, startled. The gun wasn't at my side anymore. It was pointed at his nose. His eyes told me he didn't need to see the badge.

"Police. Out." I reached in and grabbed the shoulder of the parka. He got out and I turned him around. He automatically put his hands on the car's top, flat with the fingers spread. Apparently he'd done this before. My partner was standing at the rear of the car with her hand on her gun, still holstered.

He didn't even complete one bounce off the car before he spun to the right and ran right past my partner. My left hand was clutching an empty parka and he was heading south as fast as his little feet would carry him. I took off after him as my partner scrambled to catch up.

We weaved through two rows of cars when I saw him twist his upper body toward me as he kept running at full speed. With the right training, this guy could have been a wide receiver. One of his hands was pointed back at me and it held a big, black automatic pistol. Less than ten yards behind him, I could see his trigger finger pulling the trigger. No flash, no sound, no bucking from recoil but he was pulling the trigger, over and over.

By the way, that slow motion stuff in the movies (actually adrenaline) really works. I started falling forward, aiming at his head on the way down and pulling the trigger on my Magnum. As I was falling, I saw a woman getting in a white car on the next row, directly behind him. I had already seen that a human head won't usually stop a .357 Magnum 158-grain jacketed hollow point bullet. So I pulled the gun up and to the right just as I fired, which was immediately followed by my ripping both knees out of a new pair of pants, not to mention the skin underneath. He turned back around and continued on his way, still at full speed.

I don't exactly remember it but I must have come up like a guy sliding into second base who saw he could make it to third because he'd only gained about another ten yards on me. He was heading for a mall entrance but he didn't have the gun in his pumping hands now.

He slammed his way into the mall with me a few seconds behind, gaining but slowly. Then our luck changed, his for the worse and mine for the better. Eddie was an officer a couple of years behind me but we had gotten to know one another on my old patrol shift before I transferred to SEU. Like many officers during the Christmas season, Eddie was working an off-duty job at one of the stores in the mall, trying to cut their losses from shoplifters. At that moment, Eddie walked out into the mall. He saw two guys running full speed down the mall toward him. One was a guy he didn't know being chased by a guy he did know. As the guy he didn't know flew by, Eddie stuck out his foot and tripped him. With my momentum and Eddie's head start, we landed on him about the same time. Another of the SEU guys came sliding up a few seconds later. Then came the handcuffs, the frisk search (no gun) and dragging him back outside after thanking Eddie.

Just as we got out the mall door, my partner came screeching up in the van. Jumping out with her hand on her gun butt, she fixed the suspect with a withering stare that didn't seem to wither him much. As mother used to say, a day late and a dollar short.

When the two SEU guys at the back of the lot heard the shot, they charged up to our section and got the story from my partner. One of them ran into the mall to back me while the other one started looking for the blue van. He and the other team found him prowling a few sections away and arrested him. Patrol cars were on the way to transport the prisoners and a wrecker was coming for the blue van. A patrol officer would wait by the Vette to take a report from the owner when he came out of the mall. A patrol sergeant was talking to a woman next to the white car. There was a .357 Magnum bullet in the passenger's side sun visor of her car. It had come through the open driver's side door several feet to the right of where she had been standing during the shooting. He was advising her how to make a claim to the city for repairs.

The guy's gun was found under a parked car along the route of our foot pursuit. It was a .38 automatic with a fully loaded clip in it but no round in the chamber. With a single-action automatic pistol, you have to pull the slide back to manually chamber the first round before it will fire. In the excitement of being chased by a cop with a gun, the guy had forgotten to chamber the first round. When his repeated pulls on the trigger failed to make the gun fire and I fired at him, he panicked and threw the gun away.

The female officers were reassigned back to their patrol shifts the next day.

A few days later, they held the Firearms Review Board. It had only been in existence for a couple of years. Chaired by the Assistant Chief, it consisted of half a dozen command officers who passed judgment on every shooting incident. They reviewed the official reports and interviewed the involved officer, homicide detectives, the patrol supervisor and any other necessary witnesses. I was the last one called.

I told them the story just like I'd put it in my report. They had a few questions which I answered. I was a little nervous but not overly concerned. I'd been involved in a couple of other incidents where shots were fired before there was a review board and I felt I'd been justified in firing my weapon in this incident. I knew at least two of these commanders had been involved in shootings during their careers. It helps to have people on a board who have had that experience. They understand some things that are hard to put into words. The board fell silent and the assistant chief looked around at the other members.

"Any other questions?"

A highly respected detective captain spoke up. "Yes, I've got one. Officer, where was your partner during this shooting?"

"Well sir, during the chase I saw her off to my right in my peripheral vision."

"Between the next row of cars?"

"Yes sir."

"When did you lose sight of her?"

"When the suspect drew the gun."

"And when did you see her next?"

"After the arrest."

"Did you ask her where she had gone?"

"Yes sir. She said when she saw the guy draw the gun, she thought she'd better go back to the van and get on the radio."

A couple of the commanders chuckled.

"I see. Thank you. That'll be all, officer."

About five minutes later, they told me they were ruling the shooting justified.

My partner-for-a-day resigned from the police department some time afterwards. I think she went into sales.

NOTE: Don't draw any erroneous conclusions from the preceding story. I may be a dinosaur but I'm not one of those dinosaurs who believe women don't belong in police work. I think that question has long since been answered positively. But, as the title of the story says, not everyone does, men as well as women. Although I don't have any statistics, I would assume they succeed or fail at about the same ratio.

Traffic

I was never assigned to the Traffic Division but, like most patrol officers, I've still investigated a lot of traffic accidents and written a lot of tickets. Nevertheless, all these stories aren't mine. They came from veteran traffic officers who did it all day, every day and were repeated over cups of coffee or sometimes a few drinks. A couple of them are really patrol stories but have a traffic element to them because some guys served in both divisions.

BUMPER STICKER POETRY

Big trucks and trains use air brakes. They use compressed air to slam a set of brakes on instead of hydraulic fluid like your car does. They work very well, especially for bringing very heavy things to a stop in fairly short order. Air brakes can bring a multi-ton truck to a stop in one-tenth of the distance it takes the engine to accelerate it the same distance.

A car running a red light started it all. Who the driver was, why he or she did it, and where they went will remain a mystery. Maybe it was a drunk, maybe a woman fixing her makeup in the rear view mirror or yelling at the kids in the back seat. No one saw a tag number and they could just give a general description of the car. The driver went merrily on their way and never saw the carnage they caused.

The eighteen-wheel flatbed truck was only going about forty miles per hour when he had to slam the brakes to keep from hitting the car. The driver behind him was following too closely and wasn't paying enough attention. I'm sure he would have been glad to pay any fine but he got the death penalty instead.

The bed of the flatbed truck was just below the eye level of the car's driver. When it went under the back of the truck, the bed sheared the top of the car off like a hot knife through butter. The headless corpse in the driver's seat gushed blood like a balloon full of blood with a pinhole in it.

One of the investigating officers finally found the head jammed between the truck's second set of wheels forward and one of the airbag shock absorbers. The rest of it was just their normal routine—measure the point of impact, measure the skid marks, take the photos, interview the witnesses and survivors, make the diagrams, fill out the reports. Tomorrow is another day.

The next day, the same traffic unit was back on duty, cruising up the same boulevard the fatality occurred on the day before. As they pull up to a stop light, they noticed that they're behind a flatbed truck much like the one involved in the previous day's accident. As they sit behind it with their eyes at the level of the flatbed, they see a bumper sticker just above the license plate. It read:

IF YOU CAN'T STOP
Smile as you go under

The driving officer snorts. Then his partner starts chuckling. Before the light turns green, both officers are laughing heartily, overwhelmed by the irony.

There are plenty of things to take seriously in this line of work. Contrary to what Jack Webb might have you believe, you can't take them all that seriously. If you do, the job will suffer unnecessarily and so will you.

GHETTO COP 101

Vern had a couple of years more seniority on the department than I did but he had been in the Traffic Division for several years, following his first love, riding police motorcycles. I never asked him why he decided to transfer back to patrol. I suspect it was because he intended to try to get promoted to detective (which he later did) and in those days it was easier to get promoted to detective out of patrol than it was traffic. For whatever reason, he ended up on my shift and riding with me on the eastside.

In spite of the fact that he had a couple of years on me, Vern had less experience with criminal activity. Patrol officers wrote traffic tickets but it wasn't their primary function and most of them preferred to leave the accident investigations to the traffic officers. Some traffic supervisors actually forbade their men from making criminal arrests because they considered that patrol territory. In fact, I had known of instances where traffic officers were actually punished for making criminal arrests which I considered the ultimate in chicken-shit for traffic supervisors.

So, to begin with, Vern was a little unsure of himself as to how Patrol did things on the eastside. I sympathized because I'd have been just as unsure in Traffic. So I told him to just back me up on a few traffic stops and we'd see how it goes.

So I'd make traffic stops.

"May I see your driver's license?"

"It's in my other pants-I left it at home-The dog ate it." Whatever. When he gets the idea he's going to jail if he doesn't produce some ID, he ups something, fishing license, library card, something.

"Is this your car?"

"Uh-huh."

"So it's registered in your name?"

"Uh, no, I bought it from my brother-in-law and I haven't changed the registration yet."

"Bought it when?"

"Uh, two years ago."

"Ever been in trouble with the police?"

"Who me?" A shocked look. "Nahhh, not me."

Then you check him through BR (Bureau of Records), for AW's (Alias Warrants, i.e., unpaid tickets), county, state and federal warrants, registration on the car, check for a valid DL. Invariably they came back with a record. A page or two full of burglary arrests, weapons charges, dope, stolen property, robbery, manslaughter, murder, the whole spectrum.

Over a dozen traffic stops, the same scenario played itself out. Vern started following suit when he made his own stops. One night he made a stop. While he was up at the driver's window, I stood at the corner of the patrol car covering him. After a few moments, he walked back to me. He had this startled look on his face.

"This guy's got a valid driver's license and he says he's been in trouble with the police."

He was so stunned he just wanted to tell me about it. So we got in the car and ran a full check on the guy. Turns out he'd done federal time for bank robbery, served his time and was out now.

"What do you think I should do?" Vern said.

I shrugged. "No wants, no warrants, he's not on parole or probation, the DL's valid, the car's registered to him. Write him the ticket or let him go. Up to you."

He walked back up to the car and came back a few seconds later.

"What'd you do?"

"Let him go."

"Good. Now he can't say he never got a fair shake from a cop."

—AND DIVERSITY 101

I had another partner who was a former motorcycle officer. He was an Indian—not an Indian Indian but an American Indian and, like everyone else, he was subject to getting sunburned in Oklahoma summers which made him even darker than he normally was.

One graveyard shift, we got a domestic call at a well-known address in our district. It was a residence/transient hotel/whorehouse/corn liquor joint. When the residents and/or visitors got drunk enough, a dispute always arose over the price of booze or sex and there were a few decent neighbors who called the police. After enough calls at the same location, you tend to lose patience and whatever diplomatic skills you had initially.

We drove up to the call and since I was driving, it was my call. I parked in front of the house next door and walked up to the house. The front porch was dimly lit by a fifteen-watt light bulb and half a dozen of the residents were yammering on the front porch. Since the house was set close to the street, my partner didn't come up with me, just got out of the passenger side door and stood there, ready to back me up if necessary.

I walked into this cacophony of drunken, inane, personal complaints about which the law could do nothing. The radio was still broadcasting more important, urgent calls so I listened politely for about fifteen seconds and then erupted, pointing my finger at certain individuals.

"This is all bullshit. You leave—now. You go back inside. The rest of you go wherever you belong and don't come back here tonight. If I get another call here tonight, *everybody* goes to jail."

End of call.

About fifteen minutes later, we heard Cruiser Two, the eastside sergeant, get a call to that address on a complaint on an officer. We went on about our business for a while until Cruiser Two called us to meet him. We pulled up next to his car. He had an amused smirk on his face.

"I just got a complaint call."

"Yeah, we heard it come out."

"They told me one of my officers was abrupt and rude with them."

I said nothing. I got the impression he didn't expect me to before he continued.

"I asked them the officers' names and they didn't know so I asked for their descriptions. They said the rude one was white, about six feet tall, two hundred pounds, dark hair and mustache. I told them that described about ninety per cent of the police department. Then they said his partner didn't actually come up to the house and didn't say anything but stayed out by the car. They said he was a black officer. I told them we didn't have any black officers on duty in this sector tonight."

My partner was already starting to sputter. The sergeant laughed and drove off. For the rest of the night, I had to restrain my partner from going back to that house and showing them the difference between an Indian and a black man.

OKLAHOMA CITY IS CLOSED

The Organized Crime Unit got the word first. Teletypes and phone calls coming in from Barstow, Needles, Kingman, Flagstaff, Albuquerque, Amarillo, every town along Highway 66 West which hadn't been entirely transformed into Interstate 40 yet.

A California chapter of the Hell's Angels was on a road trip west and leaving their normal trail of destruction in their wake. Robberies, rapes, assaults, wrecked bars and the occasional murder.

Oklahoma City had its own home-grown bikers and they were bad enough. The primary ones were the Hangmen and the Outlaws but the police intelligence, narcotics and organized crime detectives knew who they were, where they lived and what they were involved in for the most part. Within broad guidelines, they were controlled. They were usually a relatively minor nuisance whose ranks were constantly being thinned by felony convictions but when it came down to the bottom line, they knew that the biggest, baddest gang in town wore gray shirts and blue pants.

But the Hells Angels were a different breed. They ran amok in their native California. They openly provided "security" for concerts of major rock bands and people who got out of line got stabbed or beaten, sometimes to death. They controlled conclaves of prostitution, narcotics, gambling, white slavery and God knows what else. Now a significant number of them were moving east and it probably wasn't for the scenery.

No bulletins or radiograms were issued, no press releases, it was all done by word of mouth. Detectives talked to shift commanders who advised their shifts. Sergeants made arrangements for which units would stay in their districts and which ones wouldn't.

They timed their arrival all wrong. It was late at night and the only traffic on the streets was the small percentage of citizens who worked nights. If they had spotted the two Oklahoma Highway Patrol cruisers that were driving some distance behind them, they apparently weren't bothered by it especially since the troopers hadn't bothered them. The troopers weren't using their red lights or sirens but they were using their radios.

All must have seemed perfectly normal to the bikers as they took the long, curving Western Avenue exit into downtown Oklahoma City. Until they saw the flashing red lights of two police motorcycles blocking the bottom of the exit. As several dozen choppers braked to a halt, one of the motorcycle officers got off his Harley and approached the lead biker in the double column. He gave him a curt message.

Oklahoma City is closed.

It probably provoked derisive laughter from the thirty or forty outlaw bikers confronted by two motorcycle cops, all wearing their "colors"; filthy blue jean jackets with the sleeves cut out, a skull patch on the back and an arc reading "Hells Angels" along with miscellaneous insignia on the front, various numbers, letters and wings with ominous meaning.

Then two cars pulled to the curb on the connecting side street leaving their headlights on. Cheap model four-door Plymouths, solid colors, black wall tires, small hubcaps, whip antennas mounted on the trunk, two shadows in the front seat. California or Oklahoma, they could spot detective cruisers. Then black and whites started showing up. Accident Investigation cars, Patrol cars, supervisors cars. Two half a block away at the intersection of Western and Sheridan. Then two more on Clegern, blocking the two lanes between the idling detective cruisers. Then two more west of the exit on Sheridan. And two more. Four more. Six more. Just sitting there, idling, headlights on. Two shadows in each front seat along with a long slender vertical shadow between them. Shotgun. No more laughter.

A few more words are exchanged. Then the two police motorcycles move, unblocking the exit. The two columns of bikers slowly start forward. Following the only path left open to them without running into a police car, their only available route takes them directly to the entrance back onto I-40, westbound. California, one thousand miles, thataway.

I was not present at that incident but I spent another quarter of a century on the police department after I heard about it. I never heard of anyone seeing another set of Hells Angels colors in Oklahoma City.

Homicide

CAREER MOTIVATION

It may sound strange to civilians but not all police officers are interested or enthusiastic about all areas of police work. They eventually come to realize that all these areas are necessary and important but not all those areas motivate them. I imagine everyone, at one time or another, silently asks themselves "Is what I'm doing today *really* that important/necessary/effective/pick your own adjective?"

Some guys hate to write traffic tickets but they do because it's their duty when they see someone do something illegal and potentially dangerous with a vehicle. Some guys hate to work traffic accidents but they realize it's their job when someone has done something illegal and dangerous with their vehicle that has injured someone else, physically or financially. In that respect, it's probably like any other job. Just about every day, you have to do some things you would rather not in order to do some other things you would. The same is true of all the investigative specialties. Not everyone wants to work in the Youth Bureau or Property Crimes.

It has been said that there are no draftees in Homicide. That stems from the fact that, at least in those days, when someone got promoted to detective, they went wherever the opening had been created after all the veterans had been shuffled around according to their transfer requests. It's a budgetary thing. But nobody landed in Homicide by accident.

To get in that unit, you had to work for it. A creditable record of arrests and a record as an "active" officer in patrol would help get you promoted to detective but that wasn't enough to get in Homicide. Just putting in a transfer request and sitting back waiting for it to happen wasn't enough. You had to beg, plead, wheedle, call in favors, convince other Homicide detectives, supervisors and commanders that you wanted in there more than you wanted to eat, drink or make love to the Playmate of the Month. You had to convince them that you wanted nothing more than to work an endless supply of nights, weekends, holidays and overtime, be on call 24/7, work front-page-important cases in the glare of media spotlights and Supreme Court scrutiny, testify in court on your days off in the most intense trials in the criminal justice system, be cross-examined by the best defense attorneys money can buy, leave your family at Thanksgiving dinner or on Christmas morning to work 8, 12, 16, 24 or 36 hours straight when necessary, jump on a plane on a moment's notice to go halfway across the country without being able to tell your family when you were coming back because you don't know and so forth and so on. Fortunate timing and luck can also be important factors as they were in my case. When you got down to the nuts and bolts, it wasn't that glamorous. It was just very hard work. If anyone ever landed in Homicide by accident, I never knew about it.

The Detective Division was staffed by a skeleton crew on weekends. Just one guy in some units, none in others. Of course, if necessary, we had the entire Police Department at our call but usually the entire detective complement would fit in one car on a weekend.

One summer morning I was working the weekend duty in another detective unit. They did important and necessary work but I was beginning to learn that I wasn't that interested in it and therefore not very good at it. I was in that unit because that's where the detective retired from whose position I was promoted into. As I said before, a budgetary thing. A friend of mine was working the weekend in Homicide. Ordinarily he would have been down to have coffee with me but I hadn't seen him this morning so evidently he was busy. I took a break from my paperwork and wandered down the hall to see what he was doing.

Predictably, he was working on a fresh case. Reports and crime scene photos covered his desk. As he told me about it, I browsed through the evidence.

A man had been out early one morning throwing his newspaper route. He had the newspaper bundles in the back seat of his three-door hatchback car. He would park the car in a residential block, grab the necessary number of papers and walk the block to deliver the papers to the proper houses on his route. Since the residential areas were virtually deserted at that hour, he left the car running while he was gone. He came back from one block and his car was gone. He frantically called the police. Frantic because that morning he had been home alone with his two kids so he took them with him in his car to deliver the newspapers. Behind the newspapers in the back seat, under the hatchback, were a sleeping six-year-old girl and her three-year-old brother.

The patrol shift fanned out in all directions. It didn't take them long to find the car but it had been too long. They called in Homicide.

My friend had cleared the case. A kid, a teenager, had been roaming the area that morning. He happened onto the idling car and jumped in for a short joy ride. He didn't realize there was anyone else in the car. The extreme rear of the car under the hatchback door had been invisible behind the stacks of newspapers in the back seat. When he got through with his joy ride, he put a match to the newspapers in the back seat to destroy his fingerprints and any other evidence that he had stolen the car.

Homicide had run a test on a similar junk car with the back seat full of newspapers out at the Fire Department training area. They even videotaped it for the D.A.'s Office. The car went up in seconds. The fire was hot enough to melt the glass.

While he was telling me all this, I was looking through the crime scene photos. The car was a blackened hulk. The two small charred bodies in the back were lying one atop the other. Trapped between a locked hatchback and a flaming wall of newspapers and upholstery, the six-year-old girl had climbed on top of her little brother to try to shield him from the flames.

Six weeks later I was in Homicide.

DIFFERENT

"You're sure you've got to do this now?"

"My paycheck is $48.12 light. The credit union held out an extra payment they shouldn't have and, yeah, I need that $48.12. OK?"

"OK, OK."

"Even so, it'll take me at least one more pay period to get it back."

The two young officers looked at the directory next to the elevator in the City Services building. Accounting and Finance, second floor. The one who was $48.12 poorer punched the "2" button.

The receptionist's counter was directly in front of them as they exited the elevator. The poorer one bellied up to the counter while his partner idly read the posters on the bulletin board.

After the officer explained his problem, the receptionist picked up the phone, dialed an extension and told him someone would be with him in a minute. Incredibly, it wasn't much more than that when an accounting supervisor appeared. She listened patiently to his story and then produced a form for him to complete. As he filled in the blanks in the form, she glanced at their uniforms and began to make polite conversation.

"My cousin is a policeman."

"Really? What's his name?"

She told them.

The officer glanced at his partner who, having overheard, shook his head. "Don't know him, ma'am."

"He's a detective."

"We've only been on for a little over a year. We don't know many detectives. What unit's he in?"

"He's in Homicide."

The two officers glanced at one another again but it was a different kind of glance this time. The woman caught the look.

"What?" she said, looking at both of them quizzically.

The one filling out the form looked hesitantly at his partner before replying.

"Well ma'am, no offense but those guys in Homicide are different, even for cops."

HOW DIFFERENT?

The call came out late one night not long after Christmas. When the Homicide night shift car arrived, everything looked normal from the street. Christmas tree lights shining through a front window, frosted windows, a light dusting of snow on the dead grass in the front yard, almost a scene from a Christmas card or a holiday-themed painting. Everything except the black and white patrol car parked in front of the house, enveloped in its own smoky exhaust condensing in the wintry air, yellow crime scene tape running from one fender to a tree on the other side of the yard, a shaken young patrolman sitting speechless in the front seat, his older partner standing on the front porch writing the Crime Scene Log in his notebook. He was also guarding the crime scene from unauthorized entry but no one in their right mind would want to go in there unless they had to. Or it was their job.

One Homicide guy automatically started walking around the exterior of the house while the other went to the porch and had himself entered into the log. When the detective went in, the patrolman stepped into the doorway just to get some of the warmth coming from the interior. He didn't want to go in any farther. He'd already been in far enough.

"Body's in the back bedroom." The detective just nodded without looking up.

The detective started writing in his notebook as he was surveying the front room. Massive blood splatter on the north wall. Not just blood but blood with chunks of meat and hair in it. More on the floor. And the ceiling. And the furniture. A broken wooden shaft like a tool handle leaning against the wall behind the door, the first two feet of it dripping blood. The Christmas tree in one corner sparkled with multicolored lights and glistened with several feet of garland. Except it wasn't garland. It was someone's intestines, looped and strung over the branches.

The detective began absently humming a familiar lilting tune as he wrote.

It's beginning to look a lot like Christmas—

The patrolman just shook his head and stepped back outside. It wasn't that cold.

SIX TO THE LEFT

One of many ways the Homicide guys are "different" is the range of specialized knowledge they accumulate over the years; knowledge that isn't good for much except investigating deaths.

They acquire a whole new vocabulary, some of which can sound impressive to the uninitiated; post-mortem lividity, rigor mortis, scleral petechiae, exsanguination, stellate wounds, echymosis, autolysis, stipling, cadaveric spasm and much more. They also get to know the medical names for a lot of bones and muscles, usually the ones that most frequently get broken, shattered, slashed, punctured and sustain various other damage in usually unsuccessful quests for survival. Mind you, they rarely spice up their conversations with these terms, they just learn them so they can keep up during autopsies and while making the follow-up reports.

Since this is America and moreover southwest America, they gain a wide knowledge of gunshot wounds and the weapons that cause them. Countries like the United Kingdom, Japan, Canada and others even send some of their police officers and forensic scientists to our country to learn about them. Some American cities have more gunshot injuries and deaths in a single year than some countries have in decades. As a result, the average patrolman with a few years on the job in a large American city knows more about gunshot wounds than experienced investigators in many other countries. The average American homicide detective can usually glance at a gunshot wound and tell you whether it was probably made by a pistol, rifle or shotgun. If a pistol or rifle, he can estimate the approximate caliber, the velocity of the round and whether it was a full metal jacket, soft point or hollow point round. If a shotgun, he can tell if it was loaded with birdshot, buckshot or slugs and the approximate gauge. He can give a fairly good estimate of how far the gun was away from the victim when it was fired. Sometimes he can tell even more.

The barrels of rifles and pistols are rifled with spiral grooves to give the bullet more speed, stability and accuracy. When the bullet comes out of the barrel, it is marked with this rifling. The grooves chiseled into the bullet are called, naturally enough, grooves. The raised portions that separate the grooves are called lands. Depending upon the make of weapon, the rifling is given either a right or left hand twist. Homicide guys carry a lot of this information around in their heads, especially for the guns they most frequently encounter.

Larger caliber Smith and Wessons usually have five lands and grooves with a right hand twist but the Smith .22 has six with a right hand twist. Most Colts have six with a left hand twist. Iver Johnsons have five to the right, a High Standard .22 has six to the right and so does a Titan .38. This knowledge is usually the special domain of the police ballistics examiner but occasionally it is of immediate use to the detective. Not as often as TV and movies would have you believe but it does happen.

Bob and Jerry got the call. A shooting, victim lying in the street. DRT. Dead right there. Bob works the scene, Jerry looks for witnesses. Jerry doesn't have much luck. The victim is a Mexican male in his twenties and the area is primarily Hispanic. Lots of illegals. Nobody saw anything, heard anything, knows anything. Everybody was in the bathroom. About all he learns is the guy had a girlfriend he'd recently broken up with. That and a few people heard a car leaving the area. No description, just a car engine. Naturally nobody knows the ex-girlfriend's address but he gets some pretty specific directions to her upstairs garage apartment. It's only a few blocks away so they agree Jerry will head over there to check on her while Bob finishes the crime scene.

Bob checks the body. The guy was hit once in the ten ring, right through the pump. Looks like a medium caliber, .38 or .357 Magnum. The victim has an entrance and exit wound so it's a through-and-through shot. Walking around the body in widening circles, incredibly he finds the bullet. It's lying in the street about twenty yards away from the victim. The guy had a nice muscular chest and back that absorbed a lot of the round's energy and it just fell to the ground after punching a hole through his heart. Squatting over the bullet, Bob rolls it over with his pen tip just enough to count the lands and grooves. Six with a left-hand twist.

A lot of guns have six lands and grooves with a left hand twist but the most popular and numerous are Colts. And we don't positively know yet that is the specific bullet that went through the victim but when the odds are on your side, you play them. He gets on the radio to Jerry who is just pulling up at the girl's apartment.

"We might be looking for a Colt, .38 or .357. If it's a .357, it's probably loaded with low-power .38 ammo."

"Clear. I'm 10-97."

There are two cars parked in front of the garage apartment. As he keeps his eye on the upstairs door, Jerry casually brushes his hand across both hoods as he walks by. Both hoods are warm, warmer than the day's sunshine would account for. Neither car has been here very long.

Jerry walks up the stairs. The screen door is closed but the inner door is open. A Hispanic girl and a black guy are sitting on a couch facing the door. Lying on a coffee table between the couch and the door is—a Colt Trooper .357 Magnum. That's what we call probable cause. Jerry opens the door and walks in.

Case closed. It was all over but the paperwork.

The young lovers got in a squabble because the Mexican boyfriend caught the Mexican girlfriend screwing around with the black guy. They broke up and the boyfriend told the girl he'd "get her" sooner or later and he'd get away with it because no potential witnesses would tell the cops. She figured he was right so she asked her new boyfriend for some protection. He was an armed security guard for the local school system so he loaned her his Colt pistol while he was on his days off but told her he'd need it back by the time he went back to work on Monday morning.

The girl kept the gun overnight. The next day she decided she would be unarmed after one more day so she went over to the ex-boyfriend's house to settle it. Seeing him walking out of the house, she drove up and stopped in the street. He walked over and when he got close enough, she let him have one round in center mass and drove home. She had just put the gun on the coffee table when her new boyfriend showed up to get his gun back. He didn't believe Jerry's story until Jerry broke the Colt's cylinder open and showed him the six .38 ball cartridges with one fired. The black guy was more than cooperative. He knew his gun was impounded as evidence and he'd be fired as soon as he showed up for work without it, not to mention when the bosses found out why he didn't have it. Apparently whatever the girl was giving him wasn't worth the aggravation she was causing him.

WELCOME TO THE CLUB

For most of the 1970s, the Homicide Unit had plenty to do. They were tasked with investigating all sex crimes from rape to sodomy to indecent exposure. They also investigated all non-fatal assaults (on the theory that the victims might die later and if they did, it was too late to go back and do it right) and kidnappings. Although Robbery was officially tasked with investigating extortions, Homicide guys ended up helping on most of those as well. In addition to all that, they got down to their specialty—dead people.

The watchword at that time was "If it's dead, we work it." What that meant was that if a person died when not directly under a physician's care (i.e. in the hospital), Homicide worked it unless it was a traffic fatality. And they worked traffic fatalities in conjunction with Traffic officers if it was proven to be a deliberate case of murder or manslaughter, just using a vehicle as the weapon. So Homicide detectives showed up not just for every homicide but for every suicide, accidental death and natural death in private homes or businesses. Occasionally someone was murdered and had the house burned down on top of them to cover up the crime and destroy evidence. After the Medical Examiner autopsied a few "fire deaths" that had bullets in them, the Homicide guys were trained in arson investigations and started going to all fire deaths as well.

So if a guy accidentally got caught in the conveyor belt system at a box-making plant and got chewed up, Homicide was there. If a ninety-year-old cancer patient died at home in his bed, Homicide was there. If people died from burns or smoke inhalation in a house fire, Homicide was there. If a baby died from Sudden Infant Death Syndrome in its crib during the night, Homicide was there. If someone had a massive heart attack while sitting on their toilet, Homicide was there. Plus all the fatal and near-fatal shootings, stabbings, beatings, etc. etc. In a city of nearly half a million and a metro area of nearly a million, there were then only twelve detectives who specialized in death investigations. They saw a lot of dead people on a daily basis. Experience came rapidly.

Most new Homicide detectives got a short grace period. Teamed up with a more senior, experienced partner, they got walked through the basics. I'll show you how to investigate a crime scene and you do the next one. I'll show you how to interpret the signs of death on a body and you do the next one. I'll show you how to interview witnesses and you do the next ones. I'll show you how to interview a murder suspect and you do the next one. I'll show you how to make your reports and you do the next ones. I'll show you how to file the charges with the District Attorney and you do the next one. I'll show you the rules of testifying in court and you do the next one.

The new guys work the normal 8 A.M. to 4 P.M. day shift for a few weeks. Then about every other month they spend a week working the 7 P.M. to 3 A.M. night shift. Finally, when they get to a point where they know a little about what they're doing and have gotten some self-confidence, they have to spend a weekend working the Detective Division desk—taking the walk-in complaints, making the proper reports, notifying the proper units. The weekend duty is usually the culmination of the week they spend on twenty-four hour call for anything that dies. That week usually rolls around every six weeks. If there is a death, you leave the desk duty and go out on it. One of the Robbery or Vice guys takes over the desk for you. If you need help, you call your partner. If you need more help, you call the backup team on call. If you need enough help, you call out the whole unit. But not until you're overwhelmed.

So the new guy shows up bright-eyed and bushy-tailed at 8 A.M. Saturday morning, feeling pretty fortunate that he didn't get called out on a Friday night killing. He gets through one hour and two pretty conventional walk-ins before everything goes to hell in a hand basket.

Three kids are dead in a house fire. Robbery gets the desk and he goes to the scene. It's a ramshackle little house on the southeast side. No phone, no gas, just water and electric for utilities. A couple of hours of tearing up thin, worn-out carpet and looking in vain for accelerants, checking the electrical outlets for arcing leads to tracing the fire to an electrical space heater that caught the thin linen curtains. The parents made it out but the three kids died from smoke inhalation. That's a small consolation. From his patrol days, he'll never forget the smell of roasted human flesh. He'll smell it many more times but not today.

Just as he's leaving the house fire, he gets another call. An apparent natural death on the southwest side. A sixty-four year-old man with terminal cancer died in bed during the night. A short investigation shows nothing suspicious to either him or the Medical Examiner's Field Investigator. That's merciful since there's another call waiting at a north-side car dealership.

In the service area, several mechanics are working on cars. One calls out to another to toss him a special screwdriver from his tool kit. It's a big screwdriver, over a foot long and weighing several pounds. The mechanic tosses it to his buddy but his buddy misses the catch. The tip of the screwdriver hits him in the right temple and he collapses. No break in the skin, just a faint dime-sized contusion but he's dead. A tragic accident.

He goes back to the station and is looking forward hopefully to going home at the rapidly-approaching 4 P.M. but it's not to be. As he walks in, the Robbery guy who relieved him tells him about a homicide call. A shooting in a bar on Southwest 29th. Usually only hardcore boozers are drinking in the middle of a Saturday afternoon.

There are a dozen witnesses so he has patrol take them all to the station for questioning. He calls his partner to go to the station and start the interviews while he works the crime scene. Four o'clock comes and goes without even being noticed.

Four hours later, they've got a suspect identified but not in custody. Teletypes and wanted notices are sent out statewide with special attention to the towns where the suspect has relatives or known connections. Finishing the reports and drawing up the information to file state charges of murder on Monday take it up close to midnight.

They're just getting ready to go home when the phone rings. It's the night shift unit. They're out on another homicide, there's no suspect in custody and the case is going to belong to the day shift guys in the morning anyway so you might as well go to the crime scene and see everything for yourself right from the start.

Going through the motions on that one takes you right up to dawn. Back to the office, splash some water in the face and finish those reports. At mid-morning, another call comes in. The suspect from yesterday's bar shooting is in custody in a small town about eighty miles away. Idiot went to his mother's house and the local cops saw his car there. They want to get him out of their jail as soon as possible. Road trip.

The only good thing about official road trips is highway patrol troopers who understand. When they see two guys in suits speeding in a cheap, solid color four-door sedan with black-wall tires, small hubcaps and a long radio antenna on the trunk lid, they usually instinctively know (a) you're a driver who's been trained to drive at high speeds and (b) you're not out here running the highways for entertainment. So it's about an hour down and an hour back. The small-town cops have the guy's property all bagged up, he's fed and ready to go so the turn-around time is about ten minutes including giving them a quick rundown on the murder and getting everybody's name so you can send them commendations. They also get a free trip to the city to testify in court.

When you get back home, an interview with the suspect leads to a confession (the victim asked for it and got it, according to him) and more reports. The state charge is changed to show these new developments. Just as those reports are half-way finished, the partners get separated again. A baby is dead down in the Flats and an Iranian student has walked in claiming he was kidnapped and tortured by SAVAK, the Shah's secret police. He says they cut his arms and legs and stuck Coke bottles up his butt. Right here in River City. It smells like crap (no pun intended) but you've got to *prove* it's crap.

Three hours later, you've wrapped up the SIDS death from the Flats with another report yet to be made. No criminal charges but another report needs to be sent to the Department of Human Services to check out the living conditions in the home to protect the other kids. Your partner is laughing about the "tortured" Iranian. In the first place, the cuts are old and look self-inflicted. Second, it looks like whatever was stuck up his butt was consensual and he's looking to get it on the record that he hasn't violated the Koran. Third, he wants the police to hire him as an "undercover agent" to infiltrate the local cells of supposedly-militant expatriate Iranian students. The smell of crap is now overwhelming but it still requires some reports just to document it.

Your partner finishes his reports and heads home after eighteen hours of overtime that he might or might not get paid for. You're just starting your reports when you get called out again. A suicide. A bed-ridden old woman with lupus shot herself in the head. Since it's a one-man job, you tell your partner to go on home. With a little bit of luck, you might get home in time for the 10 P.M. news.

No such luck. You, the Crime Lab officer and the M.E. go over the crime scene. The equally-old husband is crying his eyes out but things aren't adding up. The bullet is embedded in the bedroom wall, having gone all the way through her head. She was obviously in bed when shot but the angle of the shot is wrong. There's no abrasion in the right place on what was supposedly her strong hand which the gun is lying near on the bed. Her non-resident daughter says she didn't have enough strength to crack an egg. The husband finally admits he helped her shoot herself to put her out of her constant pain.

He has to go to jail but the daughter can bond him out immediately. You know the DA will knock it down to an Aiding and Abetting a Suicide charge because it was truly a mercy killing and the old guy probably doesn't have a year left anyway. Sometimes you get a feel for these things when you spend so much time around death. But the scene still has to be photographed, measured and reported in full anyway.

The final reports have to be made on nine deaths, two arrests and one complete waste of time. These are wrapped up about 4 A.M. The new guy heads home after 45 hours in the same suit, underwear and socks while living on black coffee, cigarettes and drive-through burgers. About an hour of sleep and a hot shower precedes showing back up at 8 A.M. Monday morning to get back to work on the unsolved killing from Saturday night.

As he drags himself in the office and plops down in his chair, he sees that someone has put a small statue in the middle of his desktop. It's a chromed statue of a guy holding a golf club in his teeth and bending it into a U-shape in frustration. A small inscription on the wooden base reads "WELCOME TO HOMICIDE."

THE FIRST LESSON IN LAW SCHOOL

The defense attorney had to force himself to resist rubbing his hands together and betraying his eagerness to cross-examine the next witness. This was his first murder trial and he thought he'd come up with a strategy—attack the cops' thoroughness in the crime scene.

The Homicide detective took the stand, raised his hand and took the oath. The prosecutor then led him through his examination of the crime scene. There were no questions about the arrest and questioning of the suspect. The next witness, his partner, would testify to that. The prosecutor rested and the defense attorney stood up. Approaching the witness stand, he handed the witness a photograph.

"Detective, you have identified this as an accurate photo of the crime scene taken by the Crime Lab in your presence?"

"Yes sir."

Carefully turning so both the detective and the jury could see the photo, the attorney began pointing at different areas of the photo with his pen. "And this is the victim's body lying in his kitchen?"

"Yes sir."

"And it hadn't been moved yet?"

"No sir."

"And what are these?"

"Pools of blood and blood smears on the floor next to the victim's body."

"And you personally directed the collection of all the evidence in the room?"

"I did."

"And you had Crime Lab officers collect samples of all the relevant evidence?"

"Yes sir."

Now he had him. Now for the *coup de grace*. With a dramatic flourish, he carefully pointed to a single red blob on the wall at the other end of the kitchen, clearly more than a dozen feet from the body.

"Did you take a sample of this blood?"

"No, sir."

"Why not?"

"It wasn't blood. It was ketchup."

The attorney sneered. "And how do you know that?"

"The color and consistency weren't quite right for blood."

"But how could you be certain without testing it?"

"I tasted it." He touched a forefinger to an imaginary spot in the air and put it on the tip of his tongue.

The silence in the courtroom was deafening. The lawyer had violated the first lesson he was supposed to have learned in law school. Never ask a question if you don't already know the answer.

"No further questions," he mumbled.

NOTE: This incident occurred in the pre-AIDS generation before there were blood-borne pathogen policies or latex gloves were a standard feature at every homicide crime scene and it was a fairly routine occurrence for detectives and crime lab techs to comb barehanded through pools of blood looking for fragments of bullets, bone, teeth, brains, contact lenses or other evidence.

NOTIFICATIONS

Rookie homicide detectives learn the job the same way old homicide detectives did—by watching the veterans. If your partner calls in sick, you just hang around the office and go out with whichever team catches something interesting that you might learn from.

The detective cruiser pulled over to the side of the rural road near the farthest edge of the city limits. The lone scout car guarding the crime scene didn't even have its overheads on. There was no traffic, no media, no witnesses, not even a building within sight. The two veteran partners explained the scene to the rookie as they examined it.

The beat-up old pickup was pulled over at the side of the road next to a telephone pole. The tires on the passenger's side were in the drainage ditch, really just a shallow channel next to the road's surface. A spool of yellow nylon boat cord was in the pickup's bed. A penknife was lying next to it. The man had cut a length of it off and looped it over one of the climbing stanchions on the pole. He had climbed up on the pickup's top because the indentations from his feet were still visible on the sheet metal as were the dusty tread prints that matched his shoes. He had then tied the other end of the cord around his neck and jumped off.

The man had probably been about six feet tall when he had jumped. Now he was closer to NBA-size. The neck was incredibly elongated, the head cocked at an unnatural angle, the face purple and bloated with the tongue lolling out.

"That's what happens when the neck breaks," one of the veterans explained to him. "With no bones holding the head and torso together, the skin just stretches under the weight of the lower body."

After they took some Polaroid photos, they cut him down, severing the cord above the knot. The rest was thorough but fairly routine. Wallet, identification and a little money in the guy's pockets. No robbery. The driver's license photo matched the guy's face except for the deep purple color and the pickup's tag was registered to the victim. No other wounds on the body except for the deep ligature crease around the neck. Sometimes you find scratches on the neck above the noose but not in this one.

"Automatic reaction," one of the veterans said. "If they haven't figured out a way to tie their own hands, the body naturally resists the strangling of the cord until he passes out. Survival's a strong instinct even if you've consciously decided to end it. But not this time. Busted neck. Might have crushed the spinal cord. If he even kicked once, it was just nerves jerking."

Check his record. A few drunk arrests, some minor dope. No warrants outstanding. Ninth grade education, no wife, no kids, no job address. Parents live on a farm a few miles farther south. No suicide note. There usually isn't. Wait for the M.E. Ship the body. Impound the pickup. Just one thing left.

"The lousiest part of the job, bar none," they told the rookie. "Got to notify the next of kin." The veterans got in the front seat of the cruiser while the rookie sat in the back. They talked as they drove.

"Some of the guys are a little unsympathetic about some of the notifications," one of the veterans said over his shoulder.

"Yeah." The driver laughed. "Like when Jerry went to tell the wife of that guy who died in a gunfight with a cop. The cop got shot, too. She comes to the door and he asks her if she's the widow Brown. She says 'I'm not a widow' and he says 'Yes, you are.'"

"Or the story about the guy who's been beheaded. His wife comes to the Morgue and the cop grabs the head by the hair and holds it up. He says 'Is this your husband?' and she says 'No, he was taller.' So he raises the head up about six inches and says 'How about now?'"

As both veterans laughed, the driver spoke. "That never happened."

"I know," his partner said. "But it's a good story, isn't it?"

"You ever made a notification yet?" the driver asked the back seat passenger.

"No," the rookie answered, knowing what was coming.

"Well, you might as well do something to earn your keep today. You make this one."

Just then the cruiser turned into the dirt driveway of the rural farmhouse. As the driver turned the engine off and a cloud of dust settled over them, a woman opened the screen door and stepped out on the front porch. She watched them expectantly with the air of someone who rarely received visitors, even more rarely men wearing suits and ties. Since they were being closely scrutinized, the two men in the front seat kept their faces appropriately somber.

"What'll I tell her?" the new homicide detective said.

"Just tell her to have her kid stop hanging around 149th and Air Depot sticking his tongue out at people."

The rookie coughed violently into his fist to help him recover his somber expression before he got out of the car.

THE REAL POLICEMAN II—GINGER

The black and white patrol car idled along slowly on the dirt road, crawling along at only a few miles per hour. The radio crackled only infrequently this early in the morning hours. At 4 A.M. the large city park was deserted and pitch black. After checking the known parking holes for lovers and finding them deserted as well, the officer pulled the patrol car over to the side of the road and stopped.

Turning the radio up so he could hear it outside of the car, the officer stepped out of the driver's side. Walking in front of the car through the glare of the headlight beams, he unzipped his trousers as he stepped off the road beside the right front fender. As he began urinating into the tall grass by the roadside, he looked up at the full moon and gave a deep sigh of relief. The sigh was a response to the release of the warm liquid in his full bladder as was the slight shiver in response to the small drop in his body temperature it caused. The sigh also signaled a small release of tension at having completed most of another night on graveyard with a full moon without having caught one of the unique types of calls that the full moon seems to generate. Probably nothing to look forward to now until the morning rush hour.

As his gaze wandered down to correct the aim of his stream away from his highly polished boots, he focused on a shape lying in the weeds.

"JEEEEEZUZ!"

The urine stream stopped instantly, like shutting the gate of a dam as he reflexively took a long step backwards until his buttocks hit the car's fender. Zipping his pants up hurriedly, he reached in the passenger's side and got his flashlight out of the front seat. Stepping back to the front of the car, he shined the light over the shallow ditch beside the road. His mind started recording details, noting that the woman's body was laying face down, the dress still intact. Kneeling and stretching to avoid getting any nearer to the body than he had to, he gingerly reached across the white forearm and long dark hair to feel for a pulse in the carotid artery of her neck. No pulse and cold.

"Baker 7 to headquarters. I need a Homicide unit, lab unit and the medical examiner to the southwest corner of Washington Park."

Homicide Team Two got the case. The Homicide Unit had recently started the team concept under the theory that there was more work that needed to be done on a homicide than two men could accomplish efficiently. So they went to three-man teams.

Being the prima donnas they were, the Homicide Unit had some partners that worked well together and some that hated one another's guts. So the supervisors added a third man to each stable pair of partners they had, the third man either coming from one of the unstable pairs or one of the new men.

Team Two consisted of Wayne Thomas, Jay Olson and Ray Beyer. Thomas and Olson were one of the stable teams. Thomas was a fifteen-year veteran with eight years in Homicide and a reputation as one of the best interviewers in the unit. Olson was an eleven-year veteran with three years in Homicide. He usually did the crime scene investigations and canvassed for witnesses. Beyer was a newly promoted detective just about to reach his sixth anniversary with the department. Not long in Homicide, he was still learning from his more experienced partners.

Since there weren't any witnesses to interview except the patrol officer and he would file his own report, all three detectives concentrated on the crime scene. The patrol officer had already explained his presence in the deserted park to one of the detectives, also explaining the possibility of urine splatters on the body. Grinning, the detective told the story to his partners before they got down to work.

Thomas and the medical examiner's field investigator would actually examine the body, Olson would take notes for them and Beyer would walk the surrounding area checking for prints of feet, shoes, tires or any other potential evidence.

Thomas and Olson had already noticed a few inconsistencies about the victim's body. The size of the hands and feet, the thickness of the wrists and ankles, the prominent vein structure on the backs of the hands, the large pores visible on the forearms and the calves. They had exchanged skeptical glances when they first knelt over the body. Beyer didn't catch it. He had already scribbled "WF", white female, on his notepad.

When they rolled the body over, the brunette wig skewed slightly on the head. Thomas unceremoniously flipped the front of "her" dress up, revealing the penis and testicles bunched inside the athletic supporter under the panty hose.

Over the next few weeks, a lot of effort went into trying to solve the murder of John Thorn. More than the usual, in fact. Homicides of homosexual males were extraordinarily hard to solve, especially if they were secretive, i.e., still "in the closet", hid their lifestyle and most especially if they were carelessly promiscuous in their relations.

He lived in a rural community northeast of the city. His car had been located broken down on the Interstate highway several miles north of where his body had been found. Since the park area he was found in was less than a mile from the highway, it was theorized that he had been picked up by a motorist and shot once in the head before his body was dumped there. There was a little money, some credit cards and cheap costume jewelry recovered at the scene so he wasn't obviously robbed. The prevailing theory was that, in spite of the fact that photos found at his house showed that he made a rather unattractive woman, either John hit on the motorist for sex or vice versa. They may have gone to the deserted, dark area of the park to accomplish the act. When the motorist discovered that the heterosexual act he was preparing himself for was about to become a homosexual act, he reacted violently. It had happened before in this city.

In order to solve John's murder, the detectives had to get to know him as well as possible. Since John was dead, the only way to do this was to get to know him through his friends and associates. The detectives began to immerse themselves in the homosexual community. In doing so, they not only got to know John better, they got to know each other a little better. Wayne Thomas had that easy-going, non-judgmental way of talking to people that encouraged them to open up to him. Olson had ridden with him long enough and their personalities were similar enough that he had gained some of the same talent. Besides being a good team that complemented each other professionally, the two detectives were close personal friends and, away from the civilians, shared their caustic, cynical, sardonic cop's humor. Ray Beyer was a different story.

Having allegedly been quite the hell-raiser in his youth and coming from a family of hell-raisers, Beyer had reformed. He didn't smoke, drink or swear and he was heavily involved in his religion. When he was encouraged by the others to pontificate in the Homicide office, it also became clear that he was strongly homophobic.

His colleagues didn't agree with or understand the homosexual lifestyle but it was an affront to Beyer's religious principles. They were an offense in God's eyes and they were all going to Hell. So were all the Jews because they viewed Jesus Christ as a prophet and not the Son of God. Pronouncing this dogma in a room full of not very religious Homicide Detectives drew a lot of flak but that was just during playtime. The problem was it affected his work.

Homosexuals, when they are around heterosexuals, sharpen their senses. They can sense fear, panic, uneasiness and whether they are being judged. Not surprisingly, they don't respond well to people when they get these vibes from them and they got bad vibes from Ray Beyer. Thomas and Olson told him to relax and loosen up. It did no good. As Thomas told him, when they were interviewing homosexuals, Beyer acted like he had a hot poker stuck up his ass. He didn't have to be pals with them but he was supposed to get information from them and they sure as hell weren't going to open up to some cop looking down his nose at them like they were a lower life form. It still did no good.

During the course of the investigation, they discovered that John Thorn was more than a transvestite, he was a female impersonator. He frequented a gay bar called Anthony's where other female impersonators did floor shows. His stage name was "Stefanie" and Thorn occasionally took a turn before the lights himself although he wasn't up to the same caliber as the regulars. It was decided they would have to talk to everyone in Anthony's about Stefanie. Thomas and Olson interviewed Anthony and made the arrangements.

Anthony was quite a character. An aging queen with a deep tan and deeper wrinkles, Anthony was quite unabashed about his sexual preferences. In leaving the closet so far behind, he had become almost a caricature of a male homosexual. Ultra-feminine, limp-wristed and with a swish to his tush that a beauty queen would envy, he spoke in a high, sing-song lisp that proclaimed his lifestyle to all the world. No doubt he had taken a few trips down the lighted runway himself in his day but now he just ran the place, dressed in men's clothing. Anthony would make the arrangements for interviewing "his girls."

Thomas and Olson discussed between them whether or not to take Beyer. Then, with evil grins, they decided. As Olson put it, "What the hell! He wanted to work Homicide, didn't he? Well, you get paid to work them all, not just the ones you're comfortable with."

On the appointed night, the three detectives headed for Anthony's club. The two old partners rode in the front seat of the detective cruiser while Beyer sat in the back as befitted his status. He was a captive audience. He was also not fully informed. They had told him they were going to interview the people at a club that John Thorn had frequented but provided no details.

They arrived before the club was open to the public. Beyer was distinctly put off by Anthony's behavior. Anthony, automatically sensing Beyer's revulsion, laid it on thick. He made sure he directed most of his conversation to Beyer, even reaching out occasionally to touch him on the hand or forearm when making a point. He seemed amused when Beyer tried to be subtle when recoiling from his touch. The corners of his eyes would crinkle up and he would arch an eyebrow at Thomas and Olson as though thinking "*WELL!* He's flighty but pretty. I'll bring him around."

As the employees came in, Thomas and Olson began interviewing them while they were getting ready for their acts. They waited for Beyer to volunteer to interview one but to no avail. He just sat, listened and took notes, his face registering his distaste and discomfort. As the detectives conducted their interviews, they witnessed some startling transformations. Young men that looked and dressed so you wouldn't give them a second look on the street sat down in front of dressing tables. Stripping their clothes off with the same lack of self-consciousness as if they were in a football locker room, it was quite obvious they really were males. Deceptively slim forearms shaved hairless along with the legs, armpits and chests, and long, dainty fingers but males nevertheless. But as they girded their loins, enhanced their chests, applied wigs and makeup artfully, and painted their fingernails and toenails, they became young women to all outward appearances. Some of them, as Thomas and Olson privately joked, were attractive enough to fool the average guy with a few drinks in him in a dimly lit club.

At one point, Anthony approached Thomas and whispered something in his ear. Suppressing a grin, Thomas nodded. Winking at Olson, he told his partners that there were only three employees left. He'd take the first one so why didn't Olson take the next one and Beyer the last one? Both agreed, Olson because he knew he was supposed to and Beyer because he thought it would get them out of this den of iniquity that much faster. Thomas started interviewing his at one table while Olson sat down with another. Then Beyer's interviewee walked in. Thomas and Olson tried to keep their minds on their interviews while suppressing their laughter.

"Ginger" walked straight up to Detective Beyer and in a voice that struggled to stay above baritone and husky with suppressed passion said "I guess I'm yours." Thomas and Olson almost lost control when they saw Beyer start to develop an involuntary twitch in one eye. Ginger was 6'8" tall on his flat feet and even more imposing in his spiked high heels, as he was now. Neither of them ever imagined they made high heels in NBA sizes. A platinum blonde shoulder length wig framed a dark black face accented with splotches of bright red rouge and lipstick. The whole package was encased in a shimmering skin-tight gown of silver sequins that made him look like he was dancing even when he was standing still. With a deep breath of resignation, Beyer began his interview.

Finally the interviews were completed. No one had any specific information about Thorn's murder but they knew a lot more about his habits. As the trio of detectives stood up and closed their notebooks, Anthony came up to them.

"All done?" he asked.

"Yeah", Thomas answered. "I think we've got all the information we can. Now we'll see if we can use any of it to help."

"Well, you don't have to run off, you know." Anthony said. "The girls are getting ready to start the show and I'd be glad to buy you a drink. You are off duty now, aren't you?"

A flicker of panic showed in Beyer's eyes. That and a glance between his two partners settled it.

"Sure," Thomas said. "We're off duty. Wouldn't mind seeing the girls strut their stuff."

"Oh woooonnnddeeeerrfullll!" gushed Anthony, touching his fingertips lightly to Thomas's sleeve. "Just follow me and I'll see that you get the best seats in the house."

Anthony swished off through the room, sweeping gracefully between the tables and chairs that were starting to fill up with an exclusively male crowd. When he got to a table right in front of the raised stage, Anthony pulled out a chair and stood behind it. Thomas stepped in front of the chair and, grinning at Olson, sat down as Anthony pushed it under him. Olson plopped down in another of the chairs and loosened his tie as Beyer jumped into the remaining chair before Anthony had a chance to pull it out for him.

"I'll be right back", Anthony said with a wave of his hand and swished off toward the bar.

Thomas and Olson leaned back in their chairs, loosening their ties and looking around. Several pairs of men were dancing together on the dance floor to a slow rhythm coming from the jukebox. One pair, both with full beards, was kissing while they pirouetted expertly around the floor in one another's arms. Beyer was sitting bolt upright in his chair with his hands in his lap. The muscles in his jaw were flexing and he was breathing rapidly through his nose. He was obviously trying not to touch anything, acting like he was afraid homosexuality was contagious and you could catch it by breathing the same air as "them." Thomas and Olson smirked at each other when he wasn't looking.

The jukebox died out and one of the "girls" came out on stage. Covered in red sequins and sporting a flaming red wig, the female impersonator was greeted by a healthy round of applause as he broke into a very creditable impersonation of Bette Midler singing *The Rose*. Thomas and Olson politely joined in the applause but Beyer sat there like the Sphinx.

In a few moments, Anthony was back next to the table with a bar pad in one hand and a pencil poised over it with the other.

"And what can I get for you?" he said, heavily lisping his words in the most feminine manner he could manage.

"Bourbon and water," Thomas said.

"Vodka Collins," Olson said.

Anthony sidled over next to the unblinking, ramrod straight Beyer.

"And what about you, hon?" he whispered in his most ingratiating manner.

"Coke", Beyer said through gritted teeth, staring straight ahead.

Anthony gave a glance and a smile to the other two detectives, wrinkling his nose like a bunny. Leaning down a little closer to Beyer, he asked "Can I put anything in it for you?"

Thomas and Olson grinned at each other.

"Just Coke," said Beyer rigidly.

Anthony gave the other two another look and leaned a little closer to the detective who had beads of perspiration breaking out on his forehead in spite of the air conditioning.

"You're sure I can't add a little something to that for you? It's on the house." Anthony said.

Beyer scooted his chair a few inches sideways to try to regain some of his personal space but still refused to look at the old drag queen.

"*Just straight Coke, please!*" he said somewhat forcefully.

Anthony recoiled in mock offense, tapping the tip of the pencil against his pouting lips. He looked down at the intransigent Beyer, then over at Thomas and Olson, then back again to Beyer. In the most feminine lisp he could manage, he gave his parting shot.

"I *knew* you weren't a *real* policeman!"

And with a swish of his head and his butt, he headed for the bar.

Thomas and Olson, laughing uproariously, thought they were going to have to grab Beyer's arm to keep him from leaping across the table and pursuing the retreating Anthony.

JUST PUSH "PAUSE"

As a group, the guys in Homicide usually had reputations that were paradoxes. Free thinkers who were regimented. Rebels who were self-disciplined. Methodical but adaptable. The first group of hostage negotiators picked from the Department were all Homicide detectives because it was felt that they had the greatest experience in interviewing the widest range of people in all classes of society. One day they might be interviewing a CEO or a surgeon and the next day, hookers and pimps. Homicide was always a much more equal opportunity crime than Narcotics, Sex Crimes and most others.

Another paradox of their reputations was part cerebral and part Neolithic knuckle-dragger. They were usually familiar enough with cutting-edge forensic science to direct the actions of Technical Investigators on a crime scene. On the other hand, while some detectives might just issue a radiogram for their suspects and wait for them to fall into patrol's arms, when given the choice Homicide usually preferred to make their own arrests, hands-on.

Things were changing from the archaic times when they used to say that you weren't a "real" Homicide investigator until you had worked a case while half-drunk and taking notes on the back of a matchbook cover you picked up in the bar they called you out of at midnight. Although that still happened occasionally. While they usually took the trouble to familiarize themselves with the best uses of the technology available to the Crime Lab Unit, simpler technology was much slower in coming into their own hands, usually as a result of available money more than their resistance.

First came Polaroid cameras so they could take their own snapshots of a crime scene to show to other detectives who didn't have a chance to view the scene. It was a lot quicker than waiting the hours or days for the Photo Lab to process the 35 millimeter Crime Lab film. Next came hand-held tape recorders so they could dictate their crime scene notes instead of writing them in their notebooks, each in his own peculiar shorthand. Eventually the unit got videotape technology.

A new portable video camera was purchased for the unit. It would be used on unsolved cases (when a suspect wasn't immediately known or in custody, universally called "who-done-it's") or on unusually complicated crime scenes. No more Polaroids. Now the sergeant could video a scene and replay it for the rest of the unit back at the office, in living color, zooming in for close-ups on small evidence and out for wide angle shots.

The only preconceived problem was the fact that the camera recorded sound also. That was a potential problem when you were dealing with a group of detectives who were used to conversing largely with street people in street profanity. The cynical smart-asses with black senses of humor didn't help either. There was always the chance that these tapes would be played in front of a jury someday. But the detectives didn't get used to it overnight.

Thomas and Olson were on call again when the call came in from patrol. A girl found dead on a deserted oil lease north of the city. Obviously starting out as a who-done-it, the sergeant grabbed the video camera and piled in his car to follow them.

Usually one guy would work the crime scene and the other would interview witnesses or canvas the area. In this case, there were no witnesses except the guy who found the body and nothing to canvas so everybody gathered around the body. Not a building in sight in any direction, just a monotonously pumping oil well.

The sergeant videotaped the approach to the area, hoping for tire tracks, foot prints, anything they could use for evidence but the whole area was hard-packed, oil-soaked clay and didn't show anything of value.

The body was about fifty yards from the oilrig. White, female, face down, arms folded under the body, hot pink blouse, white short shorts, dark pageboy haircut with a splotch of red on the back.

"Looks like a head shot," one of the patrolmen said, stating the obvious.

Thomas was taking notes, drawing a diagram, copying shouted measurements from the Crime Lab guys and the sergeant was videotaping all of it. Then it was time to roll the body over.

When the body was rolled over on its back, the dark wig turned sideways. The sergeant was leaning over, the camera only a foot from Thomas's shoulder, to be sure to get it all.

Thomas sighed a deep sigh of resignation. He then very unceremoniously ran his hand under the rumpled blouse, inside the cups of the bra and pulled out a pair of beanbags. Having investigated several hundred murder scenes without the benefit of videotape, he then made a comment that made the sergeant wince as the camcorder recorded it for posterity.

"When are these cocksuckers gonna learn?"

CULTURE SHOCK

When I was a brand new detective in Homicide, the old hands used to tell lots of war stories and many times you could never be certain if they were telling the truth or, if they were, how much they were embellishing it. More stories would be added during my generation. There were wise cracks about the detective who found a suicide note in a fire death scene (get it?—why wasn't it burned up?). Then there was the case where a guy was found dead in a ditch next to a dirt road on the outskirts of the city with a single contact gunshot wound to his head. Since the gun wasn't there, it first appeared to be a textbook execution. Initial inquiries turned up no apparent reason why anyone would want to kill the guy but they were able to turn up evidence of recent depression on his part. After a few days investigation, the assigned detectives found that the road had recently been graded by a bulldozer. Interviewing the bulldozer driver revealed that he had been concentrating on the roadway he was grading and hadn't noticed any body in the ditch by the road. Returning to the scene, they searched the banks of dirt pyramided along the side of the road where the victim's body was found. In one pile of dirt, they found the gun which ballistics matched to the slug in the guy's head. Suicide.

There was another one where a guy was found dead in his garage. The .25 automatic pistol that had been used to kill him was on the floor near the body and the expended casings were in the right approximate location to support a suicide theory. The only problem was the guy had been shot five times in the chest. The detectives found burnt powder and abrasions on the web of his right hand from the automatic's slide, abrasion rings and stippling around the wounds, and eventually a suicide note. After interviews with his widow and children, they came up with a novel theory.

The guy decided to kill himself, wrote the note and considerately went out into the garage to do the deed (easier for the widow to clean up later). Most men shoot themselves in the head but he decided to shoot himself in the heart instead. Apparently he had a very limited knowledge of anatomy because he thought his heart was under the area where he put his palm to recite the Pledge of Allegiance. It's not. As one of the detectives put it:

BAM!

"OW! God, that hurt!"

BAM!

"Oh, hell. That's worse."

After two pretty painful contact shots in his left shoulder, he moved towards the center of his chest and ripped off three more. That got the job done.

I had heard the old hands say more than once "Anybody can work a homicide but it takes a good detective to work a suicide." After a few years in Homicide, I knew that they hadn't been kidding.

It was a warm spring afternoon. An ambulance and a "trouble unknown" call had sent an ambulance and patrol car to an area off of Classen Boulevard. The patrol sergeant called Homicide after they found the dead body.

The good news was the body was fresh, not a small consideration on a warm day. The bad news was the address was in the area of the city rapidly becoming known as "Little Saigon." Since the end of America's involvement in Vietnam and the Communist takeover, increased emigration from those areas had led to a growing Oriental population in the city. That particular area off of North Classen had been inundated with Vietnamese, Laotian and Cambodian immigrants, legal and otherwise. Many of the houses were old, cheap and small, most under a thousand square feet. I'd already worked one death in that area. A dozen Laotians living together and the only food in the house, honest to God, had been two tons of rice in hundred pound bags in a back room. The death had been from natural causes, thankfully, but it took more work than most murders because of the language and cultural barriers. Most people from that part of the world view their police as oppressors from birth and they don't easily make the transition to how the role of police differs in a democracy.

Everybody else in the office was busy so Ray and I got elected. Besides the Laotian deal, I had also worked on an expatriate Iranian who was allegedly being persecuted by the Iranian Secret Police and a murdered Mexican illegal alien. In the first case, we discovered that SAVAK wasn't in Oklahoma. It was just that this was the early 1980s and Iranians weren't real popular with some of the local rednecks. In the second case, the only saving grace was two Indian witnesses who were relatively sober and could speak English. I was beginning to feel picked on. I reflexively flinched whenever a case came down with international implications.

The crime scene wasn't reassuring. There were a dozen pair of shower shoes on the front porch and their owners were squatting on the living room floor with two patrolmen and the sergeant doing their best to keep them from babbling to each other in their sing-song native language. Naturally, nobody spoke a word of English. One of the men was covered in dirt and blood splatters.

Ray and I were directed to a room under construction, in the process of being added on to the rear of the house. The whole place smelled of fresh wood, sawdust and blood. The man's body was lying on its back in the middle of the floor. Tools and building equipment littered the floor—hammers, nails, pliers, screwdrivers, an orange drop light and several power tools.

The victim was a Vietnamese male who appeared to be in his thirties although neither Ray nor I had much practice in estimating the ages of Orientals. His condition didn't help. He was a mess. Shirtless and shoeless, he had two puncture-type stab wounds in his upper left chest, blood was running out of both ears, both his palms and wrists had bloody, ragged gashes on them, blood and brain matter protruded from a hole in the top of his head and there was a pronounced ligature mark around his neck. A pink froth of bloody foam was coming from his mouth and both nostrils. Obviously he'd still been breathing after the chest wounds punctured a lung. Splashes, sprays and drops of blood were all over the room, floor, walls and ceiling, and there were bloody drag marks leading from a two-foot-square hole cut in the newly constructed flooring. Blood was all over a Phillips screwdriver and a power circular saw lying on the floor. The victim's pants, feet and arms were also smeared with dirt.

Looking down into the hole in the floor with a flashlight was like looking into another world. In the two-and-one-half foot crawlspace under the house, some-one was in the process of constructing a series of underground tunnels under the house. The two-by-six floorboards of the house were nailed down with pole-barn nails, spikes as thick as your little finger that protruded several inches through the flooring. Closer examination showed that one of the spikes several yards away had blood and hair on it. I recall sarcastically suggesting that the case should be reas-signed to one of our colleagues who had been a "tunnel rat" with the 25th Infan-try in Vietnam. No such luck. Ray and I were stuck with it. In that event, everyone was going downtown until we could sort it all out.

While the patrol officers got enough cars to transport everybody down to the Homicide office, Ray and I went to the nearby Vietnamese-American Center and arranged for a translator to meet us down there.

Try talking to someone through an interpreter sometime. Detectives do most of what they do with words. Even with cooperative witnesses and a friendly inter-preter, it doesn't take a genius to figure out that a hell of a lot more is being said than you're being told. It's also no picnic trying to separate lies from truth while dealing with refugees from a totalitarian regime who have been afraid of police all their lives. I won't belabor you with the next few hours of excruciatingly slow, detailed interviews. I'll just give you the high points.

Everybody, including the victim's wife and brother, had been sitting in the front room when the victim's brother went to the back room. Then everybody heard lots of yelling and screaming. Running back to the rear room, they found it covered in blood but unoccupied. Everyone then commenced to run around like chickens with their heads cut off, some running outside trying to find the two brothers. Unable to find them outside, they ran back inside to the rear room, finding the living brother dragging the victim out of the hole from beneath the house, both of them covered in dirt and blood. Nobody had any logical reason why they hadn't checked down there in the first place but who's to say if the Hanoi Police would understand how I react under stress? What followed were various people running to various houses nearby until they found someone who knew how to call an ambulance. They didn't realize that some ambulance calls also automatically dispatch the cops. The living brother was babbling and nearly hysterical, vacillating between fear of us and apparent grief over his brother's death.

The upshot was we arranged for patrol to take the rest of the witnesses back home while we tried to get some kind of reliable information from the brother downtown. While we were laboring at this, we soon got a phone call from the victim's wife. In very broken English, we got the idea she had found something she wanted us to see. Putting the brother in a holdover cell, we returned to the scene with the interpreter. The victim's wife had found three letters—not one but three—from her husband, written in Vietnamese, naturally. The letters had been lying on a table they used for a desk and no one had noticed them in the recent furor.

The interpreter translated the letters for us. An interview with the now-calmer brother, consultations with the Crime Lab and the Medical Examiner, and some more interviews wrapped up a story that left Ray and I shaking our heads in disbelief.

The victim worked in the Housekeeping Department at a local hospital. A recent audit had turned up some missing stock, items like toilet paper, paper towels and cleaning chemicals. The victim's supervisor had called him in, accused him of the thefts and demanded that he take a lie detector test. The victim had vigorously protested his innocence as best he could considering the language barrier and stormed out of the supervisor's office.

Going home, he had brooded about it for a while and then wrote the letters to his wife, explaining the situation. He was innocent of the thefts but he and his entire family had been dishonored by the accusations. The only way to remove that dishonor was to take his own life. I had visions of the Japanese tradition of *hara-kiri*.

Alone, he went to the back room that he and his brother had been building. He took the Phillips screwdriver and tried to stab himself in the heart twice (he was right-handed). Being unfamiliar with human anatomy and thus not knowing exactly where his heart was, he merely inflicted two painful stab wounds in his left lung with the blunt instrument. He then rammed the screwdriver alternately into both ears, trying the skewer his brain. Again plagued by his lack of knowledge of anatomy, he succeeded only in painfully destroying his hearing and gouging some scratches in his skull. He then picked up the circular saw and tried to cut his wrists with it. As he tried to control the heavy saw with one hand, it jumped around as it ripped into flesh, veins, arteries and bones, slashing first one palm and wrist, and then the other while he tried to wield it with the already wounded hand. At this point, his brother had entered the room and pulled the saw away from him. The victim dived into the hole in the floor and scuttled beneath the house. Scrambling several yards across the dirt under the house, he saw one of the pole-barn spikes protruding several inches through the flooring. Placing the top of his head against it, he pushed his head up, driving the spike several inches into his brain and finally accomplishing his purpose. His brother scrambled down into the hole after him. Finding his brother's dead body, the brother tried to pull it back to the hole but didn't have the strength. Crawling back into the room, he grabbed the orange drop light cord and went back to his brother's body. Looping the cord around the victim's neck, the brother returned to the hole and pulled the victim back to the point where he could drag him back through the hole in the floor into the room. That was when the others ran into the room and saw them.

The brother was released and allowed to go back home to arrange for his brother's burial.

Ready for the punch line? Who stole the hospital's housekeeping supplies? The supervisor who accused his Vietnamese employee and demanded he take the lie detector test.

Wherever that maligned man is, I hope he has his honor.

THE POWER OF WORDS

One of the first lessons you learn in Homicide is to choose your words carefully, at least for public consumption. Just the word "Homicide" really gets people's attention. Someone investigating that crime has powers not accorded to other crimes. Things you say that might be taken lightly under other circumstances are taken seriously on a homicide scene. Things that you say seriously are taken *very* seriously.

That was pointed out to me on one of the first homicides that occurred after I came in the unit as a rookie. A body had surfaced in a local lake. The victim was a local gambler who, as it turned out later, had owed a lot of money to some very bad people in Las Vegas. He had been shot six times in the head and dumped in the lake. A reporter on the scene had asked the veteran detective on the case what his initial observations were.

"Worst case of suicide I ever saw."

The reporter wrote the quote in his notes and was actually going to report that the police were theorizing suicide before the detective caught him and explained that he was just being sarcastic.

A call came out at a sleazy motel near the fringes of downtown. This was the kind of place that instead of renting their rooms by the hour, the hookers stayed there, paid rent and the management took a cut of every trick to boot. The other residents were small-level dope dealers and thieves. A teenaged hooker was dead in one of the rooms and her body had been mutilated in some very creative ways.

The "owner/manager" was in his fifties but looked like he was in his seventies because of his daily diet of cheap dope and booze. He was short, fat, looked and smelled like he changed his clothes about once a week, and had a face full of grizzled white whiskers that showed he shaved about half that often.

It was after midnight, had already been a busy night in another busy week and everybody was tired. I got there at the same time as the Homicide sergeant who was just as tired as all his men if not more. As we walked into the courtyard, the owner scampered up to us with his mouth running non-stop. One of the patrol guys told us he'd been threatening them with hellfire and damnation ever since they arrived.

"This is private property. I didn't call ya. I want you people outta here right now. I'm gonna sue all of ya. I'm a taxpayer, ya know."

The sergeant glanced at him and turned to me.

"Check the register, all the records for the whole joint and interview him."

That set him off again.

"I didn't see nothin'. I don't know nothin'. I just rent rooms is all. I don't know any of these people. An' ya can't search my records without a warrant. I know my rights. I got nothin' to say to any of ya."

Starting up to the stairs to the crime scene room, the sergeant spoke wearily over his shoulder.

"Somebody put that old bastard in jail. Material Witness to a Homicide, Obstructing an Officer, Interfering With Official Process, Pandering and Hold For State Charges."

Two large patrolmen instantly started towards the old man, one of them taking his handcuffs out. All the color drained out of the old man's face instantly and he looked like he'd been punched in the gut. He leaned forward slightly and started breathing heavily. One of the patrolmen spoke to me as he pointed to the spreading stain on the front of the old man's pants.

"He just pissed his pants. Still want him downtown?" He obviously wasn't looking forward to searching the old man and putting him in his scout car. That's when I spoke to the old man.

"Want to talk to me here or in jail?"

He nodded weakly. He was a very cooperative witness.

LIFE'S CHEAP

One of the primary diversions of police work is the study of the endless complexities and simplicities of the human animal. And if you don't think humans are still animals, you haven't met enough of them. The best place for studying everyday behavior is the Patrol Division, responding to the myriad calls for service every day out on the streets. The best place for studying the ultimate behavior under stress is Homicide. There are very few people who don't consider the killing of another human being as the ultimate crime, the most serious thing a person can do. Cops can eventually get blasé about the common motives for murder like "love", jealousy, revenge, money, dope and sex. I suppose the Homicide Unit of every major police department keeps a running list of some of the more original explanations for killing people. For instance:

A man comes home to his apartment from work one day, opens a beer, takes off his shoes and relaxes in his recliner in front of the TV. His roommate comes home, goes straight to his bedroom, gets a gun and shoots him to death without saying a word, then waits for the cops to show up. When asked for his reason by the detectives, he said "Because his feet stank."

It seems the victim had a serious problem with foot odor, a fact well noted by every officer who went in the apartment. The victim, who evidently had an inferior sense of smell, compounded the problem by thinking that he only needed to change his socks and wash his feet about once a month. His roommate said "I been tellin' him for a week to wash them damned feet and he wouldn't listen." BANG!

A man sitting on a bar stool one night turned to the man next to him and shot him. Asked for his reason, he said "He harked on me."

The victim had turned his head toward the suspect on the next stool and sneezed without covering his mouth and nose. A wad of phlegm had landed on the suspect's coat sleeve. BANG!

A shooting in a bar. The bar had one of those pool tables that operated on quarters. It was common practice to secure your turn to play by "challenging" the game, putting a quarter on the rim of the pool table. The winner plays for free and the challenger pays. When your turn came, you used your quarter to pay for the game. One guy picked up the wrong quarter. BANG!

Another shooting in a bar. Bars can be very dangerous places especially between midnight and 2:00 A.M., when everyone has had several hours for the drinking to take effect.

An Oriental guy is dead on the floor and a little black guy is in custody. The Oriental guy was sitting in a booth with a very attractive white girl. The black kid made a comment to her that she could do better than the Oriental guy and he was the better choice. This Oriental guy was lean and mean, zero per cent body fat and a 99th degree black belt in some martial art.

So, to protect his lady's honor (or more likely his investment in her drinks), the Oriental guy screeches like a banshee, jumps up and strikes some kung fu poses, kicks the ceiling and so forth. The male version of a cat bristling the hair on its back.

The black kid isn't impressed. He has a degree in Titan .25 automatic. BANG!

Two brothers who live together are drinking one winter night. They become embroiled in some kind of petty, brotherly argument but the whiskey escalates it. One brother calls the other one a "cocksucker." He isn't and his brother knows he isn't but he nevertheless apparently considers it an unforgivable insult. He goes to the back bedroom and gets his loaded 30-30 rifle. When he returns to the living room, the brothers begin wrestling over the gun. Rolling around on the floor, the gun's muzzle ends up under one brother's chin. BANG!

A Homicide car is only a few blocks away when the call comes out. When they arrive, one brother is lying on the living room floor with the better part of his head missing and the other brother is calmly sitting in a chair waiting for them. While one detective baby-sits the suspect in the living room, his partner begins searching the crime scene for evidence. He walks about twenty feet down a hallway and turns into a corner bedroom. On top of the chest of drawers against the far wall is a three-inch-square piece of the victim's skull, with smoke and steam still coming off of it.

This one happened in another city but it merits mention anyway because two of our detectives were working with their Homicide Unit at the time. As in all large cities, there was racial strife. In this particular instance, it was between blacks and Hispanics. Their restrictive, self-imposed boundaries began infringing upon one another and the neighborhoods began overlapping, sometimes with fatal results.

The Hispanics were extremely and justifiably proud of their immigration to another country and the hard work they performed to achieve whatever success they had. The tangible evidence of that pride was that when they managed to be able to afford a piece of land with a home on it, they fenced it off. This was their version of the American Dream, their castle, the visible evidence of their hard work and sweat and honesty. It might be cheap clapboard or worn asbestos shingles but it was theirs and it was inviolable.

One night a black guy decided to court a Hispanic girl. Without invitation, he let himself in through the swinging gate of her father's cyclone fence that separated her from the outside world. An hour later, the cops got a call on a body lying in the street in front of that house. The black man's body had almost every bone broken. The homicide detective, admittedly not one of their better ones, concluded it had been a hit and run accident. Apparently his justification for this, which he later had to explain to his bosses, was that it had to be a car to cause these kinds of injuries.

The procedure for this department was that big cases were assigned by the supervisors to certain detectives for immediate action. The detectives laid all their other case reports on a table in the Homicide Unit. When the next shift came in, if they didn't have a big case working, they glanced through all of the others and picked up anything they wanted to work on. Unfortunately for the first detective on that scene, a couple of the department's more conscientious homicide investigators followed up his investigation with a canvas of the neighborhood. That's when the true story came out.

The Hispanic man who owned the house had heard the black man chatting up his daughter on the front porch. He was mightily offended because the man hadn't asked his permission to come on his property or court his daughter. He told the man in no uncertain terms to get off his property and he had thirty seconds to leave. It was a small yard and crossing it in much less than thirty seconds would have been no problem but nooooo, that was too simple. The black guy had to show the world that he wasn't scared or intimidated. So he spent the last half-minute of his life "styling", strutting around the yard, posturing, waving his arms, loudly proclaiming his God-given right to go anywhere he damned well pleased in "his country", and so forth.

After thirty-one seconds, the Hispanic man came off his porch and proceeded to kick the guy's ass—and everything else—out into the street. Unfortunately for the victim, the Hispanic guy was wearing steel-toed combat boots that caused so much damage that he looked like a car had run over him.

And then there are the quipsters. The ones who keep their sense of humor, sometimes right up to the bitter end. Sometimes it makes you wonder why that wasn't enough to sustain them.

A patrol car is skimming down a rural road on the outskirts of the city when he spots a pickup idling in the center of a large plowed field. The truck is new, shiny, obviously not a farm truck and the wisps of smoke coming from the exhaust shows it's running. He checks it out and finds the driver dead inside. It looks pretty standard on the surface. A single gunshot wound to the head, hard contact, powder burns around the wound, gun on the floorboard but he calls Homicide just to be sure.

Homicide comes out and checks the scene. Everything fits with what the officer told them. The body is fresh and still warm. They fish out the guy's ID. He lives a short distance away in a suburb. They go to his apartment. A bachelor pad. The estranged wife and kids are living somewhere else. The front door is unlocked. Just inside the door, a cold beer is sitting on a table. The condensation is still on the can. Under the can is the guy's suicide note, intended for the cops he knew would be the first ones in the door.

"This Bud's for you."

'Twas the night before Christmas and all through the house, the whole damned family was drunk as a louse. Well, the two little kids were sober. Mom and grandma Ruby, however, both had a nice glow on.

The stockings were hung by the chimney with care. The tree glistened with aluminum icicles in the corner. The presents were all wrapped under the tree. Nothing for Dad, however. Dad had already had his Christmas presents delivered by a process server—a divorce petition and a restraining order. No bow on top.

Mom and Grandma Ruby already had their presents, too. Dad was out on his ass and forbidden to come to his home or contact his wife and children. Which is what Ruby had harped about for years. Unfortunately, nobody was going to get what they wanted this Christmas.

The doorjamb splintered and the door swung all the way around on its hinges, slamming into the wall, propelled by a size-twelve work boot. The next sound, and the last sound Ruby ever heard, was Dad racking a shell into a twelve-gauge pump shotgun and saying "Ruby, I got yer Christmas present here!"

Mom, younger and fleeter of foot, was out the back door before the first blast. When the cops got there, Ruby was lying in the middle of the crushed Christmas tree and presents which were more red than green by then. Dad had sucked on the barrel of the shotgun and most of his head was on the ceiling. The kids were still sitting in front of the tree, crying. And that wasn't funny.

And to end this story on an upbeat note, if our last words on this earth were engraved on our tombstones, how many thousands would read "Well, just shoot me!"?

DRAMATIC LICENSE

Two in the morning. Another shooting at Thirtieth and Prospect. A place the district cops sardonically call "The Prospect Arms", only with a different definition of "Arms" than the usual one. A complex of a couple of hundred apartments that sees more violence and death every year than Dodge City did in its whole history.

The victim is an old acquaintance. Cody Mason, local dope dealer. Two bullets in the chest, apparently small caliber, already on his way to University Hospital by Sykes Ambulance. The patrol officer gives the homicide detective a knowing smirk. Sykes Ambulance is the district ambulance service. In those days, private ambulance services were parceled out on a geographic basis like wrecker services. Sykes used old red and white Cadillacs, filthy inside and out. Their patients have been known to die at the side of the road when their jerry-rigged engines break down or their recapped tires blow out or they're trying to suck oxygen out of empty oxygen cylinders. The patrolman is thinking the same thing the detective is—if Sykes can't kill him before he gets to University, he might have a chance.

A standard crime scene for the area. Pool of blood in the parking lot, no cartridge casings, probably looking for a cheap revolver, probably a .22, Clerke, Rohm, RG. Nothing on the canvass. Nobody heard any shots, nobody knows anything, nobody saw anything. "I was in the bathroom." All twelve hundred of them.

"Lake level must have dropped a foot when they all flushed together." the patrolman mutters.

The pair of detectives has been partners so long they don't even have to talk to communicate. One starts making notes on the crime scene while the other one starts driving to University.

Parking in one of the several spots permanently reserved for the cops near the Emergency Room, the detective grabs a small portable tape recorder as he gets out of the car. As the automatic glass doors open and he walks into the entrance hallway, the detective spots Cody lying on a gurney in the first trauma station. A doctor and nurse in scrubs are bent over him mumbling the usual medical jargon. Hemo-this and pneumo-that and spleno-the other. A packet of x-rays hangs off the end of the gurney. Just then, another ambulance comes screaming into the driveway, siren echoing off the concrete walls. A nurse comes running out of the nurse's station.

"Doctor, we've got a GSW to the head coming in. He's already coded once in the wagon."

"Right. On my way." Stripping off their latex gloves, the doctor and nurse both head back to the nurse's station. The detective catches him around the corner, out of Cody's hearing range.

"How's he doing, Doc?"

"Two small caliber wounds to the chest, probably .22, both through and through. One nicked a lung and he'll probably lose his spleen. Got a slow bleeder into his chest cavity and he's wheezing a little but he'll make it. We'll get around to him in a little while."

"OK. Thanks, Doc."

The detective nonchalantly strolled back down the hallway. Reaching Cody's gurney, he pulled over a vacant wheelchair and sat down at the foot of the gurney. Opening his notebook, he began writing a few notes, the tape recorder lying in his lap while he was absently humming a Beatles tune. Cody's eyes kept darting toward him but he didn't speak. After two minutes of listening to an off-key version of *All You Need Is Love*, he couldn't stand it any longer.

"I don't know nuthin'." Wheeze, wheeze.

The detective didn't seem to notice, dropping his hum an octave to try to get the key right.

"I ain't got nuthin' ta say. Don't aks me no questions." Wheeze, wheeze.

The low hum continued for another minute. The detective then shut his notebook and picked up the tape recorder. Pushing the Record button, he began speaking into the microphone in a low voice.

"Incident Number 79 dash 106438. Victim is Cody Mason, black male, DOB 7-12-48. Two small caliber gunshot wounds to the chest. The victim's body is that of an apparently well-nourished black male in his early thirties, approximately five feet ten inches tall, weight approximately 175 pounds. The victim's body has old needle marks and scars on both forearms consistent with the victim's prior record for narcotics possession, use and sale. No witnesses to the homicide have come forward or been located. Due to the large number of enemies the victim made prior to his death, it is the opinion of this officer—"

Cody tried to do a sit-up on the gurney but made it less than an inch before falling back heavily, wheezing heavily.

"What the fuck (wheeze) you talking (wheeze) about death and victim and homicide?" Wheeze.

"I figured the doc told you before he left Cody. You're a dead man."

"Bullshit." Wheeze.

"You really don't know what's going on here? They call it triage, Cody. Save the ones you can. Don't waste your time on the ones you can't."

"Hey, that's total bullshit, man." Wheeze, wheeze, wheeze.

"Afraid not. Why do you think he left in such a hurry? They just had a guy come in with a bullet in his brain and he's got a better chance than you."

"Can't you do sumpin, man?" Wheeze, wheeze, wheeze.

"Me? I'm no doctor. If he can't save you, there's not much I can do."

"Oh God, Jesus, no! NO!" Wheeze.

"About all I could do for you is take a dying declaration if you want to tell me who killed you." The detective held up the tape recorder suggestively and raised his eyebrows in a silent question.

Cody's chest was rising and falling rapidly now, his eyes ricocheting in their sockets like ping pong balls.

"It was Rufus."

"Rufus who?"

"Rufus who the hell do you think?" Wheeze. "Who's shot everybody south of Twenty-third street except you and me and now he's got me."

"Rufus Smith?

"No, goddam it, Rufus Graham."

"Dope deal?"

"Hell, yes. He couldn't pay so I was going to walk when the muthafucka fired me up."

The detective clicked the recorder off just as the doctor walked back up.

"Mr. Mason, they'll be taking you up to surgery in a few minutes so just try to relax."

Cody's eyes held still for the first time in quite a while as he stared at the doctor.

"You mean I'm going to make it?"

"Well, you might have some infection complications and the drug withdrawal won't be pleasant but yes, you'll live."

Cody's eyes switched to the smiling detective, silently hurling daggers at him.

"In Hollywood, they call it dramatic license, Cody."

All You Need Is Love, dum-da-dum-da-dum.

DE MINIMUS NON CURAT LEX

The aforementioned Rufus Graham was a legend on the eastside. He was also a legend (albeit a different kind) in the District Attorney's Office and the police department, especially in Homicide which got most of his business.

If anyone knew what the original Rufus was like, it was lost in the mists of time. The Rufus of the last couple of decades was permanently altered by the combination of cheap booze and dope he ingested daily. Whether it was the chemicals or his natural disposition, Rufus was notoriously bad-tempered and combative. And always armed.

No one really knew how many people Rufus had shot. Rufus himself probably couldn't guess within a dozen. A brushed shoulder on a narrow sidewalk, an impolite comment, sometimes just a hostile stare was enough to draw gunfire from Rufus. Suffice it to say his name was well known to every cop on the eastside, every detective in Homicide and most of the Assistant District Attorneys. If he had been a better marksman or used better equipment, Rufus would have had a higher body count than any of the Old West's gunfighters. Of course it helped that most of his victims were unarmed. Rufus wasn't looking for a fair fight.

Rufus' weapon of choice was a Clerke .22 revolver, the kind of pistol for which the term "Saturday Night Special" was invented. The cylinder that holds the bullets fits so sloppily that they've been known to fall out at inopportune moments. Sometimes the cylinder didn't line up precisely with the barrel and it blew up when it was fired. They were cheap, easily available and had another feature that was attractive to Rufus.

While Rufus might have trouble writing his name, he had a rudimentary understanding of ballistics. Most guns have their barrels precisely machined to the size of ammunition intended to be fired through them. That way the bullet is gripped by the lands and grooves in the barrel which spins the bullet in its passage, making it faster and more accurate. This made distinctive marks on each bullet that could be compared through ballistics. Not so the Clerke.

Firing a .22 round through a Clerke barrel was like bouncing a basketball down a sewer pipe. It sort of ricocheted from one side to the other until it tumbled out the end of the barrel. Naturally this made the gun very inaccurate but at the distance of most of Rufus's confrontations, that didn't matter much.

Rufus' adventures probably produced more paperwork in the PD and DA's Office for the least results than anyone else. He did occasional stints in jail for Carrying A Concealed Weapon, dope, public drunk and other minor offenses but he just came out even more ill-tempered and quickly found another Clerke. Most of his felony Assault With A Deadly Weapon and Shooting With Intent To Kill charges went unprosecuted because the victims went into hiding and couldn't be found or they refused to name their assailant, much less testify against him. Witnesses were equally reticent.

Everyone knew that Rufus was long overdue for his comeuppance and Homicide would be the first to know. And so it was when the detectives responded to the eventual call.

So there he was. Flat on his back, belly up on the concrete walk in the front yard of his most recent hovel, his heels splayed on the bottom step of the staircase, dead as a hammer. Three rounds in the heart, .22 caliber naturally.

His unrepentant killer was his latest "wife." Rufus had never shot her but he did frequently use her for a punching bag when in his cups and given his temper and predilections, it was probably only a matter of time until she ended up on the wrong end of a Clerke .22. At least that's how she had it figured. So she got her own Clerke one day. And when Rufus came home in his usual foul mood and Mama wasn't in the mood to take another ass-whipping, she blew him back out the front door. Rufus *fini*.

She was very candid in her statement. She'd been thinking about it since he left the house hours earlier. She knew the signs of imminent pain. If he came staggering up the walk, muttering and cursing, his unfulfilled rage spilling out in short punches and jabs in the air, she'd already decided her last beating was going to be her last beating. *Bang!*

The detectives put her in jail after interviewing the neighborhood. Everyone knew Rufus and knew his habit of pounding on his lady. She had a built-in defense of self-defense and her lawyer could always put Rufus on trial post-mortem, the he-had-it-coming defense. Nevertheless the detectives wrote it up just like it played out, First Degree Murder.

This wasn't New York or LA so Assistant DA's didn't come to crime scenes and take charge. The first that prosecutors knew about a homicide was when they saw it on the nightly news and the first they knew of any of the legal details was when the detectives presented potential criminal charges to them.

Detectives filed felony charges on what they called a "charge sheet" and what was legally called an "information." A blue legal-sized form that gave the name and details of the victim, suspect, location and time of the crime, and a list of witnesses along with a brief summary of the facts to which they could testify. All the reports were collected from Patrol, Homicide, the Crime Lab and the M.E. With the charge sheet on top, the packet was delivered to the ADA who was on call for homicides. The ADA then either filed the appropriate charge, a higher or lower charge, or declined to file any charges depending upon the circumstances. The ADA wrote any modifications in the charges on the front of the charge sheet and signed it before the detectives filed it.

The ADA on call the next day was Stan. He was an old hand at trying murders, a successful, flamboyant trial lawyer without a naïve bone in his body who had a very realistic grasp of the strengths and weaknesses of our criminal justice system and a well-developed sense of irony.

When the detectives entered his office, Stan was in his usual pose, hunched over his desk writing on a yellow legal pad. He glanced over the tops of his glasses without speaking and the lead detective dropped the thick packet of reports and charge sheet on Stan's desk while his partner flopped into one of the chairs. Without even looking at the reports, Stan rocked back in his chair. He liked to have cases presented to him verbally.

"What ya got?"

"Murder One."

"Victim?"

"Rufus." The detective couldn't help smirking a little.

Stan blinked once.

"Rufus who?" His tone said he thought he knew the answer but refused to be baited into any premature conclusions.

"Graham."

Stan peered over at the blue charge sheet for a few seconds and snorted once. He slid it back across his desk toward the detectives.

"Declined."

"Yeah, yeah. I know, Stan. But we should at least go over it."

Stan pulled the sheet back towards him and wrote "Declined" and his signature beneath it before sliding it back towards the detective.

"Declined."

"But Stan, it wasn't mutual combat. It was somewhat premeditated."

The ADA pulled the charge sheet back in front of him, scribbled something across it and shoved it back. The detective picked it up, reading.

"*De Minimus Non Curat Lex.* What the hell does that mean, Stan?"

"The law is not concerned with trifles."

WINK WINK

The North Canadian River that runs through the center of Oklahoma City isn't much of a river when you've seen the Mississippi, the Arkansas, the Missouri, the Red or any respectable river. The North Canadian's riverbed is a couple of hundred yards wide but most of it was dry sand with occasional clumps of reeds, grass and sagebrush. The actual river was usually a trickle running down the center about half a dozen paces across and knee deep at most. A local joke was that we had the only river that needed to be mowed twice a year. It has since been renamed the Oklahoma River and a series of dams have made it more respectable but that is now, this was then.

The call was on the riverbed just south of the downtown area. It wasn't unusual for dead bodies to turn up in the riverbed. It wasn't enough of a river to actually conceal or sink a body but homeless people lived (and sometimes died) under the bridges and several pretty rough areas bordered it so it could be a convenient dumping ground.

This one had been here for several days and it was summer so you could smell it long before you saw it if the wind was right.

Technical Investigators came in three types; veterans who knew their business and required little or no direction from the assigned detectives, veterans who weren't as sharp or motivated and required closer watching, and rookies who were being trained to document and investigate crime scenes. The one assigned today was an old veteran who had a rookie with him. The old veteran TI started expertly taking his scene photos from the perimeter with barely a nod at the detectives. One detective started interviewing the two kids on dirt bikes who had reported it while the other one slowly worked his way in towards where the body lay, checking for evidence, footprints or tire prints as he went.

Once next to the body, the detective knelt down and began scribbling notes in his notebook. It had apparently once been a white male. Most of the rest of the details would have to wait for the Medical Examiner. The summer heat, which relented only slightly during the night, had promoted an advanced state of decomposition. The corpse was literally alive with flies, maggots and other insects. The eyes were open and looked like two pools of milk, showing nothing but white.

As the detective was writing, he noticed some movement in his peripheral vision. Looking up, he saw the rookie TI standing about a dozen feet away holding his newly issued crime scene toolbox.

"Pappy said I should help you."

"OK. Come over. Leave the box there."

The rookie set the toolbox down and took several steps towards the body. As a gust of wind passed, he stopped and turned his head slightly as he got a whiff of the corpse. The detective motioned towards the opposite side of the body.

"Down here."

The rookie, breathing heavily through his mouth, knelt next to the body across from the detective.

"I wouldn't do that if I were you."

"Do what?" the rookie asked.

"Breath through your mouth. I know it helps with the smell but the smell won't hurt you. You're more likely to inhale a blowfly. One that's just been eating on him. Might not be healthy."

The rookie immediately shut his mouth.

"What do you want me to do?"

"Bag his hands."

He went back to his toolbox and retrieved a pair of latex gloves, two small brown paper bags and a roll of adhesive tape. Donning the gloves, he gingerly lifted one of the victim's hands by a shirtsleeve soaked with body fluids. As he was carefully putting one of the bags over the hand, he flinched and dropped the hand.

"Hey! Careful! Just because we can't hurt him doesn't mean we can't screw up the evidence."

The rookie had recoiled a foot and had a strange expression on his face as he answered the detective's rebuke.

"He winked at me!"

"Who?"

"Him." The rookie pointed at the corpse.

The detective smiled. "Well, if he did, he's the toughest SOB I've ever seen."

"Honest to God, I saw it!"

After a skeptical glance at the rookie, the detective looked at the body intently for several seconds, leaning slightly closer. Then he reached behind him and broke off a blade of grass. Leaning forward, he inserted the blade of grass into one of the victim's eyeballs. The grass went in effortlessly like he was dipping it into milk. After a couple of seconds, a maggot surfaced in the center of the eyeball before diving back into the protein-rich substance to continue feeding. Although the eyelid didn't move, the surfacing maggot momentarily made a dark circle in the center of the eye where the pupil used to be. The detective tossed the blade of grass away and looked at the rookie.

"Even maggots have to come up for air. Bag his hands."

Then he winked at him.

BILINGUAL

"Let's go."

Don looked up from the report he was reading. "Where?"

"Ted wants to interview Weedhopper about his testimony." We both chuckled.

"This should be interesting."

Weedhopper was Phillip Mason. He was black, sixteen years old and very much a product of the mean streets of northeast Oklahoma City. God only knew where, when and why he got the nickname. A lot of people in the neighborhood knew Weedhopper but no one but his family would have known who Phillip Mason was. He was a short, skinny kid who looked even younger than his tender years until you looked in his eyes. He had seen and experienced more things in his sixteen years than most people would in their whole lives.

Two months earlier, Weedhopper had been walking down Northeast Third Street one night when he had the misfortune to witness a murder. When the shooting started, his innate survival instincts kicked in and he jumped behind a tree but he kept looking. It wasn't the first time he'd been around shooting and it probably wasn't the first man he'd seen die. John Earl's wife had come out of the front door of their house just in time to see various street people running away in all directions.

When the cops got there, Mrs. Earl was cradling her dead husband in her arms in the middle of the street. She didn't know the names of the various pimps, prostitutes and drunks she had seen fleeing the area. She did remember the skinny kid standing across the street watching and she knew the name Weedhopper. The detectives picked him up within the hour.

Uncharacteristically, he told them all he knew immediately. Yes, he'd seen the shooting. Yes, he'd seen the suspect and, yes, he knew him. The detectives arrested Tyrone Webster a few hours later. The gun was in his car, Weedhopper positively identified him in a lineup and didn't give a damn who knew it. Gutsy kid.

Faced with the prospect of the murder weapon in his car and a witness who wasn't afraid to testify, Tyrone had confessed in very short order. That was before he had a Public Defender assigned to him and he found out what the penalty for First Degree Murder was in a death penalty state that really enforced it.

The paper trail of that evidence alone was enough to get him bound over for trial in the preliminary hearing. Now, two months later, the jury trial was going to start soon and Weedhopper was going to have to testify in court. The case had been assigned to Ted in the District Attorney's office and he wanted to interview Weedhopper about his testimony before trial.

Although a relatively new prosecutor, Ted was very popular with the Homicide Unit. He was the kind of guy the hardened detectives in that unit could call "a sweet man" without meaning anything snide by it. A near-genius IQ had catapulted him near the top of his Ivy League law class before he came back home to learn his craft in the D.A.'s Office. The thing that endeared Ted to so many of the cynical, jaundiced veteran detectives was that in spite of the horrors he read about in their reports and prosecuted in court, he still had a charming naiveté and innocence about him. Tall, thin, with a very fair complexion and thick glasses, Ted was about as white as a white man can get.

I led Weedhopper into the law library in the D.A.'s Office while my partner went to get Ted. He breezed in a few minutes later in his normal frenzied fashion, taking long strides on those skinny legs, his tie askew, a lock of hair hanging over one eyeglass lens and a huge stack of files under one arm. He dropped the files on the conference table while Don sauntered in behind him and sat down. Ted shook hands with Weedhopper and introduced himself before he sat. Don and I couldn't help smiling when Weedhopper frowned when Ted called him "Phillip."

"We're going to trial on this case tomorrow, Phillip, and I need to interview you about your testimony. All right?"

Weedhopper shrugged and casually replied "Sure" as he slouched back in the high-backed, tufted leather chair.

"Fine." Ted got out a pen and poised it over his notepad. "Now can you just tell me, in your own words, what you saw?"

"Sure. I'se comin' down The Stro' minding my own bidness when I seen Skibo come out the house. Then Dude come up in his deuce and a quarter, got out, fired up Skibo and then he booked with the piece."

Ted's frown now surpassed Weedhopper's. The poised pen hadn't moved. Ted cut his eyes at both of us and we were managing to keep straight faces.

"I see. Would you excuse us for a moment, please?" Ted got up and walked out into the hallway. Don and I followed. A dozen steps away he turned to us with a confused look.

"What did he just say?"

"He said he was coming down The Stro' minding his own business when he saw Skibo come out of the house. Then Dude drove up in his deuce and a quarter, got out, fired up Skibo and booked with the piece." I was proud of Don. He got it all out with a perfectly straight face.

Ted flashed a look of quiet desperation at me, with an 'Am I all alone here?' look in his eyes.

"What does that mean? What's a Stro'?"

"The Ho' Stro' is what they call those few blocks. It means The Whore Stroll because that's where all the hookers walk up and down to solicit their business."

"What's Skibo and Dude?"

"Skibo is the street name of the victim, John Earl. Dude is the suspect, Tyrone Webster. Those are the only names he knows them by. Incidentally, he'll be happier if you call him Weedhopper instead of Phillip."

"What did he mean about a douche and a quarter?"

That almost did it.

"He said a deuce and a quarter," I explained. "That's a Buick 225. It's the car the suspect was driving. But if you ask him to clarify that on the stand, he can't pronounce 'Buick'. It'll come out 'Brurick' and the jury won't know what the hell he's talking about."

Ted grunted as the lines in his forehead were starting to smooth out. He was furiously jotting things down on his notepad when he looked up with renewed confusion.

"What did he say about a fire and a book about peace?"

That was the last straw. We both cracked up. Since Don caught his breath first, he answered him.

"Not a fire, fired up. That means shot. He said he was walking down Third Street when he saw the suspect shoot the victim and then drove off with the gun."

Ted looked up from his notes with his trademark beatific smile as all the clouds cleared away.

"Oh. That's good."

I laid a friendly hand on his shoulder. "Let's go back in, Ted. We'll translate as we go. Don't' worry about it. A few more murder cases and it'll be like a second language to you."

THE CHICKEN SONG

Axioms of life.

Boys play.

Big boys play rough.

The big boys of the Animal Kingdom, sharks, lions, bears, rhinos, elephants, *et al*, usually have an assortment of scars by the time they reach maturity. As a general rule, the worst scars were caused by their own species for whatever reasons. No less is usually true of *Homo Sapiens*.

When detectives who are used to working hard but intermittently, depending upon trends in certain crimes, get bored, they turn their attentions to their colleagues. When they can't mess with criminals, they mess with each other. These adventures can become especially entertaining (or exasperating, depending upon which end you're on) when they are perpetrated within a group of aggressive Type A personalities with very fertile imaginations, a black sense of humor and resources unavailable to the average person.

The victims of these pranks are usually the most humorless, the most anally retentive, the most up-tight, take-your-job-and-yourself-too-seriously types. The loose-as-a-goose types got them pulled on them also but since they just laughed them off, they weren't as much fun to torture.

It might start as simply as loosening the springs on the back of a reclining office chair that belonged to someone who habitually leans back in his chair and puts his feet up on his desk. One morning he sits down and *CRASH!*—he's on his back on the floor. Hopefully he sits down before he's holding his first cup of coffee.

Some desk officers like to keep a meticulous bulletin board, every piece of paper perfectly squared and equally spaced, perhaps even arranged by date. Their desk drawers are equally well arranged. All pencils sharp, arranged by height, stacks of papers squared and placed in order, everything on the desk in a predetermined place. Sometimes it borders on an obsessive-compulsive disorder. In a psychiatrist's office, this guy would get sympathy. In the Detective Division, this poor guy is just asking for it.

One morning he comes in and his bulletin board looks as perfectly arranged and spaced as when he left the day before—except everything is upside down. Obviously miffed, he tries to stifle his frustration, knowing that every eye in the office is gauging his reaction. He counts to ten, takes a deep breath and reaches for the side drawer he keeps his pushpins in. He pulls it open with a terrific crash. In his overnight absence, the entire desk has been turned upside down, everything in every drawer replaced upside down and the desk righted again. Against his better judgment, he opens another drawer to confirm his suspicions. Another crash. A dozen detectives are at their desks but the only sound in the office is the *tick-tick-tick* of an unbalanced bottle of White-Out rolling into a distant corner.

He slowly rises, pushes his glasses up on the bridge of his nose, walks to the coffee machine and pours himself a cup of the overcooked brew affectionately known as Homicide Sludge. He then starts out the door of the office. Another detective just coming in greets him.

"Morning, Bill. How's it going?"

He smiles a somewhat tight smile but replies cordially enough.

"Every day's a holiday and every meal's a banquet."

He'll take an early lunch and return his desk and bulletin board to order while everyone else is out to lunch. He handled it well and won't be targeted again—for a while.

Most cops develop what is called "a good radio ear." A patrol cop can usually recognize the radio voice of every officer on his shift without bothering about their call sign. This is helpful when a voice breaks the silence virtually yelling *"SHOTSFIREDINEEDABACKUPNOW!"* An oblivious dispatcher will invariably broadcast "What unit calling?" and another car will say "That's Baker Four, Headquarters. Baker Five is en route to his last call."

Former patrolmen who have become detectives retain their radio ear. They can usually recognize a voice after hearing it a few times. It works on telephones too.

The phone rings and a detective answers.

"Homicide, Smith."

"Is Tony there?"

He recognizes the voice of the man's wife.

"No ma'am, he just left for lunch with his wife. Can I take a message?"

A few seconds of silence. Smith is smirking silently and the other detectives in the office are starting to chortle.

"His wife? HIS WIFE? *I'M* his wife!"

"Uh, are you black, ma'am?"

"*SONOFABITCH!*"

You can hear the phone on the other end slamming down three desks away. This is one reason why some guys don't give their name when they answer the phone. It's called "breaking in new wives." Sort of a rite of passage for the spouses. Police wives are a special breed as well. At least the ones who last.

Homicide wasn't just a tough crowd for the cops but also for their associates. Attorneys, Assistant D.A.'s, medical examiners, federal agents and others who came through the office were not immune to the slings and arrows. Some enjoyed the witty repartee and joined in.

"Hey Chuck. Does your wife still like it with the lights on?"

"Sure, just like yours does."

Others weren't so flexible and never came back after a first visit.

Once in a while, two Masters Of The Game will get in what is colloquially known as "a pissing contest." These guys can spend prodigious amounts of time, effort, imagination and even their own money on these contests. At those times, everyone else just declares a moratorium, sits back and watches.

One officer's wife answers the doorbell and gets a delivery of a dozen red roses. She smiles and opens the card. In a perfectly forged facsimile of her husband's handwriting, the card reads "Mary, thanks for the other night. You know how much you mean to me. All my love, Bill." The only problem is her name isn't Mary.

The next night the other officer answers his doorbell and there's a deliveryman with a dozen anchovy pizzas for the party.

"What party?"

"Beats me, bub, but you owe me $62.50."

The next day, officers overhear the other detective making a hushed call from his desk.

"Is this Thomas Concrete?" Pause.

"Good. My name is—" He gives the other detective's name and address.

"I need twenty yards of concrete delivered to my house tomorrow between noon and three P.M. I'm tired of mowing and I'm going to pave the whole yard so just dump it all on the front lawn. Then come to the door and I'll pay you."

The other detective is very particular about his perfectly manicured lawn. Not any more.

Some guys get careless and leave too much of their personal lives in their detective cruisers. Like their checkbooks.

The next day, a black hooker, resplendent in skin-tight, sequined Spandex and fuck-me pumps shows up at the other detective's house when it's well known his wife will be home alone. She presents a personalized and perfectly forged check to the wife for five hundred dollars "for services rendered." The hooker irately explains that the check bounced and proceeds to vividly describe what the "services rendered" were. The wife is speechless and aghast. She's only catching a few words in every sentence of the rapid-fire street talk coming at her. She thought "half and half" was something you put in coffee, a "pearl necklace" was a piece of jewelry and she couldn't even dare to guess what "up the old dirt road" meant. But she'd damn sure ask her husband when he got home.

And on and on until both bloodied contestants declare a truce. To the best of my knowledge, no actual divorces or shootings ever occurred as a result of these little Hatfield-McCoy jousts but I heard that a few came close.

The Patrol Division's fascination with snakes also manifested itself in the Detective Division. Since it was harder for them to come up with a real snake than their patrol colleagues, one of the Homicide detectives bought a fake snake. It wasn't your average toy snake, it was the king of all fake snakes.

Six feet long and two inches thick, it was solid rubber with the correct patterns molded in the back and belly. Accurately molded in green and gray patterns, it was an evil-looking thing. Beady yellow eyes and gaping jaws with a protruding red forked tongue that wiggled realistically, it weighed several pounds and even felt real when you held it. It was usually kept coiled up in the unlocked bottom drawer of the owner's desk so everyone had quick access to it.

When someone with a known aversion to the creatures was unwise enough to turn his back or drop his guard while in the office, it wasn't unusual to see the thing thrown through the air to land around the unsuspecting victim's shoulders, accompanied by a resounding (but too late) warning of "SNAAAAAAAKE!"

The practice became rarer when several guys reflexively went for their guns after setting world's records for the backwards long jump and throwing the flopping beast to the floor. Fun was fun but we didn't want to get anyone shot.

The guys went through a phase of playing the prank on the janitors. On their daily rounds, the cleaning crew would roll a large barrel into the center of the office and begin emptying the waste paper baskets into it one at a time. While their backs were turned, someone would coil the snake up on top of the discarded paper in the barrel. After the screams died down, we usually picked up the paper from the inevitably dropped basket for them.

One, however, got away from us. Seeing it in his barrel, he instantly threw the basket at the serpent as a diversion, streaked out of the door and down the hall in an Olympic-class performance. Not only that, even after being told the snake was a fake, he refused to come back to the office to retrieve his barrel and continue his rounds. Even a neutral supervisor we sent down to persuade him couldn't budge the still-trembling guy.

"Uh uh. I ain't goin' back in there. Them mufuckas *craaazy!*"

I guess he quit. I know I never saw him again.

There once was a commander in the Detective Division, another guy who took himself and his rank too seriously. He had a florid face that got even more florid when he didn't get his way. He was a nice looking guy with pretty blond hair that he kept carefully coifed, brushed back from a rapidly receding hairline. Because of the hairdo, the guys called him "Fluffy" behind his back.

He had a private office at one end of the Division. There was a master key that opened all the doors of the Division and the night detective supervisor kept it in case anyone needed in one of the offices after hours but Fluffy changed the lock on his door so no one had access to his office.

Every night between two and three A.M., the night Homicide shift held their breath because two A.M. was when the bars closed. If there was going to be a bar killing, that was usually the time. One night they had one. Patrol officers brought carloads of drunks, hookers and other witnesses down to the station along with the suspect. Witnesses had to be kept separate so they didn't compare stories so they stashed them in Robbery, Homicide, Vice, Forgery and every place except the broom closet. A few were still left over.

Some enterprising detective picked the lock on Fluffy's office and put a few in there. Interviews were conducted and statements taken for the next few hours as the witnesses were released one by one or jailed if they were too drunk to go home.

When Fluffy opened his office the next morning, there was a cloud of smoke and the ashtrays were overflowing with strange cigarette butts. He threw a fit and went straight to Homicide. The offending detectives convinced him that they had obtained a copy of the master key and, miraculously, it had opened his door.

He stormed out, loudly admonishing everyone to stay out of his office, and promptly changed the lock again. He would now know no peace for weeks.

One night, the new lock was picked and a painting he was proud of was removed. Following another picked lock, the painting was mounted in a lieutenant's' office in another unit. When Fluffy found it the next day, he retrieved his painting and stalked down the hall, threatening the bewildered lieutenant with all kinds of retribution.

Then came the *Mr. Roberts* incident. One morning Fluffy came to work and found a potted palm tree in his office. He assumed it was a peace offering from his men—until a Deputy Chief walked into his office to retrieve *his* palm tree. Fluffy had to carry the tree back upstairs to the Chief's office, listening to threats of all sorts of hellfire and damnation. Unbeknownst to him, the Deputy Chief had been prepared for this by an old detective classmate.

Then Fluffy bought his own palm tree. It turned various colors and soon died. Then he gave up. I don't know if he just couldn't see any light at the end of the tunnel in this contest of wills or he figured out that the reason his tree was so sickly was because the night Homicide shift had developed the habit of urinating in his palm tree's pot every night.

Fluffy spent a lot of time at his desk after that, blonde wisps of hair gently floating to the carpet around him.

One of these guys was a great cop. He was one of those cops that the citizens were getting a great bargain for his salary. Always a self-starter, in patrol he jumped on every hot call anywhere near him and the rest of the time he was chasing down felons. He was especially offended by armed robbers so he naturally got promoted to detective in Robbery. He quickly became just as outstanding a Robbery detective as he had been a patrolman. But the bosses eventually put him in a bad position. Going against tradition, they promoted him to supervisor in the same unit. One day you're one of the guys and the next day, you're the boss. That can be hard to handle. It can be impossible if you take yourself too seriously. It can also be hazardous. These guys know where all your soft spots are.

In one of his World War II books, author Stephen Ambrose quoted another author's succinct definition of the term "chicken-shit." He said "Chicken-shit refers to behavior that makes military life worse than it needs to be: petty harassment of the weak by the strong, open scrimmage for power, authority and prestige, sadism thinly disguised as necessary discipline, a constant 'paying off of old scores', and insistence on the letter rather than the spirit of ordinances. Chicken-shit is so-called—instead of horse- or bull- or elephant shit—because it is small-minded and ignoble and takes the trivial seriously." That also applies in police departments.

Anonymous phone calls began coming for the supervisor. When he answered, there were a few seconds of silence on the other end. Then a recording began playing. It was a version of the old big band hit *In The Mood* performed by a group of clucking chickens. Actually people impersonating chickens but it made the point nevertheless. He would slam the phone down and look around the room to see who was laughing. No one reacted so he did all he could do—turn red, light a cigarette and inhale it down to the butt in one drag.

This went on for days. Then he made the mistake of leaving his cigarettes on his desk or in a drawer when he left the office. Some enterprising soul had obtained a box of exploding cigarette loads. Mini-firecrackers too small to be harmful, they were crammed down into the tobacco. When the cigarette was lit and burned down to the load, *BAM!* What was left of the cigarette exploded loudly in a shower of tobacco fragments and shredded paper. The hapless victim was left with a stunned look and a filter tightly clenched in blanched lips. Some of them also had small pull-cords coming out of each end that could be used to tie together things that are closed so that when they're opened, *BAM!*

So several times a day, *BAM!* echoed throughout the Detective Division. The Robbery guys did their best to keep their composure but unrestrained peals of laughter came from Homicide, Vice and every other unit within earshot. The supervisor mounted his own personal investigation on both the chicken song and the exploding cigarettes, to no avail.

His nemesis began taking several cigarettes out of the pack and putting the loaded one in the back. Several safe smokes went and then *BAM!* The supervisor began locking them in his desk, not taking into account some detectives' lock-picking abilities. *BAM!* When he unlocked the desk and pulled open the center drawer, *BAM!* Light another cigarette. *BAM!* Occasionally he threw away nearly full packs of perfectly good cigarettes.

A few days later, the supervisor was coming down the hall when he heard the muted strains of The Chicken Song coming from—*his unit's office!* Looking around wildly, he tracked the sound to a briefcase on a detective's desk. He tried to open it but it was locked. Unfortunately he didn't possess lock-picking skills like some others. So he whirled and demanded of every soul in the office,

"WHERE'S SMITH?" the owner of the offending briefcase.

Greeted by a chorus of shrugs, he charges out to begin searching men's bathrooms, the Record Bureau, Dispatch, the report clerks and anywhere else his tormentor might be hiding. Unsuccessful, he stalks back in the office and sits down at his desk, casting an unblinking eye on the briefcase which is in exactly the same position it was when he left. He notices that the horrible song has finished and he assumes the tape has run out. Drumming his fingers for five minutes, he leaps up when Smith comes sauntering back in the office.

"Where the hell have you been?"

"In the jail with a suspect. Why?" Smith appeared very calm if somewhat puzzled.

"Open that briefcase!"

"Why?"

"Just open it! Now! I'll show you why! I've got you now!"

Smith shrugged his shoulders and casually opened the briefcase on his desk. The supervisor throws open the top and ruffles through the interior. Nothing. No tape recorder. No Chicken Song. Just detective stuff.

Someone had removed the tape recorder and tape during his frenzied search for Smith. He searched every desk and briefcase in the office. Nothing. He went across the hall to the Homicide office and announced his intention to search all of *their* desks and briefcases. One of the detectives announced his intention to knock him flat on his ass if he tried and that was the end of that idea. The supervisor had to take off early that day. He was developing a knot the size of a quarter on his neck.

A few days later the supervisor had a bone to pick with a chemist in the Crime Lab. He went down there looking for him but the guy was out. Leaving a message, he stalked back to his desk. He threw himself down in his chair and didn't notice the small cloud of fine itching powder as he started going through papers on his desk. He absentmindedly lit a cigarette. *BAM!*

"*SONOFABITCH!*"

As he was brushing the debris off his suit, he began scratching his hands. Then his arms. Then his face. Then his neck. Then everywhere. Then the chemist walked in. Trying to scratch everything and read the Riot Act to the chemist about the perceived wrong was too much for him. He eventually fell silent when the chemist, obviously not intimidated, loomed over the desk, said "Look, Sergeant,—" picked his nameplate up off his desk, looked at it and pronounced his last name like a curse. The chemist then continued with a who-the-hell-are-you attitude until he noticed the incessant scratching and in mid-sentence said "What the hell's wrong with you?" With that every detective in the office started laughing. Several guys from other units had come over to watch and had to make room when the chemist stormed out.

Mercifully, that was close to the end of the day. The supervisor went out to go home and his car wouldn't start. He got out and opened the hood. *BAM!*

"*SONOFABITCH!*"

After replacing the disconnected coil wire, he got back in and started the car. He put it in gear and lit a cigarette as he backed out. *BAM!* A nearly full pack of cigarettes came sailing out the window as he drove away.

His ever-resourceful nemesis had been practicing on opening the cellophane of a brand new pack of cigarettes and resealing them without leaving any external evidence of tampering. When he reached home, the supervisor got a brand new pack out of the glove compartment. Going in the house, he fixed himself a stiff drink, took off his coat and tie and sat in his recliner. Taking a mouthful of the drink, he stripped the cellophane off the new pack, took one out and lit it.

BAM!

"*SONOFABITCH!*"

THE "TOUCH"

We've already discussed the two kinds of detectives. Some want to sit on their asses, shuffle paper, wear a suit and tie, drive an unmarked car, and work straight day shift with no nights, weekends or holidays. The other kind want to catch bad guys and put them in jail.

So the Detective Division administration thought it might be a good idea to start a sort of "Detective j.g." (junior grade) program. Patrolmen who were thinking of taking the detective test could apply and be assigned temporarily to a detective detail to see if they liked it. In turn, they'd be paired with a team of veteran detectives who would keep an eye on them, teach them a few things and see how things worked out. Overall the program was a good idea. Most of the officers who aspired to become the straight day shift detectives didn't apply. Most were hard charging, intelligent, motivated young warriors but, as with any process, a few duds slipped in.

One of those duds was in Robbery-Homicide. He screwed up everything he touched, had no common sense and was a slow (if not non-existent) learner. One day he decided, on his own, to try to help on a robbery case. It involved showing a photo lineup to a victim and without going into details of legalities and technicalities, he screwed it up royally, compromised the investigation and made a bad situation worse.

Exasperated almost beyond control, one of his senior partners got right in his face about it.

"Some parts of this job are pretty straightforward. Some you can learn from books, classes or more experienced partners. But some areas require a certain touch." He emphasized the "touch" by gently rubbing his thumb across the tips of his fingers about an inch from the guy's nose. "Some of it can't be taught or learned. It's instinctive. Either you've got it or you don't. *AND YOU DON'T!*"

The guy went back to patrol, tried a few transfers and eventually resigned, probably to the betterment of the PD. But a lot of guys did have the "touch" and it manifested itself in many unique ways.

Bill and Sam were working nights. Not normally partners, they'd never worked together before but both were veteran, well-respected homicide investigators. When he worked days, Bill had most recently been working the desk in Homicide because he was next up on the sergeant's promotion list and they didn't want him to get involved in any long-term cases just before he got promoted out of the Detective Division.

A shooting came out at 23rd and Eastern. The victim's lying in the middle of the intersection, dead as a hammer, and the unknown suspect drove away. The uniformed guys have corralled about a dozen witnesses and it apparently started over a typically serious matter—which driver would yield the right of way from a left turn.

Sam starts investigating the crime scene while Bill starts talking to the witnesses. Although meticulous about details, Sam doesn't take long because it's a pretty simple scene. The victim is shot once in the head, close range, small caliber pistol, probably a revolver since there's no cartridges lying around, his stalled car is registered to him and he has money in his pockets so there's no robbery. Victim has a misdemeanor record for drunk driving and marijuana possession so he's not a major player among the available vices. While the Crime Lab guys finish up the photos and measurements, Sam joins Bill in the car.

Bill's interviewing the witnesses separately, having them sit in the back seat one at a time so they don't give each other ideas. It doesn't look promising. On those occasions when you can get a witness to tell you the truth, their eye witness statements can be notoriously inaccurate. But Bill is taking a unique approach.

"What kind of car was it?"

"A Chevy, I think."

"Are you sure?"

"No."

"OK. What color?"

"Dark blue, maybe."

"What about the tag? Oklahoma?"

"Yeah."

"You sure?"

"Yeah."

"Letters and numbers?"

"I'm sure the first letter was 'X'. Don't know about the rest."

OK. Next witness. Same routine.

"I think it was a Buick, about ten years old. Dark green, maybe. Oklahoma tag. I'm sure the last number was a six."

Sam sat there and listened to Bill go through all the witnesses, scribbling in his notebook. They could only describe the suspect generically as a black male about thirty, dark complexion, over six feet tall, over two hundred pounds, dark pants and light t-shirt. Finally, the last witness leaves. Bill is studying his notebook by the dim interior light and Sam is studying Bill.

"Time to make reports and a radiogram?" Sam asks.

"No. Let's try something." Bill replies, flipping to a fresh sheet of the yellow legal pad. "Make of car. I've got Chevy, Olds, Pontiac and Ford but two of them were pretty sure it was a Buick. Most thought it was at least ten years old."

He writes down 'Buick, late '60s, early '70s.'

"Color. I've got maroon, dark blue and dark green but three thought it was dark brown."

He writes down 'dark brown.'

"All thought it was an Oklahoma tag. All but one was sure the first letter was 'X'." He writes down 'Okla. X'.

"I've got E, F and T for the second letter but two were pretty sure it was an 'L'." He writes down 'L' after the 'X'.

"Three were sure the first number was '1'. Two were sure the last number was six. One was sure the second number was seven because that's his lucky number. One was sure the next number was four because that's how old his kid is."

Sam silently raised his eyebrows while Bill continued writing. Bill is well known for his eccentric Ouija-board attempts at figuring out a system to beat Las Vegas in various gambling ventures on his vacations.

Bill reaches for the radio microphone.

"374 to headquarters. Need a 10-28 on current Oklahoma tag X-Ray Lincoln 1746."

"You really think this is worthwhile?" Sam asked.

"What else you got to do at 1 A.M.?"

Sam shrugged. He had a point.

"374, your tag checks to a 1967 Buick, Albert Mason at 2116 N.E. 16th Terrace."

"Headquarters, can your run BR on that subject?"

A few minutes passed while the dispatcher called a clerk in the Bureau of Records.

"374, Albert Mason, black male, DOB 2-12-48, 6-2, 210 pounds, dark complexion, prominent scar on left side of chin, multiple arrests, convictions for ADW Firearm in '67, 6 years OSP, CCW in '74. No current wants or warrants."

So Albert was a convicted felon who shot and wounded someone in 1967, did six years in the Oklahoma State Penitentiary and was then arrested for Carrying a Concealed Weapon in 1974.

While Sam kept quiet and humored him, Bill started the car and drove to the address less than a mile away. A dark brown 1967 Buick was parked in the driveway of the small frame house. The license tag number 'XL-1746' was clearly readable from the street by the light of the bare bulb porch light. Bill parked in front of the house next door and got out with Sam following. As Sam approached the three concrete steps up to the small porch, Bill put his palm on the Buick's hood. He nodded at Sam as he joined him on the porch. The hood was still warm from a recently running motor.

Standing sideways on either side of the door, both of them unsnapped the holsters under their suit coats as Bill knocked.

The door opened. A dark black man opened the door. Six feet-two inches tall, 210 pounds, a light-colored scar on the left side of his chin, he was dressed in rumpled work pants and a white t-shirt. Neither officer drew his weapon since the man's hands were visible and obviously empty. Neither reached for his badge, either. When two white guys in suits show up on a doorstep in this part of town after midnight, everyone over the age of two knows they're cops.

Bill spoke through the screen door.

"Albert, we're from Homicide."

"Is he dead?" Albert replied.

That's what lawyers call a "spontaneous admission." All that was left was collecting Albert, the RG .22 revolver with one fired round lying on the coffee table, impounding the Buick and completing the paperwork.

While Bill was finishing his arrest report, Sam was shaking his head. "Damnedest thing I ever saw."

THE GREEN-EYED MONSTER—WITH A LEAD PIPE

The call came from St. Anthony's ER. A beating death, the nurse said. She didn't know any more, just told us to talk to Doctor so-and-so when we got there. At least the timing was right from our point of view. For a change it wasn't half an hour before the end of the shift or in the middle of the night. It was right after our morning's first cup of coffee.

We were there in ten minutes. Without a word, the head nurse ushered us into the trauma room with the nude body. No badge-flashing or any of that TV crap. Plainclothes cops and ER people recognize each other right off the bat. When there's a recently dead body in the ER and two relatively healthy looking guys in conservative, off-the-rack suits show up, carrying a notebook in one hand and bulges under their coats on the other side, it doesn't take Sherlock Holmes to spot them.

The victim was a black female in her thirties or forties. It was a little hard to tell which. There's an old racist myth that black people can't be bruised. Cops know differently. This woman was bruised from her ankles to her eyebrows. No obvious open wounds, cold to the touch. Dark lividity on her backside so she died lying flat on her back and hadn't been moved for at least a few hours afterwards. The stiffness of rigor mortis was present so we were about eight hours from the time of death. Except for the rigor, trying to lift her arms or legs was like trying to lift a wet, rolled up towel. The adult human body has 206 bones. This gal probably had about 300 now because half of the originals were busted.

Doctor so-and-so said her husband had called the ambulance and rode in with her. He was in the waiting room and hadn't been notified yet since even the medics considered him the prime suspect.

He looked angry when we approached him but not with us. We told him she was dead and he still looked angry but with a little sadness mixed in. He was very meek and easily agreed to come to the station for an interview. The Miranda warning made no difference. The interview rapidly turned into a confession, the confession of an angry man who wants to talk.

They had been legally married for four years, no kids. They lived about three blocks from the hospital. They lived in a ground floor garage apartment with another apartment above them. The upstairs apartment was occupied by a single black man.

Our suspect was a long-haul independent trucker with no prior arrests. Just a hard working guy who hauled whatever he could from coast to coast to get by.

He worked the long routes because they paid better and his wife could stay home without having to work.

He hadn't been due home for at least another day but he'd driven twenty hours straight to get home early the night before. He hadn't called ahead so he could give the wife a pleasant surprise. He parked his rig in a shopping center parking lot a couple of blocks away and walked to his apartment. Going inside, he called for his wife but got no answer so he went over to the refrigerator to get a beer.

One of the problems with the apartment was there was a foot-wide hole in the ceiling above the refrigerator. The hole corresponded to a hole in the floor in the upstairs apartment. As he was getting his beer, he heard his wife's strained voice coming through the ceiling along with the screech of tired bedsprings.

"Oh, yeah! Oh, yeah! Come on, baby! Come on! Stick it in my ass!"

He described as many of his feelings as he could with a limited education. Jealousy, betrayal, fury, humiliation, embarrassment, but mostly depression. He took his beer and walked outside. Instead of going upstairs, he walked to a row of beer joints a little over a mile away. He drank heavily for the next five hours. He then walked home, still in a funk but with the depression gradually being overwhelmed by the fury. As he neared his apartment, shuffling along in the gutter with his head down, he stumbled over a piece of lead pipe about a foot long. Considering it an omen, he picked it up.

When he walked in the front door, his wife was standing at the stove, cooking something. She turned and gave him a huge smile, just like everything was normal.

"Hi, baby!"

He walked over, shook the lead pipe under her nose and said "See can you stick *this* up yo' ass, bitch!"

He admitted that a huge domestic quarrel ensued and he hit her with the pipe "a few times." He said she was continually pleading with him to stop, saying she'd been seduced by the man upstairs because she was so lonely while he was gone so much of the time but she really loved only him. Between the blows, she maneuvered him toward the bed, saying she wanted to show him how much she missed him.

He said he finally relented and they went to bed. They had sex and he went to sleep. He said when he had awakened this morning, she was lying next to him but she was cold and wouldn't wake up. Then he called the ambulance.

The Medical Examiner confirmed that she appeared to have had voluntary sexual relations more than once in the few hours before death. He said he wouldn't have normally thought a woman with her injuries could voluntarily have sex but his job had taught him that people could do some remarkable things when trying to save their lives. So had ours.

Overall, a damned shame and a waste. An honest, hard-working man, a lonely woman, an unrepaired ceiling and a lead pipe in the wrong place at the wrong time. All wrapped up before quitting time.

ANOTHER KIND OF ROOKIE

The call came to us from a patrol unit *via* a citizen. It was in a rural, sparsely populated area in the far northern area of the city. A passing motorist reported a pickup pulled off on the shoulder of the road, idling with the driver slumped over the wheel. Patrol checked the driver, he was dead and there's blood all over the seat and floor. Call Homicide.

A narrow, two-lane asphalt road, unpaved shoulder, nothing around for several miles except cattle, horses and oil wells. The driver is wearing a jogging suit and running shoes but he's fat. Too fat to be a jogger. Soaked with blood from the waist down and a couple of inches sloshing around on the driver's side floorboard. No billfold, money or credit cards so maybe a robbery. Shot once in the crotch, small caliber, probably a .22, no stippling or powder burns, shot probably came from the passenger's side of the pickup. It didn't happen here. The transmission is in Drive and he ran into a rain culvert which stopped the truck but it didn't cause much damage so it was coasting with a dead man at the wheel. The bullet hit the femoral artery and he bled out but he had time to drive for a few minutes before his heart started trying to pump air.

Patrol has already checked the license plate and we've got a name and address. We go to the house and meet the lady of the house. She lives there with her husband. From the photos on the mantle and her description of his truck, he's our dead driver. When we tell her what's happened, she's upset but not prostrate with grief. She lets us look around the house while she's composing herself. She says he left several hours earlier to go jogging. We mention diplomatically that he doesn't look like a jogger. We also mention that they occupy separate bedrooms. Given a little understanding, she admits that she and her husband haven't had a sexual life for many years and she suspects he's homosexual. He's the service manager at a nearby car dealership, it's his day off and for the last few years he seems to enjoy hanging around with teenage boys. He had his billfold when he left and usually carries several hundred dollars in cash on him.

At the car dealership, several people say they suspected his sexual leanings but it hadn't caused any problems so they ignored it. Most of the employees are older but there's one teenaged mechanic apprentice, an 18-year old named Jimmy. Jimmy's not here today because he called in sick. He's never done that before.

Jimmy lives with his parents. At their house, an unsuspecting mom and dad invite us in and call Jimmy out from his room to talk to us. Under mom and dad's scrutiny, Jimmy sweats, shakes and generally folds up like a cheap suit. He admits his involvement and says he'll tell us the whole story later, by which he means away from mom and dad. We arrest him and take him downtown.

Jimmy refuses a lawyer and says it was all Johnny's idea. Johnny, also recently 18, is his best friend and comes up to the dealership to have lunch with him occasionally. The service manager has been flirting with them and they picked up on his sexual orientation. Johnny had the idea for Jimmy to lure him out in the country where they would "accidentally" come upon Johnny with his "stalled" car. Then they'd rip him off. He'd flashed his billfold in front of them before. The service manager wouldn't report it because they could say he tried to get them to perform homosexual acts with them.

Jimmy gets the service manager to pick him up on the corner a block away from his house and they head out into the country. Jimmy suggests a route to a place where he'd be "comfortable" and they pass Johnny's falsely stalled car. They stop to pick him up but when Johnny gets in, he pulls a gun. The victim takes a swing at Johnny and Johnny fires a shot at him reflexively as he's recoiling from the punch. They take his billfold, jump out and the victim drives off. The boys get in Johnny's car and take off.

Jimmy tells us where to find Johnny so we picked him up and impounded his car after we booked Jimmy. They're both virtual virgins, just a little marijuana on their juvenile records. In the interview room, Johnny wants a lawyer so we let him call Legal Aid. We start making reports while we wait on the lawyer.

A couple of hours later, the front desk calls us and tells us Johnny's newly court-appointed lawyer is here. He introduces himself, gives us his card and we escort him back to the interview room.

My partner and I are both casting odd glances at each other. Working Homicide, you run into a lot of lawyers but there's a fairly limited pool that will take on murder defendants so you get to know most of them. Neither one of us had ever heard of this guy so we decide to test his mettle. He's in his thirties, balding, thick glasses and much more cordial to us than we're used to from defense attorneys. When we ask him if he has any weapons in his briefcase, he looks surprised and pops it open immediately for our inspection. Again, not your usual defense attorney reaction.

When we get to the interview room, we walk in right behind him and sit down while he's introducing himself to Johnny. We actually did it just to mess with his mind a little bit because we fully expected him to ask us to leave while he talked with his new client but he didn't say a word. He just sat down, pulled a yellow legal pad out of his briefcase and looked at us expectantly. We both managed to conceal our surprise, gave Johnny his Miranda rights again and started questioning him.

"Johnny, you should know we've already arrested Jimmy and he's given us a full statement. Told us all of it."

Johnny takes a deep breath, drops his head, slumps in his chair and the neon light on his forehead lights up that flashes "I surrender." By the way, only cops can see this light.

The lawyer is scribbling on his legal pad and hasn't said a word yet.

"Where's the gun, Johnny?" The lawyer's head came up.

"I tossed it out about 150th and MacArthur."

"Where did you get it?"

"It's my uncle's. He doesn't know I took it."

"Where's the billfold and money?"

"I tossed the billfold with the gun. The money's hidden in my trunk."

"Was there any special reason you shot him where you did, you know, because of what he was?"

"No, man, I was just trying to get away from him."

The lawyer had stopped writing when the gun was first mentioned. He'd been listening intently ever since, his only reaction being blinking faster and faster. By now he looked like a frog in a hailstorm.

"Uh, could I talk to you officers outside?"

"Sure." We got up and went outside with him.

"What is this all about?"

"Didn't they tell you when the judge appointed you?"

"My office just got a call from the presiding judge's chambers. I guess he told my secretary but I forgot to ask her."

My partner and I exchanged a poignant glance.

"Mr. Smith, this is a first degree murder case."

"*MURDER?*" I hadn't thought he could blink any faster but I was wrong.

"Mr. Smith, do you specialize in criminal defense work?"

He almost sobbed when he said "*No! I create trusts!*"

"Well, your client just confessed to a premeditated murder, killing a man in the commission of an armed robbery. A death penalty case."

"*DEATH PENALTY? I don't try cases! I don't go to court!*"

"Well, you're damned sure going to court now."

My partner decided to take pity on him. Both of them actually.

"Listen Mr. Smith, why don't we stop this here until you can find Johnny an experienced defense lawyer? We can give you some names."

"But you said this was a death penalty case."

"Technically, it is. But there's a lot of what you guys like to call mitigating circumstances. I doubt if it would go that far."

"Thank you, detective." The poor guy looked like he hadn't broken a sweat since law school but he was wiping his forehead with a soaked handkerchief now.

"I'd pay a little closer attention to those court appointments next time if I were you."

Mr. Smith got Johnny one of the best defense lawyers in town. After the D.A. checked with us about the case, he pled him out to Second Degree Murder for 25 years. Johnny probably did about a third of that. Jimmy got less.

I never saw Mr. Smith again. I'll bet he did a great job with trusts.

PARTY HEARTY

Some cops party all the time. All cops party some of the time. Patrol and Traffic had their moments. In warm weather, the police parking lot north of the headquarters building became a meeting place for the officers getting off duty after the Swing or Four Shifts. The parking lot was unavailable to the Day and Graveyard shifts because you couldn't have a decent party there at 7 AM or 3 PM when those shifts came off duty. At 11 PM or 2 AM, that didn't apply. Someone produced a few cases of beer and here we go. Gun belts came off, then shirts and there was a parking lot full of guys in blue pants, shiny black boots and white v-necked t-shirts telling war stories, bitching about various supervisors, comparing lies about their sexual prowess and occasionally punching each other out. Sometimes a girlfriend or groupie stopped by for sexual liaisons. After LAPD officer Joseph Wambaugh published his allegedly-fictional novel *The Choirboys* in 1975, these impromptu parties became universally known as "choir practice."

When the police parking area was inconvenient, these soirees adjourned to a deserted city park or a lake or one of numerous bachelor apartments with a rotating occupancy depending on who was in or out of their domestic bliss at any given moment. These were the apartments where a dispossessed cop could show up at any time of the day or night, carrying only his uniform, a frying pan and a pillow and have a home for as long as he needed.

Some units had more of a reputation for partying than others. In Patrol, it was usually the east side officers. Guys who had to fill out Uniform Replacement forms to replace bloody or torn uniforms or came in with bullets missing from their loop loaders more often than others worked harder at having fun. In Traffic it was the motorcycle jocks. Guys who risked being permanently crippled on two wheels every day had a similar attitude. In Detective, it was usually what one commander termed the "more active" units. Special Projects, Narcotics and Robbery all worked at it.

But Homicide tried to develop it into an art form. Work hard, party hard. That was the work ethic. A diet of stress, fast food, long hours, lots of overtime, missed holiday celebrations, having your successes and failures trumpeted on the nightly news and the front page, being publicly cross-examined by the best defense attorneys money can buy, toxic-waste coffee, and, during the breaks, whiskey. When it's controlled, the price can be headaches, heartburn, constipation, ulcers, high blood pressure, screwed up blood chemistry, insomnia and hangovers. When it's not, the price can be burnout, premature graying and/or baldness, alcoholism, sexual promiscuity, early heart attacks and divorce. When they work hard, they work harder than most. And when they party—legends are made.

In the late 1970s, soaring homicide rates encouraged homicide investigators from some medium-sized cities to travel to larger cities to try to learn from their larger problems.

Two homicide detectives traveled to Houston, Texas, to gain some insight in what to do if their homicide rate rose from 100 to 600 annually. At the time, Houston PD was having more than their share of problems. Several officers were under indictment for various crimes and the local FBI office was reviewing all Houston PD's officer-involved-shootings in five-year increments for civil rights violations.

The visiting detectives were teamed up with Houston Homicide teams to ride with them and go on their calls with them. They thought it a little odd that all the Houston guys kept asking to see their gold badges, always remarking on what good looking badges they were. Riding around, the Houston guys were always asking them about war stories and homicide procedures in their city. They thought the Houston guys just wanted to reassure themselves that the visitors weren't "political appointments" and really knew something about what they were doing. The guys were a little standoffish but Homicide is a tight clique wherever you go.

They rode on all three shifts and it seemed that whenever they got off, the Houston guys always went to a cop bar. Always invited, the visitors always joined them, feeling it would be rude to refuse. This happened every night for a week. A lot of whiskey was passed, a lot of war stories were told and a lot of sleep was lost by all.

Finally the partying every night relented and the Houston guys seemed a lot more relaxed and open around them. That was when they found out what had been going on. The Houston people thought they were undercover federal agents, planted among them to investigate them from the inside out. Asking how they had passed the test, they were told that part of it was their cop stories which had the ring of unrehearsed believability. Another part was their language. Since they like to view themselves as "a cut above," most federal agents can't swear with a street cop's natural, fluent profanity. Another part was the automatic way one of them had reacted when spotting and apprehending a car burglar they surprised in the commission of his crime. But the final, acid test had been "You guys had to be cops. No Fed can drink like that."

Robbery/Homicide Conferences were well attended. Several were held throughout each year in various cities. Most were productive. Classes and lectures were held on the latest advances in technology and detectives from the various cities presented their more interesting or unsolved cases in lectures. After the lectures, other investigators came forward with ideas the other people might use to advance their cases. After the lectures and classes subsided, most met in various bars, clubs or motel/hotel rooms for drinks and war stories. This too had a purpose. Much valuable information was passed and many lessons learned during these informal bull sessions. And then there were the actual parties. Again, legends were made.

One year, the conference was held locally and was attended by one of the DA's secretaries. Tall, blond and very fond of cops, she was known as "Big Bird" after the character in the kid's program *Sesame Street*. That particular year, Big Bird had a lot to drink at one of the parties and seemed to be setting her hat for one of our colleagues in Homicide who was matching her drink for drink.

No actual direct evidence was witnessed and no confessions were made but the next day, Big Bird called in sick and didn't show up for work. No one had heard from our friend but it was a scheduled day off for him so that wasn't unusual. Until mid-afternoon when a call came into the Homicide office.

"Homicide, Smith."

A weak voice on the line said "Trace this call and come get me."

Laughter, other guys getting on the line.

"Where are you?"

"I don't know, dumbass. That's why I want you to trace the call."

The guys who went and got him at a local motel said he looked like hell. "Rode hard and put away wet" was the phrase they used, as I recall.

Late one night, a patrol car got a call at a local hospital. The front lawn of the hospital had three large footlights that illuminated the front of the building. Three drunks were sitting in front of one of the lights and the hospital people were afraid to approach them.

When the cops got there, they realized these weren't what they had expected. Instead of three old homeless guys, they were confronted with three young guys in suits and ties. One of them was on his hands and knees, puking his guts out in front of one of the lights. The other two were studiously examining the expelled stomach contents and trying to decide what he'd eaten for his last meal. Recognizing the homicide investigators, the patrol guys took them home.

One guy was legendary for his huge capacity for beer. After downing about half a truckload of beer one night, caught up in the fervor of the party, he switched to vodka screwdrivers. Then he *really* put on a show. When he left, apparently he had a hankering for some tacos and stopped at a fast food place. Satisfying his hunger, he decided a nap would be in order before he went home. The next morning, the front seat of his car was covered in crushed taco shells. No word on whether the suit ever got clean after rolling in a couple of dozen smashed tacos.

Another one wandered into a suburban living room filled with startled strangers watching TV, sat down in a chair and cheerfully asked "Ya'll got anything to eat?" Looking around at the unfamiliar faces in the unfamiliar surroundings, he quickly figured out he was in the wrong house and gracefully left.

Two others left a raucous party and were getting ready to leave in a pickup truck. The truck's engine kept turning over but wouldn't start. They decided that priming the carburetor with some gasoline might be a good idea. Getting a gas can out of the rear, they popped the hood open and proceeded to pour some gas directly in the carburetor. Later rumors had it that they poured gas until the carburetor overflowed. With the air cleaner still off, they then tried to start the truck again. The engine turned over and then backfired. A jet of flame shot up from the center of the engine and sprayed flaming fuel all over the engine compartment. When others at the party came outside to see what the noise was, both guys were busily throwing handfuls of dirt under the hood.

NOTE: Some of these people drove their personal vehicles while off duty and under the influence of alcohol. This was several decades ago, before that was as serious an offense as it is now. Even though the legal penalties and fines were considerably less than now, it was against the law and, like everyone else who does it, they risked those penalties. Unlike everyone else, they were also risking their jobs. No, their job is not an excuse for this behavior but it might be a reason. None of them ever hurt themselves or anyone else during these incidents.

A TOAST

The bartender at the Police Club knew something was different as soon as the two detectives came in because they sat down at the first two seats at the bar, only a few steps inside the door. She reflected on what an education this job had been in the last few years.

Before she took this job, the only contact she'd had with cops was on the few occasions when they'd written her traffic tickets. But the last few years had probably qualified her for a college degree in psychology. Without even overhearing the conversations, she could tell which ones were having trouble in their marriages, which ones were respected by their peers and which ones weren't, which ones were cheating on their spouses, which ones' spouses were cheating on them and the reasons they were at the club on that particular night. There were party nights, celebration nights, therapy nights, stress-reduction nights and decompression nights.

With a police department of nearly a thousand officers, she didn't know all their names and didn't even try. She identified them mainly by their drinking habits and their assignments. She could identify the problem drinkers, the social drinkers and the periodic drinkers. The instant they came in, she could separate them into the categories of happy drunks, belligerent drunks, combative drunks, amorous drunks, sloppy drunks and controlled drunks.

These two were Homicide detectives, partners and usually happy drunks who only patronized party nights. Sometimes they'd come in for a single drink right after four o'clock when most of the Detective Division got off duty but mostly they showed up when the entire Homicide Unit took over two tables pushed together next to the jukebox. That they sat at the bar sent an ominous message. They had last been in on Monday afternoon for one of their single-drink sessions. This was Wednesday and they were wearing the same suits as on Monday, the starched shirt collars wrinkled and a little wilted, the ties loosened and askew. Their faces were flat and expressionless. They'd been working one of their occasional 36-to-48 hour days.

These were hardened men who lived in a violent world. She'd heard them telling stories that even shocked other cops. She'd heard them talk about having to stop at the hoses in their front yards and wash brain matter off their shoes before going in their homes. They'd learned that lesson the hard way after one of their kids asked what the funny smell was in daddy's closet. About having to show their badges to their dry cleaners because they were always bringing in clothes with bloodstains on them. About having to throw clothes away after working a fire death or a decomposing corpse because no dry cleaner could ever get the smell out.

She smiled pleasantly and approached them.

"What'll it be?"

"Scotch and water," the stocky one said.

"Scotch, a double," the dark-haired one said.

"No water?" she tried amiably.

He smiled wanly at her. "The ice will provide the water."

If you give it time to melt any, she thought. She sat the drinks in front of them. They both fulfilled her silent predictions. The stocky one took a healthy pull on his drink and sat it back down. The dark-haired one emptied his on one long series of gulps.

"Again."

While she was fixing the second drink, she noted another difference. They weren't talking. No chat, no small talk, no war stories, no laughter. Just two silent men looking into their own unblinking eyes in the mirror behind the bar. She also noticed that there wasn't anything strained or uncomfortable in the silence between them. They weren't angry or shy, just two close friends who were very tired, lost in their own thoughts and knew each other so well they didn't need to speak them.

"Again."

In the few seconds she'd been observing them, the dark-haired one had poured down his second drink. She fixed his third and he took a third of it in the first gulp.

She was right about how well they knew each other. The dark-haired one knew his partner would go home tonight to a loveless marriage and fall asleep in his recliner in front of the TV. Long after his wife had gone to sleep, their dog would wake him up by licking his feet. Then and only then would he go to bed.

The stocky one knew his partner would go home tonight, slowly inserting his key in the front door and lifting up on the doorknob so it wouldn't squeak and wake anyone when he went in. He'd spend the next hour sitting in the dark next to his son's bed, his hand on the boy's back, feeling him breath in the sleep of innocence.

And they'd both be back at work at 8:00 A.M. the next morning.

The dark-haired one raised his glass toward his partner.

"To Michelle."

The stocky one touched his glass to his partner's and they both emptied them. The dark-haired one slid off his bar stool, tossed a bill on the bar, placed his hand on the stocky one's shoulder for a second and went out the door.

The bartender looked after him as she spoke to the stocky one.

"Another?"

"One more."

Setting the drink in front of him, she asked "Who's Michelle?"

He answered in an emotionless monotone that belied the horror in his words.

"Monday's killing. Little girl. Multiple skull fractures. X-rays looked like a jigsaw puzzle."

"Who killed her?"

"Her father. Kept shaking her to make her stop crying. She was 33 days old. Had broken ribs that were inflicted within a week of her birth."

"How could you tell that?"

"Autopsy. They were starting to heal."

"Where was the mother?"

"Doing dishes in the kitchen, watching TV, listening to the baby scream—for three weeks."

The bartender could feel the tears starting to well up in her eyes as she looked into the detective's tired eyes. She shook them off as she looked at the front door.

"Is he all right to drive?"

"Yeah. Believe it or not, sometimes you can't drink enough to get drunk."

POPCORN

Two other detectives, call them John and Jim, flew to Los Angeles but on more traditional Homicide business. Interviewing witnesses and suspects who had fled from a local killing. Two LAPD Homicide detectives were assigned to help them locate the locals, check records, get warrants and drive them around the unfamiliar streets. After a long day of detective work, they all decided to adjourn to the bar in the visitor's motel and relax a little.

Like true professionals, the first few drinks were tossed down in a single, long swallow. Evidently having known a cop somewhere in her past and recognizing the signs of Olympic-class drinkers, their waitress kept them coming. The inevitable comparisons of departments, policies, procedures, commanders, department politics, pay, benefits, promotions, war stories and groupies lasted late into the night. Around midnight, after a very respectable eight hours of drinking, the two LA guys excused themselves. They had to get up early and go to work the next morning. They told the two out-of-towners they'd be by the next morning to take them to the airport for their flight home. John and Jim decided to close the place down and continued drinking for another two hours before they settled their tab and staggered out.

John just wanted to go back to the room and pass out but Jim wanted to eat. John tried to dissuade him but relented under his insistence.

"Nahhh. Do you a world o' good. Give yer stomach somethin' to work on besides th' whiskey."

They went into the motel's restaurant where both ordered a traditional breakfast. John ordered black coffee but Jim insisted on a tall glass of cold milk. While picking halfheartedly at his plate, John told his partner he was nuts for drinking the milk while Jim lustily cleaned his plate.

"Nahhh. S'good for ya. Coats yer stomach. Prevents ulcers."

Sated, they staggered across the parking lot to collapse in their room.

The next morning's wake-up call came far too early. Jim got up and stumbled to the bathroom for his morning constitutional while John lay on his bed, fighting off waves of nausea and feeling like he was tied on top of a running helicopter rotor. Jim had failed to close the bathroom door and John was soon inundated with Jim's bathroom noises echoing off of the tile walls and floor.

"Nnnnnnnnnnnnnnnnnngggggggggggggggggggggg!" A staccato of flatulence followed the strained grunt.

John rolled over on his side, facing away from the bathroom and tried to shut out the sounds.

"Nnnnnnnnnnnnnnnnggggggggggggggggggggg!" This one was punctuated with a splash that sounded like someone dropping a brick from shoulder height into a bucket of water. Writhing in agony on his bed, John was covered with a wave of incredible stench wafting out of the open bathroom door. He summoned all his strength for one plaintive plea.

"Close th' door, fer Chrissakes!"

No answer.

"Nnnnnnnnnnnnnnnnnnggggggggggggggggggggg!" Another tidal splash.

"Oh Jesus, please, take me now," John whimpered in pain. The smell permeating the entire room was causing contractions from his bowels to his throat. But no mercy came from his partner.

"Nnnnnnnnnngggggggg … RRRRROOOOOWWWWLLLLLFFFFF!" The sounds coming from the bathroom were different now. Someone was spraying a garden hose into a metal container and dropping golf balls in it at the same time. Another wave of odors rolled out of the bathroom and mixed with the other smells. A different stench. The acidic smell of vomit.

"Rrrrrrrrooooooowwwwwllllllllffffffff!"

Using all his reserves of strength, John rolled over to his other side. He tried to take his mind off of the sounds and odors now assaulting all his senses. Not only could he hear, smell and taste it in the air, he swore he could see the waves of odor coming towards him. He tried to take his mind off of the horror enveloping him. Where's my gun? I wonder if I could reach it without getting up? I wonder if I've got the strength to pull the trigger? Just once?

While John was trying to decide whether he'd shoot Jim or himself, he heard shuffling footsteps and a moist, sloshing sound behind him. He painfully twisted his head around to look over his shaking shoulder.

Jim was standing a few feet from the bathroom door. His underwear was still down around his ankles which accounted for the shuffling, hobbled foot-dragging. Swaying slightly, he was shakily holding a round, metal trash can in both hands and staring down into it. From a hole in the bottom of the can, a cloudy cord of thick yellowish phlegm trailed back into the bathroom. Jim's watering eyes were hazily trying to focus on the chunks of congealed milk floating in the vile mixture in the can.

"Did we eat any popcorn last night?"

John puked in the bed.

Tactical Team/Hostage Negotiations Unit

HEAD GAMES

The Minnesota Multiphasic Personality Inventory (MMPI) is a psychological test developed in 1940 at the University of Minnesota. It consists of over 500 questions to be answered true or false. The questions range from the seemingly innocuous to the bizarre. They seem to be very interested in how you feel about your mother and whether you're concerned about having black, tarry bowel movements. Some of the questions are repeated at various intervals to see if you answer them the same way every time. I'm not sure if the reason for this is to see if you're lying or just have a short attention span. At any rate, I guess that most psychiatrists and psychologists think it's just great. I'd also hazard a guess that most cops think it's bullshit.

After the murder of Israeli athletes at the 1972 Olympics, many American police departments began forming Hostage Negotiations Units and SWAT (Special Weapons and Tactics) teams to deal more efficiently with hostage situations and barricaded suspects. Our Tactical Team was formed in the early '70s and negotiators were added in 1979. Before that, those situations were usually handled by the first two cops to arrive at the scene. One takes the front door, the other takes the back door. Are you *coming* with us or are you *going* with us? The Tactical Team/Negotiator approach was an improvement, both for officer safety and suspect survival.

Our first negotiators were all detectives from the Homicide Unit. The prevailing theory was that they were all veteran officers who were successfully making police work a career, they were volunteers for one of the most high-profile and stressful jobs in the PD, they were used to working under pressure and thinking on their feet in life and death situations, they were experienced investigators and thus, interviewers, and they were used to talking to the widest possible range of people. Hookers, thieves, drunks, college professors, CEO's, doctors, lawyers and everybody in between seemed to pass through Homicide sooner or later as a victim, suspect or witness.

The department found out that some larger PD's were also employing full-time psychologists to assist in these situations. Since there weren't enough hostage/barricade situations to occupy them for a full 40-hour week, they started working on the cops. Screening recruit applicants, interviewing officers after they were involved in line-of-duty shootings to assess their psychological well-being, marriage and divorce counseling, assessing their stress levels and tolerance, and so forth.

The cops, naturally, took it as a threat. If you didn't show enough remorse after shooting a suspect or if you showed too much remorse, they could banish you to a desk somewhere. If a cop needed to talk about his marriage(s), divorce(s), kids, step-kids, ex-kids, finances or stress with someone, it was usually with his partner, either riding around in the car or at a cop bar after the shift. It wasn't a perfect system but it never got you fired, demoted, transferred or taken off the streets against your will.

So the department hired a psychologist. And a lot of funny stories ensued.

The first one they hired was a gentle soul. Apparently he'd never known any policemen before and thus had a somewhat idealistic view of them that couldn't have been farther from reality. He sat around waiting for cops to start filing into his office to tell him their troubles. When that didn't happen, they sent him out on a hostage situation one cold winter's day.

An armed multiple murderer had run from the cops and was trapped inside an old lady's house where he had taken her hostage. The negotiator's biggest hurdle was that the guy thought he'd killed a cop and would be assassinated if he surrendered. He had fired at a cop and the cop went down but he wasn't hit, he just slipped on the ice. Telephone negotiations progressed normally until a commander thought to diplomatically ask the psychologist if he had anything to offer. He did, all of it totally worthless unless he'd had the suspect duct-taped to his therapy couch. He was then ignored until the suspect's surrender was arranged. He listened while the Tactical Team commander gave his men their instructions for the arrest.

The suspect had agreed to surrender to an officer he knew from past arrests. The old lady was to stay inside the house. The suspect was to open the door, lay his gun on the porch and walk out into the front yard with his hands held high above his head. The officer would walk to meet him in the yard and handcuff him. This would guarantee his safety. The entire scenario was talked over thoroughly with the suspect and he agreed to every aspect of it.

Preparing for all contingencies, the cops had to consider that the suspect might have more than one weapon and he might decide to try to shoot the officer he was supposed to surrender to or even try to take him hostage. With the psychologist listening, the Tac Team commander instructed his sniper, "If he drops his hands below shoulder level, kill him." This wouldn't be much of a challenge since the sniper would be behind a tree about 25 yards from the suspect. Tac Team snipers routinely practiced with their .243 Winchesters with telescopic sights from a distance of 200 yards and could put rounds in a bull's-eye the size of a quarter from that distance all day long.

The sniper took up his position behind a tree at the corner of the house the negotiators were using as a command post. The psychologist strolled out on the porch a few yards from the sniper to watch. The negotiator called the suspect and told him to come out. The front door opened slowly and a hand reached out, gently laying a revolver on the concrete porch. The door opened the rest of the way and the suspect stepped out. The officer taking the surrender stepped out into the open at the front of the yard. The suspect raised his hands above his head and started walking toward the officer.

His rifle laying across a thick branch and his unblinking eye peering through the telescopic sight centered on the suspect's head, the sniper was as immobile as a still photo. Suddenly, the psychologist saw a flicker of motion. The sniper's right forefinger gently caressed the trigger and a barely audible whisper escaped his lips.

"C'mon, asshole, drop your hands."

I never talked to the sniper about it and I don't know what he was thinking. Maybe he was thinking about the old woman and young boy the suspect had brutally murdered in the last couple of days. Maybe he was thinking about the death penalty moratorium our state was still under. Maybe he was thinking about this human predator living out his life in relative comfort in a cell at taxpayer's expense. Maybe he was redefining his own definition of justice. I know he wasn't an unstable, naturally bloodthirsty man thinking about himself. He made it through a long career without killing anyone in spite of numerous opportunities and later received several promotions.

The suspect kept his hands up and was arrested without incident but a perfectly horrified psychologist resigned not long afterwards.

The next psychologist the department hired was tasked with giving psychological exams to the hostage negotiators. The Chief wanted to know if his negotiators were liable to snap under the pressure of a hostage situation or were susceptible to the Stockholm Syndrome, a psychological phenomenon where hostages (and sometimes negotiators) over-identified or over-sympathized with their suspects, tending to go to extreme measures to protect them.

The negotiators were not impressed. These men had already served for years in a patrol car and most had survived one or more gun battles. Each had won promotion, worked their way into Homicide, investigated hundreds of dead babies, dismembered hookers and everything else imaginable, and more than a few things that were not imaginable. They had also all successfully negotiated several hostage situations and seriously doubted anyone's ability to judge their psychological wellbeing other than their peers.

The first test was the MMPI. By previous collusion and without even reading the questions, one of them answered all the questions true, another answered them all false and the third one alternated his answers between true and false. The resulting profiles would probably have fit Adolf Hitler, Ma Barker and their illegitimate son. The psychologist, no fool, quickly figured out he was being had.

The next test was an oral interview. He soon discovered that the answers alternated between being flip and sincere but it was difficult to tell which was which.

"Do you think you could kill someone if you had to?"

"Sure, who do you want killed?"

"How do you feel about killing?"

"There's nothing wrong with killing as long as the right people get killed."

He finally gave up. His final report to the Chief of Police noted, fairly kindly, that the hostage negotiators were some "unique individuals" and all were "basically stable enough" for these duties. He also concluded that all the negotiators were highly resistant to the Stockholm Syndrome and one was "totally immune to it." The Chief put the report away and made no changes in his negotiators.

WELCOME TO THE DARK SIDE

The Tactical Team and Hostage Negotiations Unit are conducting their monthly training session. A few classes at the Training Center, then an equipment check, some practice assaults and role playing situations. They don't know it yet but they've got a little surprise in store for them today. An unannounced visit from the Chief of Police. And the Chief has a few surprises in store for him as well.

A career traffic officer, the new Chief is widely known as a gentle, decent, unassuming man, even possessing an unusual degree of naiveté. Dignified and religious, he has somehow remained relatively untouched by the cynicism and hard edges a quarter century in police service can give a man.

The reason behind his visit is an "attaboy" for the troops, to show his official appreciation for the successful conclusion to several recent hostage situations. A successful conclusion meaning no one was hurt—officers, suspects or hostages.

He's never confronted these men in their natural habitat before. He's used to seeing them in flawless, sharply pressed uniforms with shiny boots and polished brass or conservative business suits. Today will be a new kind of epiphany for him.

At first blush, it's obviously not a normal police training class. No sharp uniforms in here today. No orderly rows of silent, attentive officers taking notes with a supervisor standing at a podium up front. The podium is vacant and there is a moderate din from everyone talking at once.

They're sprawled around the room, rocked back in chairs, feet up on the tables, a couple of them sitting cross-legged on top of the tables. The uniform of the day is an eclectic mixture of blue jeans, camouflage military pants, scuffed combat boots, sneakers, cowboy boots, t-shirts and the occasional baseball cap. Some have just come off of their days off and have several days' growth of beard. Unless you knew them personally, lieutenants and sergeants are indistinguishable from detectives and patrolmen. If they had an unofficial motto, it might be "Hope for the best but train for the worst."

Animal strolls in with a fresh Styrofoam cup of black coffee. He's a shotgun man on one of the assault teams. Two hundred and fifty pounds of mostly muscle, a grin that could send chills up a bad guy's spine and a nickname that is well-earned. He's already killed two armed felons in the line of duty and seems to be doing just fine without any psychological counseling. But the most unsettling thing for the Chief is the slogan on Animal's t-shirt. It reads "Kill 'em all and let God sort 'em out."

The rest of the room is no more comforting. A group at one table consists of the team snipers and a couple of negotiators. One of the snipers is wearing a t-shirt that reads "When I kill, all I feel is recoil." He's drinking coffee out of a cup labeled with the Latin phrase "*Rubicundus Nebula.*" The Chief jovially asks what it means.

"It means 'pink mist', Chief."

His puzzled expression begs an explanation.

"It's what's left behind when a .243 rifle slug goes through a head at three thousand feet per second."

As the smile turns wooden and he moves away, the men return to their prior conversation. They were discussing hand and arm signals for face-to-face confrontations between a negotiator and a hostage taker. The negotiator's t-shirt has a bull's-eye on the back and the legend "Surrender or die."

"If he's getting more aggressive, I'll scratch my left ear and back up a step. If he's right on the edge of losing control, I'll scratch my right ear. Then you take him out."

The Chief rushes through a short version of the "job well done, keep up the good work" speech and hurriedly exits stage left. He never came back.

PHASE TWO

The call is at one of the older three-story office buildings on the outer edges of downtown. It's one of those calls that, in spite of the seriousness, a cop can't help but be struck by the irony.

A man charges into his lawyer's office in high dudgeon. He has paid his lawyer $15,000 to get him out of a felony charge. No one knows how he came up with the money and no one wants to know, least of all the lawyer. In spite of the fact that the man is guilty, he's highly offended when he's convicted. Released on an appeal bond, he steams about it over quite a few beers until he blows a gasket. He drives to his lawyer's office and charges in waving a pistol and demanding his $15,000 back. The secretary abandons the office posthaste and calls the cops.

Patrol evacuates the building, the Tactical Team sets up a perimeter and the negotiators set up their communications equipment. Elevators are shut down and every hallway, stairwell, door and window is covered. The negotiator's technical man works with the telephone company to isolate the lawyer's phone lines. If anyone picks up the lawyer's phone, the only person he can contact is the negotiator a few offices down the hall. None of the other phones in the office will work. The lawyer's office is totally isolated from the world.

The primary negotiator makes his call. Predictably, the lawyer answers. The negotiator gives the lawyer a very short speech on how to act to best stay alive and then asks to speak to the suspect. His name is Ray.

It quickly becomes apparent that Ray isn't the brightest bulb in the room and the beer isn't helping any. The conversation follows a very predictable pattern. Ray is loud, mouthy and confident he's in charge. Threats to kill the lawyer, "If you charge in here, everybody dies", demands to get his $15,000 back, the lawyer doesn't have the money, impasse. Eventually, the negotiator agrees to get the $15,000 from a local bank and get it to Ray but only in exchange for the lawyer. He keeps calling the lawyer "Bob" to reinforce in Ray's boozy mind that his lawyer is a human being, not some anonymous stranger.

True to his word, the negotiator gets the money. He then calls Ray back and tells him they need to make detailed arrangements for the exchange—the money for the lawyer. They finally agree on a plan. A Tac Team officer will put the money on the floor in front of the lawyer's office door. The lawyer, with Ray right behind him, will pick up the money and give it to Ray. This is so Ray won't have to expose himself to the Tac Team's assassins he believes are licking their chops to kill him. Ray will then let the lawyer go. The negotiator asks to speak with Bob so he knows exactly what he's supposed to do.

It has long since occurred to the good guys that Ray might very well keep the money *and* the lawyer so they plan for that. While the negotiator is on the phone with Ray so he can't see out in the hall, a young and muscular Tac Team officer slips into the vacant office across the hall from the lawyer's office. Another Tac officer, covered from both ends of the hall, lays the money on the floor in front of the lawyer's door.

When the time for the exchange comes, the negotiator calls Ray and tells him the money is in place. Watched carefully by the officer in the darkness across the hall, the lawyer's front door slowly opens. The lawyer is peeking out with Ray right behind him with a gun in his back and the other hand holding his coattail. The lawyer steps out, picks up the packet of money and as he was instructed by the negotiator, quickly turns and throws it back into the office.

In the same instant that Ray is grabbing for the flying money, the Tac officer steps into the hall, grabs the lawyer and throws him bodily into the office across the hall, follows him in the same motion and slams the door.

A few minutes later, the primary negotiator calls again. Ray picks up the phone with an entirely new demeanor.

"Hello, Ray?"

A very subdued Ray said "I guess now we go to Phase Two?"

The negotiator couldn't help laughing at the resignation in the man's voice. He has figured out that he's all alone in the office, with $15,000 he can't spend and no hostage to shield himself. He has a .22 pistol and he's surrounded by a small army with shotguns and machine guns. All dressed up and no place to go, as they say.

Ray was completely convinced the Ninja warriors would burst in on him now and machine gun him into shreds. He happily threw his gun out and submitted to an arrest he thought he'd never live to see.

FIRST, YOU HAVE TO GET THEIR ATTENTION

There used to be an old joke about a farmer who was trying to plow his fields with a new mule. The mule sat down and refused to pull the plow. The farmer's wife suggested he walk up and down the rows so the mule could see what he wanted him to do. The silent farmer's response was to go up to the farmhouse and pick up a short two-by-four piece of lumber. Walking back to the field, he hit the mule between the eyes with the board as hard as he could. The mule snorted, shook his head and stood up. Just as the farmer's wife was starting to berate him for his cruelty, he walked behind the mule, picked up the reins and the mule started pulling the plow. His puzzled wife asked "How did you get him to do that?"

"First, ya gotta get his attention."

A man and his wife get into a domestic dispute. He's had a few drinks and things get out of hand. He grabs his pistol and thumps her over the head with it before throwing her out of the house. She calls the cops from a neighbor's house, telling them the couple's two kids are still in the house. The Patrol guys call Tac and Hostage. With a very low profile and keeping everyone out of the potential line of fire, the Tactical Team evacuates the surrounding houses and sets up a perimeter. The negotiators set up their equipment in a house also out of the line of fire.

The primary negotiator calls the home telephone. The man answers. The negotiator identifies himself and asks if the kids are all right. The guy says "Sure. They're watching TV and eating cookies." He asks to speak to one of the kids and the guy refuses.

"Hell, no, you can't talk to my kids. You talk to ME!"

Okay. He asks the guy to come out and talk to him. The guy refuses. He doesn't have anything to say to the cops. He slams the phone down.

The negotiator calls back. The guy irately explains that he's in his own home, his home is his castle and by God, they can't come in and he won't come out. He has the right to drink in his own home and to keep and bear arms so that's that. He slams the phone down again.

The negotiator calls back again. He tries to explain that the guy has committed a crime by pistol-whipping his wife and throwing her out of the house. He snorts at the idea.

"That? Oh hell, that's just a family fight. None of your business."

"I'm afraid it is. She wants to sign a complaint against you and prosecute you. And we can't just drive off and leave an armed man who's been drinking and shown a tendency for violence alone with two kids." The man isn't convinced.

"Bullshit! My house, my gun, my booze, my kids. Go away."

All this time, the Tactical snipers have been watching through their scopes, gathering intelligence and relaying it to the command post. The kids are in front of the TV in the living room. When the phone rings, the guy answers it at the kitchen table, gazing out the picture window at his seemingly empty back yard. He seems very relaxed and nonchalant.

The primary negotiator and the SWATCOM negotiator discuss it. SWATCOM is the secure radio link between a negotiator and the Tac Team leader who has similar contact with each of his men. The primary decides the guy isn't taking them seriously yet. The guy can look out his windows or doors and see nothing unusual except that there are no people and no traffic. That needs to change. It's called "manipulating the suspect's stress level." The SWATCOM negotiator calls the Tac Team leader.

"In sixty seconds, have one of your guys in the back yard show himself."

"Roger. In sixty."

The SWATCOM negotiator nods to the primary who dials the phone again. The man picks up on the third ring.

"I'm getting real tired of this. I've told you and I've told you and I'm getting tired of it. I guess you're just a little slow—*JEEESUS CHRIST! A GUY IN A SKI MASK WITH A MACHINE GUN JUST RAN THROUGH MY BACK YARD!*"

"Mr. Smith? Did you think I was the only one out here? Now I hope you realize the seriousness of this situation. We need to discuss it in detail."

He came out peacefully a little while later.

SHOWTIME

Middle of the afternoon, middle of the week, middle of a busy shopping center, less than a block from a busy interstate highway. The only good thing about the call was it was at a fast food restaurant that was separated from all the other businesses and had what the Tactical guys called a large "kill zone", i.e. a relatively large space around it separating it from other buildings.

Two white guys in their early twenties with pistols had come in but it didn't sound right for a robbery. They started running people out of the place and most of the employees and customers didn't hesitate to hit the door running. But after interviewing them, we found out there were a couple of employees missing, apparently still inside.

Tac set up their perimeter and the negotiators set up their phone equipment in a drive-through bank about a hundred yards away. It also had the advantage of an entrance on the side away from the restaurant and windows on the side toward it so they could see the scene.

The primary negotiator made his first call. No answer. He kept it ringing. It's very hard to ignore a ringing telephone for any length of time. Suspects had torn them out of the wall or shot them or taken them off the hook before but they were hard to ignore. But it had been done. A cop killer once hid under a bed for three and a half hours while a phone rang constantly.

Snipers couldn't see any movement inside from their positions. Assault Team members around the outside of the building reported that they could hear the phone ringing inside.

In the midst of all this, some genius among the city fathers decided to send an Assistant City Attorney out there to advise on the liability situation. Some kid in his twenties showed up flashing a bar association card and was directed to a uniformed captain on the perimeter. He proceeded to inform the captain that he was in charge here and was to be informed of all actions taken in advance. He then asked where the command post was where he could be out of the summer afternoon heat. The captain, silently unimpressed, directed him to the bank building where the negotiators were set up. The captain also pointedly neglected to inform the Juris Doctor that he was in charge of crowd control and what happened inside that perimeter was strictly in the control of a couple of detectives wearing headsets and half a dozen patrolmen wearing black fatigues and ski masks.

The lawyer was escorted to the bank building and an officer told the negotiators who he was. The primary negotiator, leaning back in his chair and appearing a lot more relaxed than he was, struck up a casual conversation with him since he wasn't doing anything but listening to a phone ring a hundred yards away. He first explained that if things started happening, like a phone being picked up or the sound of gunshots, he was to sit down and shut up immediately. The lawyer looked a little chastised but sat down and sipped coffee.

Meanwhile the SWATCOM negotiator talked in a low voice on his headset, relaying information back and forth with the Tac Team leader. Every once in a while, he would tell the primary what was going on or more accurately, what wasn't. No movement inside. No sounds from inside except the phone ringing. The two negotiators, who had worked together for many years, communicated mostly with raised eyebrows, quizzical looks, shrugs and subtle hand signals while the lawyer sipped his coffee, completely oblivious. Some of the SWATCOM guy's talking was in police codes and signals that the lawyer couldn't tell if they were directed into the headset or to the other negotiator. The other negotiator, however, did know and the lawyer was too proud to ask what they meant.

It was eventually decided that they had waited long enough and tried everything they could. The fate of two hostages was unknown and Tac recommended a forcible entry. The Tactical commander and both negotiators agreed. All this took place over secure radio headsets and no one told the lawyer anything. The SWATCOM negotiator subtly raised his hand to the primary with all fingers spread out. Five minutes. The primary nodded.

The SWATCOM negotiator listened to the Tac Team talking to each other. Snipers scanning for targets and sightings. Shotgun men lining up out of sight along a solid brick wall. One man with an automatic weapon paired with each shotgun man. At our request, the highway patrol was stopping traffic on that section of the interstate highway until further notice.

Four minutes. Three. Two. One. Lock and load.

Both negotiators took their headsets off and the SWATCOM guy unplugged his so the Tactical network would come over the speakers in the control unit. The primary lit a cigarette and turned to look out the window toward the restaurant.

"It's showtime!"

The lawyer looked at both of them with a puzzled expression.

"Huh?"

WHUMP!

The concussion from the flashbang grenade rattled the windows of the bank building even a hundred yards away. For an instant, the light inside the restaurant was brighter than the midday sun. The entire building instantly filled with thick gray smoke which almost as quickly rose to about waist level. The speakers from the radio/telephone set crackled to life.

"GO, GO, GO!"

Sounds of glass shattering and metal twisting.

"One and three right!"

"Two and four left!"

Silence. A long minute.

"One clear!"

"Three clear!"

Shots. Seven of them. The negotiators could tell they were .223's from the Tac Team's M-16's, not handguns.

Silence. Another long few seconds. Then two more shots. This time they were handguns.

"One suspect down!"

"Two suspects down!"

"Report!"

"One clear."

"Two clear."

And so forth, until all had reported in.

The lawyer sat open-mouthed, watching smoke pour out of the building as the negotiators walked out toward the restaurant.

It turned out that the two suspects were escaped mental patients and our Tactical Team didn't kill them. The shots they fired were to blast out a one-way glass, a little "recon by fire". Although we could never be sure (no one to interview), the suspects apparently had some kind of elaborate suicide pact. One killed the other and then killed himself. The two employees inside had barricaded themselves in a back room and were all right.

The Assistant City Attorney was gone when the negotiators came back to pack up their gear and no others came to hostage situations.

NOTE: In spite of the previous stories which highlight a black sense of humor, jocular attitudes and Draconian measures exhibited by the officers involved, I wouldn't want anyone to misinterpret something. To the best of my knowledge, no law enforcement agency forces anyone to become a Tactical Team member or Hostage Negotiator. They are all volunteers and veterans. This is no job for rookies. They are all highly motivated, well trained and highly disciplined. They fully understand the gravity of the responsibilities they are asking for and take them *very* seriously.

It's all about saving and protecting lives; barricaded suspects, hostages, hostage takers, innocent bystanders and police officers alike. Insomuch as the hostage takers will cooperate, that objective is always primary in everyone's mind and they have a high percentage of success.

The most frequent misconception conveyed from Hollywood productions is that every hostage situation is a contest between the Tac Team and the negotiators to see who can use their talents to solve the situation first. The guys in the black ski masks are just salivating at the mouth, eager to charge in and use their weapons while the negotiators are anxious to trade themselves for the hostage(s) or shield the hostage taker from the mean old Tac Team with their bodies. That is all crap.

Everyone works together, everyone trains together, works under the same command structure and is trying to achieve the same results every time. Even three decades ago, all these people had instantaneous communications and it was a rare moment when anyone on the team didn't know exactly where everyone else was, what they were doing and intended to do.

Let's just say that there are a lot of people alive today in all five of the above categories because of the professionalism and restraint of these officers.

Sex Crimes

EVERYBODY DOES IT

The Homicide night shift was in the office. It was a weeknight and had every promise of being a quiet night, at least until the bars closed at 2 A.M. They were caught up on all their cases so they were using the temporary lull to catch up on paperwork.

It was nearing midnight when Ken came in leading a man in handcuffs. Ken was a Sex Crimes detective. Although the Sex Crimes Unit didn't have a night shift per se, there was no telling when Ken was going to be out amongst them so his appearance was no particular surprise. His prisoner was a white man, mid-forties, pudgy, cheaply dressed. He was handcuffed behind his back and Ken was holding onto the cuffs.

"You guys mind if I park Spud Butt in here for a while? I've got five more in holding cells."

"Damn, Ken" one of the Homicide guys responded, "Super cop, ain't we?"

"Just a wealth of riches tonight, guys. You know what they say about Sex Crimes."

"Yeah. Everybody does it. Just park him over there." The Homicide detective gestured toward a vinyl-covered chair in front of the empty secretary's desk.

As Ken led the man past them to the chair, the other detective turned from his desk.

"What did you call him?"

"Spud butt. Got him at Mercy ER. He came in for a procedure. Seems he likes to stick potatoes up his ass and one went in too far. One of the docs I work with on kids gave me a call on the off chance he might be good for one of my open cases."

When the Homicide guy quit laughing he said "Potatoes? Like new potatoes?"

"Nah. The baking kind. Big ones. With eyes and sprouts and stuff."

The other detective sniffed the air.

"Jesus. What's that smell?"

Ken grinned evilly. "He wears diapers. Stretched his asshole out so far it won't close up all the way again, you know? Guess he's got a leak."

"Good God. What have you got waiting in the holdovers?"

"One's a church janitor. Patrol responded to a light in a church after hours. When they peeked in a side window, they saw the janitor screwing a stray dog. A terrier, I think. Used furniture polish to lube him up first."

More laughter, shaking of heads and comments.

"Is the dog under 18?"

"Can the dog pick him out of a lineup?"

"Did the dog consent?"

"Maybe the dog was teasing him?"

Ken was laughing with the rest of them.

"And it's not even a weekend. What else you got?"

"Got a twelve-year-old girl in the juvenile holdover for an interview, her stepfather and two cousins under arrest. Also a fifty-six year-old school maintenance guy."

"Bad night for janitors. Child abuse?"

"And then some. Seems dad and the uncle have been molesting the girl since she was six. She made the mistake of telling a janitor at her school about it so he started taking his turn in the janitor's closet between classes. She finally upped it to a teacher who called it in."

No laughter this time.

One of the detectives gestured towards Spud Butt. "You get a lot like this?"

"What's a lot, ya know? Hell, this is nothing. I was talking to a guy in a Sex Crimes unit in Texas last week. He told me about this call he got to an ER. This guy brought his roommate in screaming his ass off. He dies before they could get him on the table. Internal bleeding. Seems they'd been taking turns sticking a live eel up each others butt."

"An *eel*?"

"Yeah. Thought it'd be something new, I guess. Anyway, eels are slippery so it got away from him and wriggled up in there. Well, eels can't back up in tight spaces. No reverse gear, I guess. And they've got teeth. So the eel just started eating his way out. He said the M.E. recovered the eel alive during the post."

Momentarily speechless, several seconds passed before the silence was broken by one of the Homicide guys.

"You think that really happened?"

"Hell, I don't know. You know, you'd think doing this job would make you one of the least gullible people on the planet but I've seen so much by now, I'll believe almost anything's possible."

"I'll take a good old gut-slinging killing any day."

Narcotics

THE INVISIBLE MEN

My partner and I were sitting around the office one afternoon doing paperwork when one of the Sex Crimes detectives came in. He was working on a case on which he could use our help. The kind of help best provided by cops who don't look like cops, the department's "invisible men."

A few weeks ago the detective had investigated a reported rape in the northwest section of the city. A man had broken into a woman's home, waited for her and raped her when she came home. It hadn't been a brutal or sadistic rape and other than the rape itself, she suffered no other physical injuries.

The Friday night after the rape, the man had called the victim back at her home. He had told her he wanted to "see her again." He had then asked her if she had liked it, if she had been satisfied and other things, spilling his deviant psychology over the phone. The victim, a smart lady, played along with him, agreeing it hadn't been too bad but he had frightened her pretty badly and she'd have to think about whether she wanted to "see him again." She told him to give her a few days and call her back. She then immediately called the detective and told him the whole story.

The detective arranged for a legal wiretap on her phone. Because the guy was telegraphing his predictability, the detective didn't expect the guy to call back until the next Friday night but he kept close tabs on her throughout the week just in case. This was the next Friday night.

The Sex Crimes detective was going to spend the evening at the victim's home waiting for the expected phone call. He wanted us to be nearby, checking pay phones and just watching for suspicious characters fitting the suspect's description which we could do with a lower profile than he could. My partner, a master narc, had shoulder length graying hair, was skinny and even managed to look like a heroin addict. In fact, his nickname was "Junkie." I was much less convincing but still looked a little unsavory with a couple of weeks beard stubble, ratty jeans and a faded old Army fatigue jacket with the sleeves cut out turning it into a vest. Our car was a beat up old Chevy Nova, faded orange that rattled and smoked like the junker it was. Its only modifications were the police radio hidden in the glove compartment and the twelve-gauge shotgun we carried under the front seat.

We agreed to randomly patrol the area because we figured this guy would want to be close if he called back. When not patrolling, so as not to been seen too often, we'd wait in a supermarket parking lot a few blocks away.

We did more waiting than patrolling because there wasn't anything outstanding about the suspect. White male in his thirties, average height, average weight, bland clothing description. We didn't want to burn ourselves by being too visible. After a few very boring hours, the Sex Crimes detective called us on his portable radio. Speaking softly, we knew he would be near the victim while she was on the phone.

"He just made contact. I can hear traffic in the background so it's probably an outside pay phone."

We started checking all the outside pay phones within a three-block radius of the victim's house. After a couple of minutes, he called back.

"He wants her to meet him at the convenience store at 36th and Penn."

This was only two blocks from the victim's home and we were less than a block away. We gunned the car a little and pulled into the parking lot in less than a minute. There were two pay phones in front of the store and a guy who fit the description was talking on one of them. Just as he hung up the phone, our radio crackled again.

"He just hung up."

Junkie leaned over below the level of the dash to speak into the microphone. "Got him spotted. He's going inside. We're on him."

The guy walked over and walked in the store. We got out and followed him in. Several other people were in the store but none of them took any notice of us. That was when I learned that you can walk around among a group of people with a gun in your hand, doing nothing to conceal it except letting your arm hang naturally down by your side and most people will never notice it. Amazing.

The guy walked to the back of the store and kept looking towards the front door but looking right past us like we weren't even there. Perfect. I went down one aisle and my partner went down the other. Then, with no one else close by, I pushed his face into the Slurpee machine and grabbed one arm while Junkie grabbed the other arm and stuck a .357 into his temple. A softly spoken "Police. You're under arrest." did the job. Contrary to the Hollywood versions, these things aren't always screamed at the top of your lungs when you don't want to attract undue attention. I cuffed him and we turned him around to lead him out.

When we turned, we saw the clerk standing behind the counter with both arms stretched upwards as far as they would go.

"Jesus, please don't shoot me!"

My partner showed him a badge and told him to relax. When you're in an undercover job and thinking in cop mode, sometimes you can forget other people see you as just two scruffy guys with big guns.

As we headed for the front of the store, the Sex Crimes detective came in, grinning.

"I knew you guys were in here."

"How?"

"When I pulled up in front, there were about six people trying to get out the front door at the same time. It looked like a Three Stooges scene."

We then noticed that all the other people who had been in the store were gone. The Invisible Men had struck again.

THE TRUTH, THE WHOLE TRUTH AND NOTHING BUT THE TRUTH.

The Federal courtroom was packed. What little room not taken up by lawyers, defendants, witnesses, cops and Deputy U.S. Marshals was overflowing with spectators. It was, as the courthouse wags said, the "biggest trial in awhile."

Johnny Lee's dope ring had been taken down, lock, stock and barrel. It had been the largest and most successful narcotics operation in the southwest region but with tendrils that ran from Chicago to Los Angeles, from Mexico to Colombia. The DEA, ATF and state narcs had all had a hand in it but their main contribution had been federal money, federal warrants, federal racketeering statutes and jurisdictional niceties that uncomplicated things like state and national boundaries. The operation had been started and primarily run by the local city narcotics unit.

Now, after a year and a half of wiretaps, stakeouts and surveillances, Johnny Lee and dozens of his minions were under arrest. Palatial houses, luxury cars, expensive boats, bank accounts and all their contents had been seized in three states not to mention tons of dope. The narcotics would be destroyed after it was used as evidence. The rest of the property now belonged to the federal government and the money from their sale would be deposited into the budgets of half a dozen federal, state and local law enforcement agencies.

It was the beginning of the second week of Johnny Lee's trial for violating the RICO statutes, the federal racketeering laws. Johnny Lee was the first one to be tried. Cut off the head and the rest of the body will collapse. If he were convicted, his lesser associates would start scrambling to make all the deals they could to lessen their own time in jail. Some already had.

Federal court is different from state court. The decorum is much more somber, restrained and dignified. Circus atmospheres are not allowed. A federal judge, secure in the warmth of a lifetime appointment, reigns supreme with an iron hand from his raised podium with armed Deputy U.S. Marshals standing by to enforce his edicts instantaneously. Only slightly less dignified is the panel of jurors seated to one side who must sort through the selection of truths, half-truths and lies they will hear throughout the trial.

Today it was Arthur's turn to testify. Arthur (NOT Art!) was one of Johnny Lee's lesser street lieutenants. Many of the suspects had answered a knock on their doors to be confronted by several men in business suits. A piece of paper had been handed to them and they had heard the litany "We're federal officers and we have a warrant for your arrest." Arthur's arrest had been a little different.

Some of the arrest locations were centered in an area where arrests had caused riots in the past. It was decided that a lot of trouble could be averted with an initial show of force that would discourage outside interference, what the military calls a quick surgical strike. During the coordinated raids to pick up all the suspects, Arthur had been followed to a convenience store by an undercover city narc in a Corvette. The narc had then radioed his location to an unmarked undercover van that contained an assault team of other narcs wearing blue body armor with "POLICE" emblazoned across them in foot-high bright yellow letters. He had been arrested when he came out of the store. He agreed to testify for the prosecution in return for a reduced sentence.

The court clerk called Arthur's name and he sauntered in, using his normal *Yeah-I'm-bad* jailhouse stroll. Directed to the witness's chair, he sat down before he was directed to stand and take the oath. He did and sat again. The courtroom was so silent that his right foot could be heard idly tapping the floor. This was the first time Arthur had been in court when he wasn't the defendant. Unlike those occasions, this time he *had* to testify.

The prosecutor conducted his examination, establishing that Arthur was a twice-convicted felon, sold narcotics on the street and forwarded a large percentage of his profits back to Johnny Lee. Then it was the defense attorney's turn. He had decided to impeach Arthur's testimony by attacking the legality of the arrest. If Arthur had been arrested illegally, he wouldn't need to make a deal with the prosecution and could recant his testimony. However, it seems he either hadn't interviewed the witness well enough for the line of questioning or Arthur was too stupid to grasp it.

"Were the officers who arrested you in uniform or plain clothes?"

"I dunno."

"What do you mean?"

"I dunno."

"Do you mean to tell me you didn't notice whether the officers who arrested you were wearing uniforms or not?"

"No."

The attorney was getting a little perplexed at Arthur's befuddlement.

"How were the officers dressed who arrested you?"

"I dunno."

"They arrested you and you didn't even see them?"

Arthur kept looking over at the judge like he was afraid of violating the courtroom decorum but he was getting exasperated also.

"Look, alls I know is I went to the Seben Eleben to get me an' my ole lady some malt liquor an' hot links an' when I comed out, all I seen was a bunch of white boys wif guns jump outta this van yellin' 'Motherfucker, hit the ground!'. An' you don't see a lot wif yo face pushed into the parkin' lot, if you get my drift."

The silence was deafening. It started in the jury box. A juror's shoulders started shaking and he tried to cover it with a somewhat strangled cough. Then another man started snickering through his nose. A black woman in the spectator gallery started a low, throaty laugh. One of the cops in the front row was turning red in the face, pretending to lean his head on one hand but holding the hand firmly over his mouth. Then the judge started laughing. With that, the whole courtroom exploded in barely contained hilarity. The lawyers, the cops, the jurors, the witnesses, everyone was howling and doubling over with tears rolling down their cheeks.

And no one in the courtroom doubted that Arthur's testimony was *exactly* what had happened.

And Finally

THE S.T.O.P.S. UNIT

When I started writing this book, I didn't exactly intend for it to have "a message" *per se*. If it does, however, I guess it would be that cops are basically just like any other large group of people. There are some special things about them due to the influences of their jobs and the people they associate with as a result but basically they share the same strengths and weaknesses as any other large group of people.

Most of them have strong personalities but some don't. Most are dedicated but some are lazy. Most of them have great integrity but some are moral cowards. Every now and then, a physical coward even turns up. Most are honest but some are corruptible and a few are corrupt. Most of them are smart but some are stupid.

Now, we're all human. Smart people sometimes say and do stupid things, and stupid people sometimes say and do smart things. As my uncle used to say, a busted watch is right twice a day. But there are aberrations and then there are behavioral patterns.

Stress and frustration are inherent parts of police work. They come in many different forms, some external and some internal. That doesn't just mean where you feel it but also its place of origin. Probably the worst forms are the internal kind generated from other cops, usually supervisors, commanders and staff administrators. This is probably universal among the ranks until you become the Chief of Police. Then your frustration and stress comes from the city manager, mayor and city councilmen.

There is, and always will be, a lot of bitching about how much things have changed since "the Good Old Days." Never mind that selective memory clouds the fact that not everything was good about the Good Old Days or that common sense tells you that some of the changes are for the better and even if they're not, they were nevertheless necessary due to the realities of changing times.

We used to bitch about the promotional system we dubbed "the good old boy system." The administration gave tests for the various ranks that a blind chimpanzee could score at least fifty per cent on so everybody who took it got on a promotional list. But the Chief didn't have to promote people in the same order they scored on the test. He promoted whomever he wanted to promote and didn't have to justify it to anyone. Under that system, although we didn't necessarily realize it at the time, there was a pretty good chance that the sergeants, lieutenants and captains that came from it were good cops with experience, integrity, common sense and weren't micromanaging megalomaniacs. There was always the occasional wild card but the odds were on our side.

Then a system was created that was written into labor contracts—a system that entailed difficult comprehensive tests, personnel evaluations and assessment centers. Then people started getting promoted who were good test-takers and gave polished presentations before a group of assessors who didn't know them. When they were promoted, some of these people lived up to their hoped-for potential. Some, however, couldn't make a decision in the field if you gave them a week's warning and held a gun to their head. Others had spent years hiding from enforcement duties behind reams of paper. Their most frequent evaluation from their peers was "Wouldn't make a pimple on a policeman's ass." It's a far cry from talking about what you'd do if you were in charge of a hostage situation for twenty minutes in a classroom and doing it in real life. As one old saying went, "Screwing and fighting—anybody can *talk* a good one." There's also a problem with trying to respond to real situations with a memorized checklist or the Policy and Procedures Manual under one arm as opposed to thinking on your feet.

Then the bad choices started gaining ground on the good choices. Then the bad choices began outnumbering the good choices. Then it became commonplace for some commanders to start stacking the deck with their pets and the supervisory ranks began filling up with ass-kissers, yes-men (and women) and those who spent more time worrying about getting promoted to the next highest rank instead of doing the job they were presently occupying.

Another problem was a breakdown in the chain of command. If a sergeant orders a patrolman to do something, he damned well better do it as long as it's not illegal. The same is true when the lieutenant gives orders to the sergeant and the captain gives orders to the lieutenant. But when you get into the appointed ranks, the ones above captain, the ones for which there are no tests except who the Chief wants in that position, there is a tendency to *negotiate* with commanders about what they should do within their division or their bureau.

As most people who have been in a supervisory or managerial role know, most people require minimal supervision assuming they had some competency in the first place. They just want to know what the rules are and be allowed to do their jobs within those guidelines. On the other hand, there are always a few too stupid to understand the rules or who think they're so special that the rules don't apply to them. These people require more of a supervisor's attention and it can be trying and tedious to deal with them every day. That applies whether you're a sergeant supervising a patrolman or a major supervising a captain.

As a result, some supervisors and commanders were allowed to run amok with little or no controls placed upon them by their superiors. Depending upon the level of their megalomania, these people could seriously degrade or even totally destroy the efficiency and morale or both of entire units.

Many years ago, a small group of off-duty officers of various ranks were debating these frustrations over some drinks. They began theorizing about forming a new unit to solve these problems. After a few more drinks, they actually came up with a set of written guidelines. What follows is a copy of those guidelines.

"S.T.O.P.S.

Systematic **T**ermination **O**f **P**olice **S**tupidity
Providing Incentives In Police Performance
By-laws and Guidelines

I. ORIGIN AND PURPOSE

The STOPS Unit is a clandestine unit within the Oklahoma City Police Department. It is made up of a classified number of police officers dedicated to, as the name indicates, the systematic termination of police stupidity within that organization.

II. EXECUTIVE COMMITTEE

The organization will be headed by an Executive Committee that consists of the Commander, the Assistant Commander and the Action Officer.

III. MEMBERSHIP

There shall be no limit to the number of members but the stringent qualifications will keep the membership relatively small. The names of members will be confidential and will not be revealed to non-members.

IV. QUALIFICIATIONS FOR MEMBERSHIP

Prospective members must;

1. Be a fully commissioned Oklahoma City Police officer.

2. Be recommended to the Executive Committee by a member in good standing and seconded by another qualified member.

3. Have a relatively unblemished reputation for a lack of professional stupidity. Personal stupidity (within reasonable bounds) concerning sex, money or alcohol will not be considered as disqualifying.

4. Have a reputation for a black (or at least very dark gray) sense of humor.

5. Have a proven, documented ability for physical violence.

6. Have the ruthlessness of a starving wolverine.

7. Have an excellent memory and history of carrying and avenging grudges. Any proven tendencies of leniency, mercy or forgiving and forgetting will be considered as disqualifying.

8. Have the prerequisite upper body strength, eye-hand coordination and guile to accomplish the duties of membership.

V. TRAINING

Before becoming fully qualified members, applicants will be trained in the following areas:

1. Stalking and ambush techniques.

2. Cover and camouflage.

3. Physical evidence eradication.

4. Batting practice.

VI. MEETINGS

Meetings will be held once a week at a local bar to be decided by quorum. After a minimum of three (3) alcoholic beverages per member, the meeting will be called to order by the Commander. The Action Officer will report on old business and the floor will then be opened for new business.

Emergency meetings may be requested by any member by contacting a member of the Executive Committee and briefing him on the nature of the emergency. The Executive Committee officer will then either approve or deny the emergency meeting.

VII. METHODOLOGY

Any member in good standing may collect information on any officer of the OCPD, regardless of rank or assignment, who is continually committing acts of professional stupidity that adversely affects the administration, reputation or operation of this department. This evidence will then be presented to the Executive Committee. A majority vote will then decide which of three courses of action will be taken:

1. MOTION DENIED-INSUFFICIENT EVIDENCE

This may be reconsidered if additional evidence accumulates in the future.

2. MOTION GRANTED-CAUTION RECOMMENDED

If it is felt that the offender can be salvaged by learning from his mistakes and altering his behavior, a single warning will be sent. This will consist of a STOPS memo reading "CAUTION-The STOPS Committee is considering you for future action!"

3. MOTION GRANTED-IMMEDIATE ACTION CANDIDATE

Upon adoption of this motion, a member will be selected by a quorum of the Executive Committee. This member will be informed of the identity of the Immediate Action candidate.

The member will then select a STOPPER from the Armory. Unless unusual circumstances exist, the STOPPER will consist of a 36-inch Louisville Slugger baseball bat made of oak or other suitable hardwood with the core drilled out and replaced with asphalt. The member will then, with the least possible delay, arrange a private meeting with the candidate by appointment or ambush.

After insuring there are no witnesses and facing the candidate squarely, the member will place the STOPPER against the head of the candidate with all available force. Although no warning will be given and no words spoken by the member, ideally the candidate should have an instant to realize he is being STOPPED but not enough time to cry out or evade the blows.

The minimum number of blows will be applied until the member is absolutely certain that all life signs have been extinguished. A reliable indicator is when the top of the candidate's head has been beaten down level with his shoulders.

The member will then thumbtack a notice to the candidate's chest reading "This person has been STOPPED!" The member will then leave the area without being seen after ensuring that no incriminating evidence is left behind. The STOPPER will be returned to the Armory after being cleaned and polished.

VIII. CITATIONS

Members will be eligible for the following citations:

1. THE LOU GEHRIG AWARD-For 10 STOPS without leaving evidence.

2. THE PETE ROSE AWARD-For being investigated for a STOP and convincing investigators that he's innocent when he's guilty.

3. THE HOME RUN AWARD-For 3 STOPS performed by a single blow each.

4. THE YOGI BERRA AWARD-For performing a STOP on the wrong person (but one who would have had to be STOPPED eventually) and getting away with it.

5. THE HANK AARON AWARD-For performing a STOP on a black candidate.

6. THE BEARDED CLAM AWARD-For performing a STOP on a female candidate.

7. THE PRINCE OF DARKNESS AWARD-For performing a STOP on a candidate while he begs for his life, offers bribes, promotions or transfers, and attempts to shield himself behind pictures of his family."

Of course, it was all just a facetious diversion to alleviate frustration. Looking back on it though, it wasn't that bad an idea.

Glossary

Relevant portions of the Police Ten Codes and Signals in use during the period covered in this book;

10-4—Roger, affirmative or informally abbreviated to the word "Clear."
10-6—Busy, out of service, unable to respond to calls.
10-8—In service, ready to respond to calls.
10-15—Prisoner in custody, on the way to jail.
10-20—Location.
10-22—Disregard last transmission.
10-28—Check registration on license number—.
10-29—Check stolen on license number—.
10-97—Arrived at location of call.
10-98—Leaving scene of call, call completed, back in service.

SIGNAL 7—Dead body.
SIGNAL 8—Mental patient.
SIGNAL 30—Traffic accident with fatality.
SIGNAL 76—Traffic accident without injury.
SIGNAL 82—Traffic accident with injury.

978-0-595-48357-0
0-595-48357-7

www.ingramcontent.com/pod-product-compliance
Lightning Source LLC
Chambersburg PA
CBHW022245290526
45785CB00015B/246